MAIDEN VOYAGES

The **Institute of Southeast Asian Studies** (ISEAS) was established as an autonomous organization in 1968. It is a regional centre dedicated to the study of socio-political, security and economic trends and developments in Southeast Asia and its wider geostrategic and economic environment.

The Institute's research programmes are the Regional Economic Studies (RES, including ASEAN and APEC), Regional Strategic and Political Studies (RSPS), and Regional Social and Cultural Studies (RSCS).

ISEAS Publishing, an established academic press, has issued almost 2,000 books and journals. It is the largest scholarly publisher of research about Southeast Asia from within the region. ISEAS Publishing works with many other academic and trade publishers and distributors to disseminate important research and analyses from and about Southeast Asia to the rest of the world.

MAIDEN VOYAGES
Eastern Indonesian Women on the Move

Catharina Purwani Williams

LSEAS

Institute of Southeast Asian Studies
Singapore

First published in Singapore in 2007 by
ISEAS Publishing
Institute of Southeast Asian Studies
30 Heng Mui Keng Terrace
Pasir Panjang
Singapore 119614
E-mail: publish@iseas.edu.sg
Website: http://bookshop.iseas.edu.sg

The responsibility for facts and opinions in this publication rests exclusively with the author and her interpretations do not necessarily reflect the views or the policy of the publishers or their supporters.

ISEAS Library Cataloguing-in-Publication Data

Williams, Catharina Purwani.
    Maiden voyages : Eastern Indonesian women on the move.
    1.   Women travelers—Indonesia—Nusa Tenggara Timur—Anecdotes.
    2.   Women travelers in literature.
    3.   Women migrant labor—Indonesia—Nusa Tenggara Timur—Anecdotes.
    4.   Women alien labor—Indonesia—Nusa Tenggara Timur—Anecdotes.
    5.   Women domestics—Indonesia—Nusa Tenggara Timur—Anecdotes.
    I.   Title.
    II.   Title: Eastern Indonesian women on the move
G465 W72   2007

ISBN 978-981-230-393-6 (soft cover)
ISBN 978-981-230-394-3 (hard cover)
ISBN 978-981-230-568-8 (PDF)

Typeset by Togaware using LaTeX.
Printed in Singapore by Utopia Press Pte Ltd.

in memory of my mother Yoni,
who taught me how to learn. . .
AMDG

You're in the right place. *You are in the right place if you are merciful. You are in the right place if you struggle for justice. You are in fact in the right place if they persecute you, or insult you, you're in the right place. It's about social location. It's about where we choose to stand. The Beatitudes is not a spirituality, it's a geography* (Boyle 2002).

Contents

PART THREE REFLECTIONS

List of Figures

List of Tables

List of Boxes

Preface

This book explores women's mobility in particular geographical, social, and cultural contexts. I am captivated by women's travel as a way of opening a space of inquiry about Eastern Indonesia's spatial relations. Examining practices of travel provides insights into contemporary social and cultural processes (Clifford 1997; Kaplan 1996; Tsing 2000). This book emphasizes how travel situates Eastern Indonesian women at the intersection of ethnicity/place, class and gender politics. I investigate theoretical issues of travel within feminist geography frameworks, in which interpretations of place and ideologies of Self are problematized. The field research focuses on contemporary rural women and was conducted mainly in parts of East Nusa Tenggara and while travelling on boats in the region.

Women from Eastern Indonesia travel by sea along three routes: inter-island, to urban centres and travel overseas. Their travel stories are analysed to magnify the step of *"langgar laut"* or crossing the ocean. This local term represents negotiations of a range of social boundaries. Boundary is employed as an analytical tool to understand women's engagement in mobility to overcome exclusion from various social categories. My analysis grounds women's micropolitics of place in their journeys and nests it in the larger, macro-scale politics of place. The result points to the significance of the history and local specificity in both enabling and constraining the women's mobility. Travel highlights the mutual constitution of spaces and women's subjectivities.

My study on women's mobility moves beyond the dominant economic approach to migration. It highlights the liminal space of travel, allowing re-imagining of identities, new subject positions and subjectivities. Women travellers forge a range of scales of relations and push boundaries. I suggest that these strategic movements raise interesting theoretical issues concerning women's mobile subjectivity. My conceptualization of women's travel takes into account subject, subjectivity and local specificity, aiming to contribute to an understanding of women's mobility and spatial relations in Eastern Indonesia.

Acknowledgements

The journey of writing this book has had its turns and crossroads and I was grateful that many accompanied me in unfolding other women's journeys. My greatest debt is to the women of East Nusa Tenggara who welcomed and shared their life journeys. Very special thanks are due to the Australian National University, particularly to Professor Katherine Gibson, Professor Hal Hill, Dr Deirdre McKay, Professor Peter Rimmer, Dr Andrew Walker, and my staunchest supporter and friend, Brigid Ballard. A visiting fellowship from the University of New South Wales at the Australian Defence Force Academy with the support of geographers from the School of Physical, Environmental and Mathematical Sciences is gratefully acknowledged.

In East Nusa Tenggara I was fortunate to know the extended family of the *Societas Verbi Divini* (SVD) with their hospitality, particularly Br Rufinus Rehing, Fr Victor Bunanig, and Fr Philipus Tule. The sisters of Ursuline, CB, CIJ, including Sr Yerona CIJ, all enriched my fieldwork through their networks and care. They offered insights, shelter and companionship — *terima kasih seribu*.

In Jakarta, for their generosity of spirit, I am profoundly grateful to David Marwoto and Riani Budi and the rest of the family, Novin, Suwati, Alix, Usada and Restu. Thanks are also extended to all those who inspired and cheered me from the sidelines, including Dr Hadi Soesastro, Dr and Mrs Thee Kian Wie, Dr Mari Pangestu, Dr Haryo Aswicahyono, Medelina Hendityo MA, and Dr Tubagus Feridhanusetyawan and friends in *Keluarga Ex Kolese Loyola* — AMDG — in particular Fr Markus Wanandi SJ. Triena Ong and Rahilah Yusuf of ISEAS, Singapore were very helpful with the publication of this book, and Emily Brissenden designed the cover — thank you.

Last but not least, my deepest thanks to Graham my husband who shared this journey, providing harmony and balance. For a sense of wonderment, I thank our children Sean and Anita. To say more would be too little. Another part of my journey unfolds.

Part One

Departure

In Eastern Indonesia gender is an important category that stratifies social groups. Women's access to mobility is influenced by their position in social relations. I begin by situating myself in the research project and then locating the Eastern Indonesian women in the geographical, economic and political situations of East Nusa Tenggara. Women's travel represents efforts to negotiate their position in spatial and social relations. Such representation does not change the dominant discourse of social categories or boundaries, however it does open a new space for women's shifting roles.

CHAPTER 1

Women, Space, and Travel

Introduction

xploring the mobility experiences and subjectivities of women travellers in the context of a developing country, this book aims to contribute to the theorization of women's travel. Routes of travel are significant in tracing contemporary social and cultural processes (Clifford 1997; Tsing 2000). The routes of travel by Eastern Indonesian women are varied and so are the outcomes. This book focuses on groups of young women travellers from Eastern Indonesia. It analyses the ways these women through their travel have created a subjective space enabling re-imagining identity and subject positions in a larger scale of social relations.

Travel, traveller, and travel stories have formed the heart of geography as a scientific discipline for centuries (Domosh 1991). In the context of Indonesia, travel is a visible part of the recent economic and political changes that have taken place in the country. Women's travel is a component of these national and regional transformations or the macropolitics of location, and is interconnected to multi-layered social relations. Travel also reflects a range of specific local, social and cultural changes. A question that motivates my research concerns these forces of change in relation to women and space; why and how has travel preoccupied women of Eastern Indonesia? More specifically, I address three inseparable concerns: the distinctive characteristics of women's voyages; how women's travel not only reflects and reproduces but also resists gendered space; and how the space of travel allows women to shift subject positions and subjectivities.

Indonesia is the setting of my research. The country's recent political and economic changes provide a window through which we can gain a perspective on the flow of people, and of women in particular. My choice of Eastern Indonesia as the regional focus of the study follows one of the classic interests of human geography in its concern for the region, the area or the locality (Massey 1984, p. 2). My own familiarity with the people, language and culture is, of course, an advantage. Eastern Indonesia, in particular the province of East Nusa Tenggara, attracts my interest for a number of reasons. It is known as a place at the margin. The region has been described as the Outer Islands, with a relatively low transport penetration indicating that it is a "peripheral region" (Rutz 1976, p. 161), and "the least integrated and most underdeveloped of Indonesia's provinces" (Drake 1989, p. 221). Described as a "fractured region", it also lacks resources — in particular good soils, forests and mineral wealth (Hardjono 1994, p. 179; Hill 1996). In the last few decades, however, there have been improvements in infrastructure and physical networks in Eastern Indonesia (Williams 1999). Nevertheless, places are linked in unequal ways and changes in transport connections affect people differently depending on their gender, locality, and class (Barke 1986; Leyshon 1995; Massey 1995). Contextualizing women within the networks of social relations created through transport reveals how physical transport connections favour some individuals and groups over others. So the question arises as to which group of women are able to benefit from improved transport networks?

Like many other women travellers or migrants who move to seek better opportunities, I feel some affinity with those who live at the margin and shift between places or worlds (Groves and Chang 1999, p. 249). Indeed doing this research has, to some extent, enabled me to deal with and re-imagine my own marginality in being between two worlds, Australia and Indonesia; an ambiguity within a simplistic binary structure of being inside or outside a boundary. Travel allows a transient moment and space, a transcending of boundary and a re-imagining of identity between spaces. My own travel during the research was a set of experiences; it was not merely a movement to cover a physical distance between a place of origin and a destination. Travel leads to a questioning of boundaries or constructed distinctions between the familiar and a larger-scale social system (Thrift 1993, pp. 92–94).

My "field sites" moved with my travels and the women's travels. The ethnography of women's travel continually shifted in response to unexpected circumstances found on the boat and on the road. My field journey became a rite of passage, a site of personal and professional initiation and more significantly, a set of discursive practices (Clifford 1992, p. 99). In the field, I observed many women on the move. In East Nusa Tenggara, thousands of women travel through crammed ports and bus terminals. They can be seen on buses, aeroplanes, ferries, and ships. This study, however, concentrates on sea travel, because sea travel is the most commonly used and cheapest means of travel in the archipelago of Indonesia. Maiden voyages may refer to either young virgins' sea travel, or, the first sea travel. As it will become apparent in the later chapters, my study encompasses both connotations. Many young Eastern Indonesian women whom I met were travelling by sea for the first time and were concerned to preserve their purity. Thus my respondents were East Nusa Tenggaran women, many of whom I met on voyages which became sites of new encounters.

The narrative structure of women's life stories is analysed in relation to three different distances and categories of travel — inter-island, to urban centres and to overseas — and I select some dissimilar examples from the typical stories and group them according to the dynamics of the route. As a continuation of Part One (Departure), Chapter 2 provides a background to the geographic, economic and political settings of the province of East Nusa Tenggara where the main field research was undertaken. Then I address the question of how travel highlights the links between changing spaces and the constitution of women's mobile subjectivity. In Chapter 3, I analyse the context of Eastern Indonesian women's travel. First I situate women's travel within several strands of literature. Then the local women are situated in a broader structure of networks of physical and social relations. Both the literature and the social relations create a perspective from which we can analyse travel as an interplay of social structures and other contingent relations with women's agency, as also shown in the selected folk narratives. Located at the intersections of cultural, migration, and gender studies, the key converging themes of this book are that of travel and mobile subjectivities.

The three chapters in Part Two (Journeys) present a range of travellers' stories, drawing from the ethnography of women's travel. Through the travellers' gazes and accounts, I endeavour to draw out the multiple meanings of space through which women travel, given the context of their social relations in Eastern Indonesia. Chapter 4 introduces travel as an ambiguous space in relation to the local notion of propriety. In voyages women transform the physical and social space of their travel into a space of wider possibilities for behaviour. The next chapter focuses on nurses and teachers, the professional women who frame their travel to urban centres through socially "safe and acceptable" occupations. These women use the liminal space of travel to perform an idealized femininity in order to mobilize selves and thus exercise their personal autonomy. I then explore the experience of the local women travelling overseas to work as contract domestic workers. They travel abroad and their experience expands from the familiar to the alien within a larger scale of international interaction. Their travel stories contain a theme of new and wider subject positions as a route to a better position within the localized power relations.

The final chapter provides a conceptual discussion of women's travel as *langgar laut*, crossing the threshold of the ocean. I link the analysis of women's strategic mobility from the previous chapters, their micropolitics, with the macropolitics of place. Thus this concluding chapter analyses the dialectical dynamics of the local specificity of Eastern Indonesia as manifested in women's travel with the broader politics of place.

Methodological approach to travel

Seen as a classical ethnographic project, travel has changed significantly in its natures and patterns (Siikala 2001, p. 1). There have been concerns about the inadequacy of methods originally developed for studying supposedly small-scale societies which have now become mobile, influenced by the globalizing world. One of these concerns relates to the dramatic change in the complexities of people's movements which has not been accompanied by a corresponding shift in the ethnographic disciplinary practices of fieldwork (Gupta 1997, p. 3). Transnational movements, for instance, raise problematic representations of travellers. As Appadurai (1991) puts it:

> The landscapes of group identity — the ethnoscape — around the world are no longer tightly territorialized, spatially bounded, historically self-conscious, or culturally homogenous.... The task of ethnography now becomes the unravelling of a conundrum: what is the nature of locality, as a lived experience, in a globalized, deterritorialized world? (pp. 191–196)

Here I view my travel for this research as a continuous field, therefore this ethnography is not limited to specific localities. I include marginalized blurred boundary areas, such as the materiality of the boat and the ship, that often "slip out of the ethnographic frame". The discourse of ethnography ("being there" in the field) is usually separated from that of travel ("getting there") (Clifford 1997, p. 23). However, in my study, both processes are more appropriately integrated into one ethnography of women's travel. Thus my own travels became the basis of my engagement with many Eastern Indonesian women, as I participated in a wide range of voyage experiences. I also stayed in and observed a number of the home and destination communities to which the women belonged, and this offered insights into their identities at home/away. Clifford (1997) asserts that spatial practices of fieldwork provide an enormous advantage for in-depth understanding through intensive participant-observation. In this project, my journey in field research in Eastern Indonesia became the basis of my qualitative inquiry and is constituted here as an ethnography of women's travel.

I work from a non-essentialist position, and my approach to the ethnography of women's travel is a partial view of dynamic representation. This position does not entail an all encompassing perspective or representation of Eastern Indonesian women moving between places. Ethnographic presentation offers "partial truth" because "much of our knowledge about other cultures must now be seen as contingent, the problematic outcome of inter-subjective dialogue, translation and projection" (Clifford 1986, p. 109). In this context, my book explores individual women's travel through stories, life histories, and my participation in their travel and daily practices. The abstraction and representation are situated in the historical perspective of localities and travellers' sites.

Travel stories I heard during my field research provide particularly striking examples of a range of possibilities of women's travel, as do my own field work experiences as a traveller. I follow a mode of inquiry grounded in the social relations based on at least two interconnected levels: "an ideological, discursive level addressing questions of representation", and a material, experiential, daily-life level focusing on the micro-politics of location (Mohanty 1991, p. 21). To uncover the meanings of Eastern Indonesian women's travel, I ground the women's stories, that indicate a range of subjective experiences of space, in the context of the structural relations of geographical and historical subjects moving places. The women's stories and events I learnt and observed as I followed some of their trails by sea were signs of both the discursive construction and materiality of the micropolitics of women's travels.

Relating changes in individuals' circumstances to changes at the local and regional levels requires intense engagements with the people in the field. This, to some extent, explains the scarcity of studies on individual women's travel within a context of local social relations in Eastern Indonesia. A few studies observe physical connectivity changes at the regional level and relate these to the general picture of people's mobility (Rutz 1976). Although my experience in the field revealed the relatively limited connectivity of the region, this cannot be taken as evidence of lack of mobility of local women. This experience requires further fitting against the historical and geographical context of local women and the common features which bind women. I do take into account the specificities and the historical contexts of the women by drawing from other historiography and ethnographic studies of some localized areas in East Nusa Tenggara.

Most of all, my own observation and study of women's travel confirms that a careful focus on individuals allows interesting insights into the underlying framework of relations in which women operate in the local context. I argue that individuals, with their situational knowledge of social relations, are affected by and respond to the dynamics of regional and local social structures, but their individual strategies of mobility are not totally determined by them.

Positionality and reflexivity

I follow critical feminist methodologies which acknowledge that my positionality and biography affect my fieldwork. This choice also produces particular mappings of and relations with women in the field, which in turn affect my representations. The methodologies require continual reflexivity throughout the research process (England 1994; Katz 1994; Kobayashi 1994; Staeheli and Lawson 1994). This reflexivity in the research and writing has offered an opportunity to examine the implications of my own gender, class, and ethnicity through the research process. At the intersection of reflexivity and inter-subjectivity lies positionality, which is central to my work (Nagar 1997, p. 208). As a researcher, I am concerned with how I position myself within the research project, given the hidden power relations in my interactions with the people in the field. Understanding my positionality involves an analysis of my location and relationship in reference to the "researched" (ibid.). Reflexivity, thus, becomes a process for making the power relations visible within the research project (Mullings 1999; Katz 1994; Kobayashi 1994; Rose 1997). To address this issue of power relations, I choose to engage in self-reflection on identity as part of the historical, cultural, and political processes, also known as auto-ethnography (McKay 2001). This analytical technique aims not only to create a space, however unstable, for theorizing travel, but also to invite others to recreate the space where the personal becomes the political and where power relations may be continually re-examined. Further reflecting on the interview as a technique in traditional ethnography, I approach my interviews with informants as encounters, where all of us participate in a discourse from our own inter-subjective locations.

My origins as a woman of Indonesian Chinese descent with strong Javanese influences do not fully qualify me as a native among the people of East Nusa Tenggara province in Eastern Indonesia. Narayan (1997, p. 23) problematizes issues for a field worker who is a native. She suggests that there is no fixity of roles but, rather, shifting identifications of a field worker in the midst of a field with its network of social and power relations. Like Narayan I found myself performing different roles and taking on a range of identities in the field. I have had continuous personal contacts with the people of the region for many years. We use the same Indonesian language, Bahasa Indonesia, facilitating our communication, and, to some extent, I can understand their nuances, quirks and subtle body language. Women telling travel stories provided materials for interpretation of not just the stories but also the more intricate, subtle, idiomatic and nuanced expressions of their views on social relations as the setting of their travel. My position allows an in-depth localized perspective, where I am able to recognize aspects of these rich cultural codes.

Undertaking reflexive ethnography, I realized that my identity as a researcher in the field was problematic (Mahler and Pesar 2006). The way I entered the field at a particular space and time influenced the way I was perceived and the extent of people's acceptance. The closer I was to the insider circle, the more depth of understanding I gained about local relations. Indeed, being "one of them" on my journey and being on the road with them was the most significant aspect of my research. Similar to Abu-Lughod (1991) who chooses to write from the vantage position of a "halfie", I can relate to the ambiguous position of being not quite an insider but not completely an outsider either. In this way Abu-Lughod (1991) is able to subvert the process of Othering by simultaneously being half an insider and half an outsider, without being bounded by assumptions of the Othering process, through making use of lived experiences of everyday practices. Throughout the field research I realized the highly unstable position of the binary of insider/outsider and I was aware of the dynamism of my position in time and through space (Mullings 1999, p. 340).

Through a one-to-one relationship with each informant and, in turn, by synthesizing a disparate range of facts, I have been able to make sense of different connections. Particularly when I focus and reflect on the interrelations between diverse informants, I have been able to see the link between the women's experiences to the wider structures and systems of their community/culture (Strathern 1991, p. 9). This has led me to envision the relational dimension of the local context of the women's travel. The central converging themes that of various women's travel and mobile subjectivities are teased out throughout this study.

CHAPTER 2

Charting the Routes

Space of inquiry

ast Nusa Tenggara, the province of origin of my informants, provides the dynamic settings of the research, and through travel I exemplify the spatiality and specificity of the local contexts. I also explore the space of my inter-subjective interactions with the informants. This micro study of travel aims to capture subjects moving through spaces at a range of different scales and forms. However, unlike a particular study of migration, it does not put specific time or administrative boundary limits on the spatial movement.

Geography of East Nusa Tenggara

Eastern Indonesia is a diverse region in terms of its physical geography and people. The physical geography has influenced both the traditional settlement patterns and the people's contemporary lifestyles. The scattered islands of the region, its hilly and mountainous areas and the dispersed small population occupying small pockets of fertile land, make communication difficult, thus creating a sense of isolation (Jones 1995).

East Nusa Tenggara province consists of 4.7 million hectares of land with 3.9 million inhabitants (Badan Pusat Statistik Propinsi NTT 2001). It is one of the least urbanized provinces in Indonesia with less than 20 per cent of the population living in urban areas (see Figure 2.1). The population density is 83 per square km and is among the lowest in Indonesia. The islands are mostly a continuation of the volcanic archipelago of Indonesia, which starts in Sumatra. The smaller outer arc of the Lesser Sundas — Sumba, Savu, Ndao, Raijua, Roti, Semau, and Timor — con-

Figure 2.1: Percentages of urban population by province, 2000

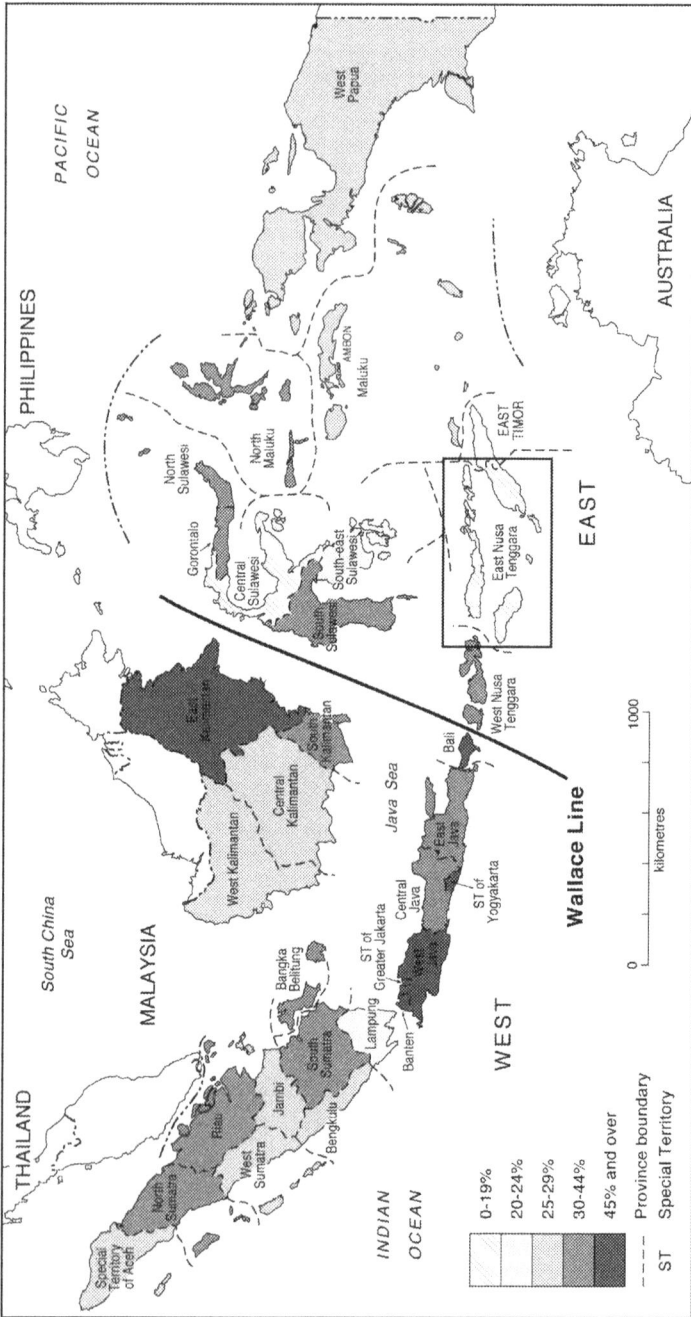

Source: Calculated from Census 2000.

sist mostly of uplifted coral and limestone. The climate of East Nusa Tenggara is semi-arid, with low average annual rainfall of 1,500 mm. The further east, the drier is the area. The islands of Nusa Tenggara are separated from Java and Bali by a deep-sea trench, which also marks a biological boundary known as the Wallace Line (see Figure 2.1). To the east of the Wallace Line, where East Nusa Tenggara lies, the flora and fauna are more similar to that of Australia than to neighbouring Southeast Asia. Forest covers 21 per cent of East Nusa Tenggara (Jones 1995).

In East Nusa Tenggara province, people live in a village setting and there are up to 500 sub-ethnic groups professing a range of religious and local-traditional beliefs. They mainly live in rural areas in the three main islands of Flores, Timor, and Sumba (see Figure 2.2). Catholicism dominates the island of Flores, and Protestantism dominates West Timor and the rest of East Nusa Tenggara. The majority (88 per cent) of the population profess Christianity, as shown in Figure 2.3. The people form multiple ethno-linguistic groups, each with a distinct cultural identity. Most people live in the lowlands to more easily access transport and natural resources. The highland settlements are widely scattered in small numbers reflecting a shortage of resources, and people there work in unirrigated garden plots (Jones 1995).

The economic and political settings

Three decades of strong economic growths from the mid-1970s to the 1990s were unexpectedly disrupted by a severe economic crisis in 1997–98. The International Monetary Fund (IMF) initial policy prescription — to overcome a reversal of foreign capital inflow combined with a weak domestic financial sector — failed to resolve the economic problems as the political dimensions of the crisis became more paramount (Grenville 2004). By 2005 the new government of President Susilo Bambang Yudhoyono (SBY) has to some extent restored the confidence of the business community in Indonesia. His government economic policies have begun to bring back investment activity, steady gains on the stock market and private capital inflow into the country (McLeod 2005).

The Asian financial crisis in 1997 triggered a crisis in Indonesia that was more severe and deeper than in other Asian countries. The Indonesian exchange rate depreciated far more steeply, with wider negative consequences for the economy and the people's welfare. The financial

Figure 2.2: East Nusa Tenggara.

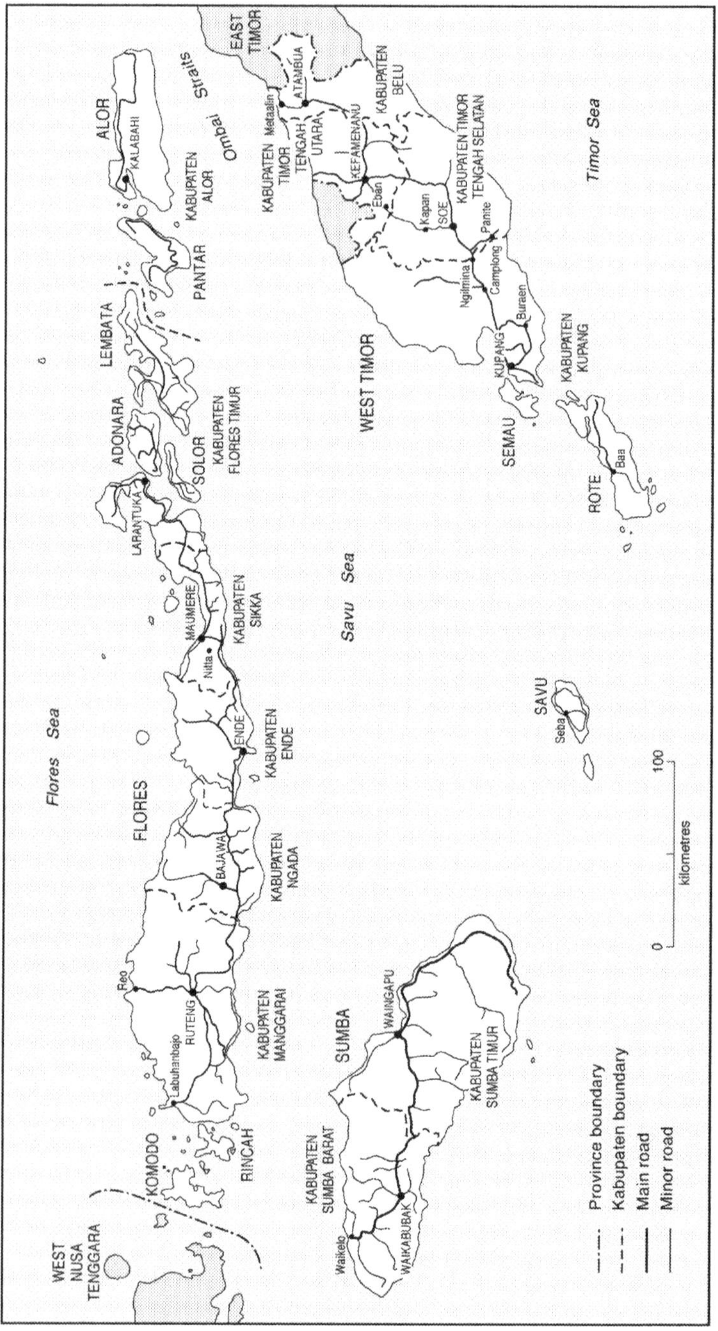

Source: The Australian National University, RSPAS Cartography.

Figure 2.3: Religious persuasion in East Nusa Tenggara, 2000.

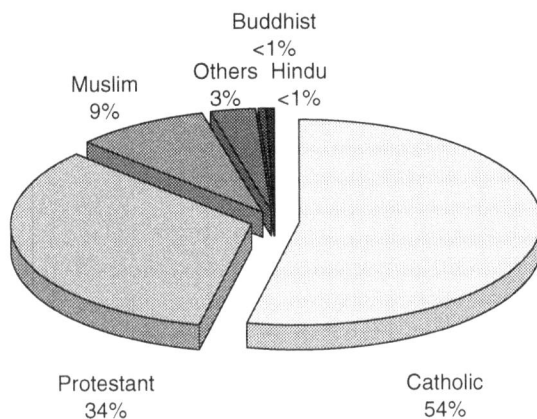

Source: Badan Pusat Statistik Propinsi NTT (2001).

system, which almost collapsed given the combination of economic and political events in 1997–98, may be understood as the consequence of a politicization of economic activities during President Soeharto's era. The social and political crisis that followed the financial collapse was centred on the rent-seeking practices of Soeharto and those connected to him. Soeharto's final failed attempt to prevent further rupiah depreciation marked an end to the value of his connections and the loss of people's confidence in his leadership. This triggered political unrest, riots, and his resignation in May 1998 (Berger 2001; Cole and Slade 1998). Sporadic riots and violence continued to occur throughout the tumultuous leadership changes of Soeharto's immediate successors, Presidents Habibie and Abdurahman Wahid. Social unrest broke out in parts of the country, involving Muslim–Christian clashes which spilled over into attacks on Indonesian Chinese (representing Christian) property (Cameron 1999).

In this period, Indonesians referred to their country as confronting *kristal* or *krisis total* (total crisis), and also *krismon* or *krisis moneter* (monetary crisis), pointing to the marked decline in socio-economic conditions. The real Gross Domestic Product (GDP) shrank by around 14 per cent in 1998. In the same period, the number of people below the poverty line was estimated to reach half the population and this proportion continued to grow as the crisis continued (Evans 1998; Cameron 1999). Since the crisis started, wages in real terms have fallen by approximately 40 per cent. The agricultural sector has absorbed some labour from other sectors as there have been large-scale movements of people from the urban areas to their rural roots in order to return to agricultural activities (Cameron 1999).

In East Nusa Tenggara province, 65 per cent of the population aged 10 years and above is recorded as economically active in the year 2000. The remaining 35 per cent includes students attending school and housewives working at home (Table 2.1).

Table 2.1: Population aged 10 years and above by type of activity during the previous week, 2000.

Activity During The Previous Week	Numbers	%
Economically Active	1,912,770	65
Worked	1,887,088	64
Looking For Work	25,682	1
Not Economically Active	1,030,357	35
Attending School	469,329	16
House Keeping	357,306	12
Others	203,722	7
Total	2,943,127	100

Source: Badan Pusat Statistik Propinsi NTT (2001).

Spatial linkages

Increasing travel by women reflects the general rise of population mobility in Indonesia (both permanent and temporary), linked to rising incomes, education and better communications and transport services. Nowadays more women enter the labour market both in formal employment in factories and industries and in informal sectors, and they often have to move to do so than in the past. This increased rate of women's participation has also been positively correlated with the broader base in the educational, industrial, and occupational distribution of women's employment in Indonesia (Manning 1998, p. 265). These trends have necessitated more mobility for women.

As Manning (1998) points out, Indonesia has undergone several periods of employment change in response to the economic policies of the day which, he argues, have benefited women. The three periods before the 1997 crisis — the period of recovery and economic boom (1971–80); the slowdown in economic growth (1980–85); and the economic liberalization (1985–90) — were similarly characterized by rapid non-agricultural urban employment growth. The boom period had recorded a particularly slow growth in agricultural employment (just over 1 per cent annually for Indonesia) and even lower growth in agricultural jobs in Eastern Indonesia. Manning (1998) contends that the reason for this slow growth in the agricultural sector was the opening up of non-agricultural employment opportunities associated with rapid urban growth and improvement in rural communications and services. In addition, the significant increase in employment in the public sector was a result of massive public expenditure in the health and education sectors, evident in the growing numbers of schools and health facilities throughout the country. This meant the creation of mostly traditionally female jobs, attracting women from other areas to migrate to find this type of work. Government administrative and social services jobs grew by almost 14 per cent annually during 1975–83 (Manning 1998), providing an opportunity for women's participation in many centres throughout the country and encouraging their movement to different regions. As East Nusa Tenggara province has the highest incidence of poverty in the country (Jones 1995), this might be a factor stimulating further travel out of this region.

Analyses of provincial migration, however, show that smaller proportion of people of East Nusa Tenggara migrate out of the province permanently relative to the other provinces. This result, produced from using census data, hides a rising trend towards temporary travel (Ananta, Anwar, and Suzenti 1997). It is these temporary travels of local women, which are not detected by either census or falling between the cracks of surveys of passengers, that are of interest to me. As I demonstrate in the later chapters, the varied motives of the women travellers and the dynamics of their trips contain social and individual meanings beyond mere physical movement.

At the physical level, transport is the means for travel. Observing transport as a spatial link between different areas not only provides an understanding of it as a means for interaction, but, at a conceptual level, it also works as a means of discussing relationships between gendered spaces and geographies of mobilities. As Law (1999) asserts:

> Attention to transport [offers] a way to link discussions of gender relations, transport systems, public and private spaces, accessibility, and the spatial and temporal organization of human activity.(p. 567)

The inter-relations between transport and interaction produce a synthesizing perspective from which to view a woman's travel as her means to express or experience power in social relations. Her travel represents both a physical movement and also a metaphorical journey where she negotiates her positions of being in the marginalized space. I expand on this local perspective in Chapter 3.

In the regional context, the degree of spatial linkage or transport connections partly determine the extent to which people in different islands and settlements can benefit from employment, education, trade, and other inter-regional relations. Social relations however do not simply arise from the provision of transport. While transport improvement changes the relative location of places in the Indonesian archipelago, Eastern Indonesian women are situated in multi-level interactions that affect their ability to benefit from these improvements.

The "shrinking" of distance affects patterns of activities and benefits certain locations and groups of women. The way in which, with improved transport systems, distances "shrink" is often referred to as time–space convergence framework (Janelle 1969; Giddens 1993). However, places are linked together in unequal ways, and changes in transport connections favour only some locations and groups of people, depending on relative position and social relations (Barke 1986; Leyshon 1995; Massey 1995). Some are able to find opportunities in the increased transport links and declining costs of travel that facilitate mobility, including transnational travels (Hugo 1999). Others have never travelled outside the region. Why? The inter-regional relations which bind the community together can be traced to relations of power (Massey 1995, p. 69). Power in Indonesia is concentrated in Java as the centre of political and administrative activities, rather than in the outer islands. As expected, the larger centres with the concentration of power have been the first to benefit from linkages provided by transport improvement (Hill 1996).

Within the East Nusa Tenggara region people do not benefit equally from national transport improvements. They may even be relatively disadvantaged because their relative location remains unchanged or even worsens with new physical connections. Within the province people face different transport problems, depending on their income levels, social status/class, and gender. This leads to the notion of the power geometry of time–space convergence, which suggests that "different social groups are placed in very distinct ways in relation to the flows and interconnections" (Massey 1993, p. 61). This means that when presented with the same transport system, both women and other social groups confront distinct accessibility problems. For instance, a wife of a subsistence farmer with a young family has many domestic responsibilities, including childcare, and may not have the time and resources to travel even intra-region. Such groups of women may only benefit from the flow of people, goods, and information offered by the network improvements in an indirect way.

Nevertheless, the advantage of transport developments in the past few decades is admitted even by the government's critics as having increased people's mobility, including that of women. In terms of the road and ferry transport improvements, Sumatra, Java, Bali, and Lombok now have a well-connected road and ferry transport system (Hill 1996, p. 215). At the local level, however, problems in road transport still exist, including intra-regional or inter-regencies (*kabupaten*) transport (ibid.). In the case of air transport, the ultimate result of the improvement is the shorter amount of time required (more destinations and frequent services) to travel, for example, from Jakarta or Surabaya to the main destinations around Indonesia. For high income groups who can afford airline costs, the country is "shrinking". In 1996, just before the financial crisis, not only did Jakarta have twenty-seven direct connections with other cities across the country, but Jayapura, Nabire, Surabaya, Denpasar, Makassar (Ujung Pandang), Ambon, Kupang, Balikpapan, Batam, and Medan had between ten and twenty direct connections with other cities in Indonesia (ABC. 1997).

At the same time sea transport has also improved markedly, facilitating a larger scale movement of people, including women. In the period 1991–95, the number of ship passengers travelling through the ports managed by the state-owned enterprises (SOEs) increased by an annual average of 18 per cent, while at the same time the passengers carried by ferry transport managed by SOEs increased by an average of 11 per cent. The lower end of the sea transport market has been served by pioneer shipping (*kapal perintis*) during the same period. In the inter-island sea transport, the passengers carried by the pioneer shipping increased by 20 per cent. This shows that the fastest growing segment of sea passenger demand is among those with lower purchasing power. The highest concentration of origin–destination (OD) sea passengers was in Java and Sumatra, whilst in East Nusa Tenggara, Kupang connections had an annual of less than 50,000 OD passengers (see Figure 2.4). So sea transport is my focus here because in Eastern Indonesia many women sojourn by ship and ferry as this is the cheapest means of travel.

Intra-regional communications within the province are conducted between the administrative *kabupaten*, which are mostly inherited from the colonial era. In the context of colonial rule in the first half of the twentieth century, East Nusa Tenggara was also known as the province of Lesser Sundas, including Timor. The divisions of Flores under colonial rule were headed by five Dutch controllers who governed through the nine rulers (*raja*) of Flores (Tule 2004, p. 33; see also Therik 1995, p. 19). Social relations within each division also contained hierarchical systems creating class boundaries, where the *raja*s (male) and their descendants had a symbolic sacred/highest position followed by other classes in the community. The five administrative divisions later became the basis of the contemporary regencies after Indonesian independence in 1945. In the recent years of the political reform era, decentralization has shifted power relations between the centre and the region, and new regencies have been created, including *kabupaten* Lembata in east Flores.

The constructions of social categories, hierarchies, and territories in relation to space emphasize the role of boundaries, often an abstract space. These boundaries are responsible for separating Self and Other (Newman and Paasi 1998). It is important therefore to situate the discussion not only within the historical and political economy of the women's travel, but also to critically locate the concept geographically (Mitchell 1997). In this book I explore and conceptualize some of these boundaries that women cross when they travel. I found in my own travels and in that of other women that the boundaries at a range of scales of space may be fluid and negotiable. One shifting boundary at a larger scale is evident in the inter-regional relations. The socio-spatial relations are specific responses to the interrelated changes in political and economic situations created by the 1997–98 crisis. These fluid relations provided the setting of my field research and this, in turn, impinged upon the way people felt about being interviewed. Some people's reluctance and anxi-

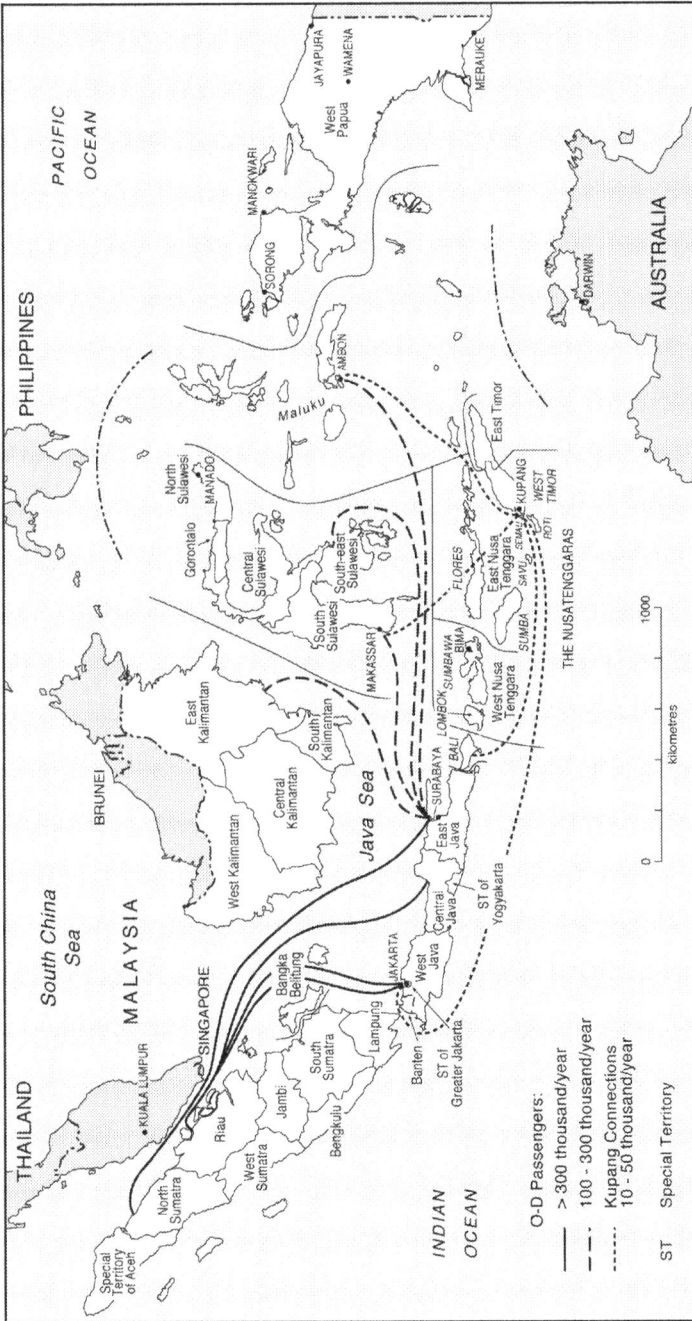

Figure 2.4: Passenger movement.

O-D Passengers:
— > 300 thousand/year
–·– 100 - 300 thousand/year
···· Kupang Connections
10 - 50 thousand/year

ST   Special Territory

Source: Calculated and mapped from Directorate General of Sea Transport (1996).

ety to be interviewed can be understood in terms of the bigger concerns they had with the uncertainties of the economic and political climates.

Fieldwork: sites of multiple journey and research practices

Within the uncertainty in the context of the political and economic crisis situation, my fieldwork, travel, and the women's travel changed as a result of unexpected circumstances. A political crisis emanating from the fall of Soeharto, resulting in social unrest in many parts of Indonesia including in Makassar and Surabaya, overlapped with my fieldwork. Between my reconnaissance trip in 1998 and the end of my fieldwork in 2000, I observed and experienced people's panics because of spiralling prices, tensions of party campaigns for presidency, and the exodus of people from East Timor following a civil war in relation to East Timor independence.

Encounters during my own travel fluctuated both in number and intensity. At times, events unfolded at a dizzying pace on the boats and in the field. From this I learned to be open, ready to adjust, to respond, and to embrace changes as my field research progressed. I began to take travel and its risks as they came, as is evident from the following story. When I did my preliminary research on media reports of women's travel by sea at the CSIS (Centre for Strategic and International Studies) library in Jakarta in 1998, I came across clippings of newspaper articles on a number of tragic sea accidents in Indonesia. Overcrowding/overloading of the PELNI (the state owned enterprise) ships is a safety hazard, leading to the sinking of ships with disastrous loss of life. Acting on advice from an experienced and caring anthropologist working in the region, on the earlier voyages I carried a newly bought life jacket with me. Later, however, I felt that overcoming a fear of drowning from shipwreck and taking the risks of travel, like many other women, was one way of being part of this space of great uncertainty. Moreover, the life jacket was itself impractical and bulky, and it marked me as "different" and privileged from other fellow travellers. So I left the life jacket behind. My sea travel provided a first-hand experience of the risks of travelling and also insights into other women's feelings including their fears.

The field

During the six months of intermittent fieldwork (1998–2000) I travelled extensively by ship, ferry, bus, other public transport, and on foot. I concentrated in three basic areas — parts of East Nusa Tenggara, Surabaya, and Makassar (Ujung Pandang). The choice of the two cities as spatial focus was based on the 1996 data on temporal (passengers) movement from the Indonesian Department of Transport surveys and permanent (migration) movement from the past census, which showed that Surabaya and Makassar were both important places of transit and destination for people from East Nusa Tenggara (Hugo, Hull, Hull, and Jones 1987; Hugo 1997).

In the field, twice I had to interrupt my field research because of personal security reasons (the university asked me to leave the field). I left Makassar when social unrest broke out, resulting in the burning down of churches, shops, and buildings including Wisma Kare near Hassanudin University, where I spent some time. Then, I flew out from Kupang on the island of Timor just in time to avoid militia activities, a few days after the East Timor independence ballot result was announced in September 1999. At this time everything associated with Australia was viewed unfavourably because of the Australian government's role in sending the peace-keeping forces to East Timor. That was also the time where I saw unusual flows of people, particularly displaced people from East Timor; however this was not the focus of my study.

In Flores, I visited *kabupaten* Ende and the surrounding villages of Nuobosi, Detusoko; Sikka and the surrounding Wolowaru, Maumere; *kabupaten* Flores Timur particularly in Larantuka; and the newly created *kabupaten* of Lembata. In Timor, I mainly stayed in Kupang and its surrounding areas. Local people were very wary of outsiders, suspecting them to be troublemakers (*provokator*) inciting religious and ethnic violence. Despite difficulties in engaging some women in the field because of the economic and political crisis, I was fortunate to be accepted readily in several women's networks. In addition to meeting my fellow travellers on the road, I started with one contact in each locality. I followed the leads which quickly branched to involve a larger number of women. The snowball sampling procedure gave me access further into the women's networks. In some cases I followed my main informants to their villages after meeting them in urban centres. The strategy of my travel as a dynamic and continuous field, constantly shifting from one place to another, required flexibility and resilience. As with any trip, I met some engaging women, only to say goodbye at the next port. The fieldwork alternated between sailing at sea and travelling on the road, to reach and dwell for a while in villages, small towns and cities.

In the women's homes in their villages, I observed and experienced the daily activities and concerns of the local women. These things I would not have encountered if I had simply stayed in urban centres — sites of their travel destinations. Homes and neutral places, such as on the ship, in a park and at a waterhole, were ideal settings for our chats and interviews. The other in-depth interviews were conducted at the more private settings of the informant's room or the room where I stayed.

However, in the port settings, interviews were not so easy because I was "out of place" – as a young middle-class woman. Such a woman would not usually wander alone at ports. Independent field research in ports, such as I did, is uncommon. Ports are out of bounds for a woman like me, except before boarding a ship. People stared at me, or worse still, port staff and the porters harassed me with their remarks, *"Mau kemana?"* they would say. This literally means, "where are you going?" But it most likely meant "what the hell are you doing here?" and often that was the tone of voice I heard.

Boundaries often became noticeable when I overstepped them. I shall never forget my sense of terror at overstepping an invisible boundary of male territory when I entered alone the Port of Perak (Surabaya). My "misfit" position, shown by my roaming around alone in the port without a legitimate reason (in their views) or a proper male escort. My presence for interviewing at the port was seen as an intrusion of the boundary of male territory. In ports, I had little success in conducting the interviews. Assumptions of a certain propriety in women's mobility prevented me from moving freely in port settings and thus hindered further progress of interactions. Many pairs of eyes belonging to men and passengers alike opened wide, following my every movement with bewilderment, pity or even confusion. Apart from the roles of a trader or a sex worker, there was not any "proper" role for such a woman traveller (without any luggage) that would fit me and therefore I was thought of as being lost. The second time around, I recruited a local male (university graduate student) to accompany me on my interviews in the port. After his first trip with me to Port of Perak, he resigned because he felt intimidated by the port's thugs. When I went back several times to Perak with a more "legitimate" reason to board the ship I did not arouse any suspicion.

Throughout the field research people often found my identities ambiguous. I am married but was frequently mistaken as a single woman because of my "carefree" travelling alone (*jalan sendiri*). I wore a simple wedding band on my finger signifying my marital status and to avoid any nuisance (not my real ring, as I was warned petty crime was on the increase because of the financial crisis). In the context of East Nusa Tenggara, it is rather unusual for a woman either single or married with no connections, to travel alone for such a long period of time on ships, bus, and other public transport. In the Indonesian context, it is strange to be a student and yet have the means to travel extensively, and this compounded local people's perplexity over my status and intention. My place of origin also caused confusion: I am an Indonesian but have lived, studied, and worked in Australia. The contacts I had at the official (national and regional) levels were from past association and work with Australian government projects. In this way, I was able to secure interviews with port authorities in East Java, South Sulawesi, Flores, and Timor.

In the subsequent formal visits to meet the port authorities, it was suggested that I would be escorted by a port official in uniform whilst doing my interviewing. Feeling grateful, I accepted the offer only to find that this strategy had its own problems. This way of surveying did not work out because people were reluctant to talk. People were apparently suspicious of everything formal and official in the then uncertain social and political climate. Under these conditions women refused requests for an interview or, at best, they were not willing to disclose information beyond basic matters relating to their current trips. They feared that the interviews might be used against them. Thus I was left to my own devices, meeting women in more natural ways as fellow travellers, or through introductions made by acquaintances. Box 2.1 contains an extract from my field notes illustrating some of the difficulties in the field.

Nevertheless I think that, because I am a woman (although I do not intend to essentialize my relationship with other women) I gained access to personal intimacy, and won the confidence of some women whom I interviewed. I introduced myself as a traveller and a student who was doing research on travellers. When I was in Surabaya and Makassar between 1998 and 2000, starting from one contact each, I was invited to social functions organized by the community of Flores–Sumba–Timor (Flobamora) and also attended their church services. Many of the women

Box 2.1: An encounter at Port Perak.

A woman over fifty years old travelled with nine members of the family, all women except two. The family were waiting for a PELNI "Pangrango" ship which would sail to Eastern Indonesia. They brought many bags, sacks and boxes containing clothes, personal effects and food, including rice. After explaining about my research project, I had a chat with her daughter and granddaughter about their upcoming trip. They agreed to pose for a photo and, as I was about to take a photograph of them, the old woman burst into her local dialect which I didn't understand but which was strong enough to stop me taking further action. In my confusion at the unexpected rebuke, I trembled and apologized profusely and assured her that I would not do anything without their consent. Apparently she was worried that I might be a journalist, who could use their photograph in the newspaper. The daughter, who seemed to understand the purpose of my interview, tried to calm her mother down in her dialect. She turned to me to apologize, saying her mother "did not understand the research," (*tidak paham penelitian*). She consoled me by opening her bag to offer me some biscuits to eat. From this encounter I learned two lessons. Firstly, as a woman I appeared as a misfit in such a location, someone who did not follow the assumed propriety of women's mobility. Secondly, people were obviously sensitive and cautious in the climate of uncertainty of the prevailing economic and political situation; they did not want anyone to take advantage of them.

Source: Fieldwork.

who belonged to this group worked in strongly female occupations, such as nursing and teaching. I was also privileged to be introduced to a Catholic nun, a matron of a hospital in Surabaya who in turn introduced me to many nurses from East Nusa Tenggara. In Makassar, I boarded with teachers who introduced me to others from the region. After several interactions and talk about travel, some women readily told their life histories, and this often included confiding their personal problems to me. Some even included me in their social networks and several times in family occasions or celebrations.

In this way, some informants became friends and invited me to come and stay at their houses. Despite usually having to cram into their already crowded houses, these stays offered me an opportunity to interact with the family and observe the household relations, providing a deeper understanding of the informants' domestic domains. In observing first-hand the dynamics of everyday lives and the family relationships, a window into the women's local relations was opened to me. I also stayed in several convents and presbyteries in Flores, being the largest Catholic missionary area in the past, the legacy of which can still be seen today. This included an interesting stay with some nuns, where I was allocated a patient room in a hospital in Lewoleba. I think, being on the road for a while, I was seen as a woman who needed to be cared for in a protected place. These stays provided different insights into both the women and the local communities. The contacts I had with the Society of Divine Words Missionary (SVD) and other Catholic religious orders quickly branched out to involve a larger number of women soon after I followed a few leads. The quality and propriety provided by the religious networks as the first contacts created trust and opened ways of engaging with the women.

The relations with my informants changed as my field research progressed. The first few moments of interaction with most of the women were inevitably rather formal, indicated by the way they addressed me as *ibu*, meaning mother, a rather conventional and respectful way of addressing a woman of some social status. However, some young women would then change my title into *kakak*, a more intimate term which literally means an older sister. This was an indication of acceptance into their circle. Some other (usually older women) would called me *nona*, a common address for a young single woman — even with my wedding band, my marital status was not always obvious, although *nona* is also used for a woman of Chinese descent in the local context. In such interactions, I was aware of the power relation between the researched and the researcher, and attempted to neutralize it. I quickly learnt that a camera, a tape recorder and papers were symbols of academia and thus of power, which might impede our natural communication. Our talks were often very personal. I opted to be flexible and, if need be, conducted the interviews in a less intrusive and informal way with semi-open-ended questions, without a questionnaire or tape recorder but only a small notepad to write down some important points. In the local setting of the women's home or parks or food stalls we connected comfortably using our common language, Bahasa Indonesia. In this study I provide my translation in the stories to ensure authenticity and a richer nuance. For example, the strong meaning of _langgar laut_ is sometimes lost in the translation. I use English spelling for provinces but keep the original Indonesian spellings for regencies (_kabupaten_), districts (_kecamatan_) and sub-districts (_kelurahan_).

In my research, ethical dilemmas of power relations encountered in doing feminist ethnographic research are embraced as challenges to constantly being aware of my interactions and relationships with my informants. In the field I was neither "an insider nor an outsider in any absolute sense, but rather an interlocutor" (Nast 1994, p. 60). I recognize the fact that my involvement and representation in this research has been based on privilege and hopefully also mutual concerns and trust (Kobayashi 1994, p. 74). My positionality as a researcher during the research process, as previously mentioned, and also in writing and representing the women's stories has been a dialogical process (England 1994). Constantly I ask myself how to incorporate their voices without reinforcing patterns of domination (England 1994, pp. 80–81). As illustrated before, my relationships with informants varied, some were intimate, others were reciprocal, some others were delicate or even difficult. An example of an incident as noted in my field notes (see Box 2.2) shows this delicate situation characterized with strong personal feelings.

I attempted to engage in inter-subjective dialogues in order to understand the women "in their own terms", allowing careful consideration of the consequences of our interactions (England 1994, p. 82). To preserve confidentiality, I use pseudonyms for personal names of informants throughout this text and when necessary I change the names of the location to avoid personal identification. In the book, images/photographs are presented mainly to show activities and locational contexts of stories, and I am aware that photographs have the potentials of both homoge-

Box 2.2: Problematizing a disclosure of intimate feelings.

The weight of reflexivity of writing up some of the ethnographic sketches of this study prompted a question on how much to reveal. I marvel how far my informants have shared the space of the intimate details of their private relationships through their stories. I found myself a little taken aback when they told me the private details of their lives and their intense emotions early in our encounter, particularly when I did not initiate that private line of conversation. Some of the informants disclosed information in much more personal detail than I had previously anticipated learning in such a short time. However I was aware that by doing ethnography, I was fully engaged in the women's lived experience and emotional feelings. I took on a role as a caring companion on the journey who was involved and interested in their personal affairs.

On reflection, this engagement may be due to an intricate combination of factors. Women may disclose personally sensitive information because they knew that I was a stranger, a travel companion only during the journey, whom they might never meet again. When the interviewer will remain a stranger in a one-off meeting with no possibilities of follow ups, the respondents are likely to open up in an in-depth disclosure (Brannen 1988). In that particular loose, transient and liminal space of travel we related with each other as companions. They also found it useful to borrow things from me, from thongs, medicines and magazines to a multi-purpose Swiss army-knife which I carried around with me everywhere. Throughout such constant interactions and many hours of conversations, an intimate familiarity with the other travellers inevitably developed.

Throughout the process of ethnography, I was aware of the unequal interaction with the informants, because at the end of the day I retained the power to walk away with the information. Reflexively, I pose questions as to how far it is ethically desirable to explore the intimate emotions of personal relationships as well as struggling with how much of the disclosure is an authentic private life. As Duncombe and Marsden (1996, p. 152) point out, the multi-layered relations of the stories that individuals tell about their intimate feelings raise problems for ethnographic research. One of the problems is how to decide which particular layer of the stories is genuinely of their concern or whether it is a superficial passing feeling only. My main problem is to find the connections of the multi-layered relations of the stories and to recognize which layer truly relates to the issues of travel that I am interested in.

Source: Fieldwork.

nizing a visual experience and also commodification of subjects. I take much care not to link a particular individual and an image describing individual story. Rather the images are a representation of their everyday life and environment. My involvement in both the daily routine and travel of the women through the technique of participant observation also implies a participatory approach to learning and research. The process of dwelling and travelling alongside those I studied necessitated a dialogue between us. In this way participant observation allows insights of inner concerns and rich textured of women's multi perspectives. The variety of these travellers and their different hidden feelings in their stories and purposes of travel are fully expanded in further chapters.

Travellers' profiles

A range of travellers' profiles with various reasons of movement reflects the variety of women's travel. The travellers I met included professionals, students, housewives, workers, and Catholic nuns. I interviewed forty-six women and surveyed another sixty-eight women who travelled by sea (see Figure 2.5). The difference between an interview and a survey for the purpose of this study is the time spent with an informant. A survey lasted not more than ten minutes, covering basic information including places of origin, destination, age, marital status, occupation, reason of travel, and whether a woman is travelling alone or with companions. On the other hand an in-depth interview involved many hours or days of interaction, covering wider and deeper relational aspects of their travel. The ethnographic material, including forty-six interviews, reflects my interest in how local culture, as a web of socially negotiated meanings, is embedded in women's mobility.

Out of the total 114 respondents who travelled by PELNI ships and ferries, seventy-nine were single women, mainly professionals and students, who were expected to have a higher mobility, compared with the remaining thirty-five, consisting of housewives and among whom eight were self-employed women. Almost one-third of the respondents were categorized as either self-employed or employed (see Table 2.2). The median age of the respondents was 27 years, pointing to the relatively higher mobility of the younger women and the significance of this particular stage of life cycle as single women. The maximum age of 60 years was that of a housewife, *ibu haji* from Ende (*ibu haji* refers to a woman who had made the Haj pilgrimage), whilst the youngest was a 15-year-

Figure 2.5: Spatial patterns of travel.

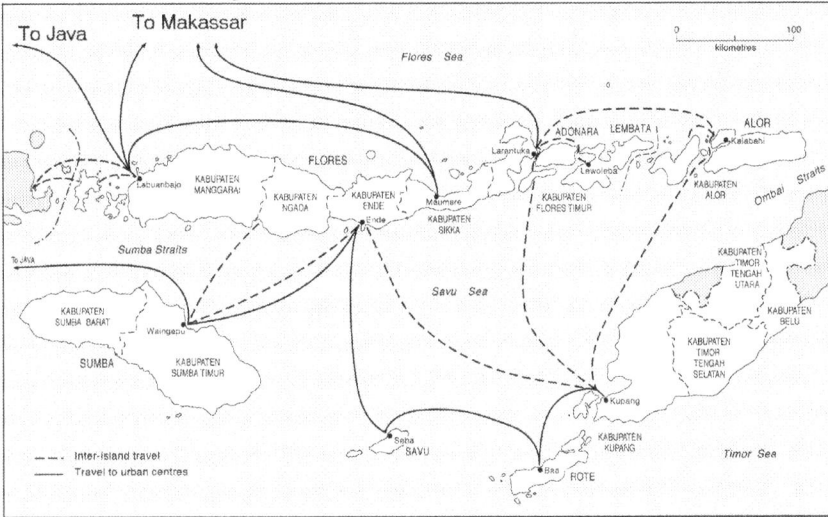

Source: Fieldwork and PELNI timetable.

old student. My observation shows that among women within a similar middle to lower income background, those who are single are relatively more mobile than others who are married with younger children. A married older woman, such as *ibu haji*, whose children have grown up, has a reduced load of childcare and housekeeping. She also enjoys fewer restrictions on her mobility, because her increased age may also allow increased ability to exert authority over kin (Dickerson-Putman and Brown 1998, p. xii).

My own travels for this research typically followed main routes based

Table 2.2: Women travellers by occupation.

Occupation	Total n	%	Travel in Cabin n	%	Travel Alone n	%
Self/Employed	33	29	1	6	25	37
Professional	29	25	10	56	19	28
Student	27	24	3	17	20	29
Housewife	25	22	4	22	4	6
Total	114	100	18	100	68	100

Source: Fieldwork.

on transport connections. Similarly, travellers of the region moved within three basic categories of destinations:

- local inter-island;

- Java and other urban centres; and

- overseas.

When I categorize the respondents by these basic patterns of travel, it reveals distinctive uses of the main routes with commonly related purposes of travel, which I refer to as dynamics of the route. I documented travellers' details using a database and this was further grouped by three travel destinations, occupations, status (married, single, widow) and style of travel (economy class or cabin/private berth; alone or accompanied). The analysis shows a connection between a woman's particular subject position with the kind of travel she undertakes. For example, professionals or financially independent women, comprising just over half of the women interviewed, were most likely to travel to urban centres. Housewives mainly travelled to visit relatives and friends on the inter-island routes. More recently, there has been an increasing number of women travelling overseas, either documented legally as domestic workers or as illegal construction or plantation labourers. I situate the individual travellers within their contexts of travel. Within this I group them in terms of distinctive dynamics of a particular route, which is related to the possibility of relations the route may generate (Tsing 1993, p. 48). In presenting the dynamic of routes, I select some dissimilar examples and anomalous stories of particular individuals. The atypical stories serve to highlight a range of mobilities and how they are grounded in materiality of localities, such as gendered and spatial organization of family and domestic life.

When asked about their reasons for travel, women gave a range of motives for their jorneys. These reasons varied from maintaining contact in the form of a mundane visit, to working, studying, or seeking a new experience and self actualization as expanded in Chapter 4. The women's travel destinations were often associated with particular motives. For example travel to urban centres was closely linked with the motive of seeking work and furthering education. Through in-depth interviews with the women I present dissimilar travel stories of teachers and nurses who had lived and worked in Surabaya and Makassar in Chapter 5. In

Flores, I interviewed returned travellers who worked as overseas domestic workers in Singapore and Hong Kong, whose stories are presented in Chapter 6. The returned migrants' stories reveal personal and metaphorical journeys, which are vividly captured by one informant, Netti, in a detailed sketch. This unusual personal cartography becomes the basic structure of the chapter. I excluded other groups of travellers such as traders and Catholic nuns, from my study, in order to limit my project and also because, separately, the smaller groups fell outside the themes that I was interested in. Although I also talked to more than 200 other people in the field to gain an understanding of their perspectives on local relations, this information is interwoven as supporting material to the stories. This information included that from state and regional government officers, academics, members of religious orders (Catholic nuns, priest, brothers), transport operators, ports authorities, ship crews, and of course members of families of travelling parties.

About half of the encounters with the respondents occurred at particular stages of their journey — on ship, in ports, and in transit. Chatting on roads and on ships came naturally, provided that my fellow travellers were in close proximity and did not get travel sickness. As a passenger on a voyage, I travelled up to four days at a stretch to spend time with other women on the same journey. While travelling and observing I gained insight into the multitude of spaces the women occupy and also the symbolic meanings of their travels by observing their mundane activities as they travelled. Not only did I investigate what the women said but also what they did (Herbert 2000) in order to understand meanings of the space of travel for these women.

Most respondents travelled in cramped lower decks because it was the cheapest and easiest way to travel. The deck/economy ticket is much easier to get than a cabin/class ticket. On any voyage on a PELNI ship, there is limited cabin space available, with only a small proportion occupied by women passengers. Out of the 114 respondents only eighteen women had ever travelled in cabins, with one girl travelling first class and seventeen others travelling in the second and third classes. The rest travelled in economy class. Personal/family income plays a role in travel, as the higher the income, the better the style of voyage. Women with stronger connections in social networks and a high-income background are most likely to travel in private cabins which afford them some privacy, security, and comfort. Moreover, the higher the ticket class on the ship, the harder it is to get a ticket because of reduced availability of the berths.

Also there is a quota for cabin space at each port, particularly in the cabins available for women. In PELNI ships, there was a strict division of cabin space based on gender. Unless one is married or a part of the family, mixed gender cabin occupancy is unavailable. Therefore it was not easy to obtain a cabin ticket for a woman because the PELNI office is then obliged to fill the rest of the space with same-gender passengers. I came across a woman who, after queueing for her cabin ticket (she obviously had the money), had to go to see the head of the ticket office to be interviewed by him to justify her travel in a private cabin. The woman was finally issued with a second-class ticket (in a four-berth cabin) after explaining that she had just had surgery and required a berth to rest on. More than half of the respondents travelling in the comfort of a private cabin were professional women, followed by almost a quarter who were housewives who travelled alone (see Table 2.2).

My own travel offered a space of new relations and a peculiar intimacy. This space of intimacy, being part of the ethical dilemma of a feminist ethnography, provides both a challenge as well as an opportunity. In one of my first voyages in Eastern Indonesia, I met a woman, Martha, who graciously shared her space with me on the deck of a very crowded ship. Not only did she literally give me a space on a wooden bench to sit on, but by readily sharing her stories, metaphorically she also created a critical space for me to start an ethnography of Eastern Indonesian women's travel. Martha's travel story, expanded on in Chapter 4, points to the significance of a notion of propriety in the context of travel. Her travel also fits at the theme of a space of liminality (from Latin *limen*, meaning a threshold). By permitting herself this ambiguous and unstable space (neither here nor there), where she could choose what she wanted to be, Martha enacted the phrase "to be oneself" (*menjadi diri sendiri*). This implied widening of roles and positions during and after Martha's *langgar laut*, or crossing the ocean. The significance of her travel was much more than simply a covering of a physical distance, it was a process of becoming.

A selected number of travel stories are presented on the basis of the three main themes alluded to in Martha's travel — propriety, liminality, and the widening of subject positions — which I analyse within the three travel routes. My writing, as previously mentioned, is framed in the non-essentialist position with very little ground for "cultural certainty and essential identity" (Tsing 1993, p. 225). Accordingly the lens of travel is used to make the diversity of women's experience visible.

CHAPTER 3

Situating Women and Their Travel

Women and travel within the literature

his chapter provides a context for discussion of women's travel by firstly identifying several strands of literature where issues of women and travel are discussed. The link between space, women's travel, and subjectivity is then explored. Secondly, I draw on social analysis and ethnographic work on localities in East Nusa Tenggara and also on collective thought in folk narratives to situate women and their travel within the local socio-cultural context. I am interested in the ways that culture, as a web of socially negotiated meanings, is embedded in a process of women's mobility. Mobility is a way in which women participate in the dynamic processes of reworking both the meanings of place and their own identities (Marcus and Fisher 1986; Silvey and Lawson 1999, pp. 124–125).

Current studies on travel and travellers extend to a wide range of spatial practices. Movements of people in diaspora, exile, transnational and inter- and intra-regional migrations, global tourism, and other flows have been classical research projects in geography. The spatial pattern associated with the social and cultural condition of post-modernity in which people depart from (a notion of) a place of origin, has become increasingly complex, thus harder to describe and analyse (Appadurai 1991; Siikala 2001, p. 1).

The vast amount of research on people's mobility reflects the significance of movements for existence. The rich migration literature encompasses a range of theoretical perspectives and scales of analysis. A systematic review of migration research produced by Silvey and Lawson (1999) shows a diversity of approaches within the migration field. Migration has been shown as a powerful force affecting identities in the context of societies such as Irish, Italian, Mexican, and Caribbean (Walter 1997; Grimes 1998; Webster 1998; Fortier 2000). This literature, located at the intersections of cross-cultural studies, diaspora studies, and gender studies, provides theoretical debates on identity in relation to space. A smaller but increasing number of more recent works on gender and contemporary migration, in which my work is positioned, pay attention to women's identities and subject positions (see, for example, Romero 1992; Constable 1997; Kofman and England 1997; Barbič and Miklavčič-Brezigar 1999; Cox 1999; Gamburd 2000; Parrenas 2001; Hondagneu-Sotelo 2001; Silvey 2000, 2001).

Migration research employing political and economic frames nevertheless dominates the work on people's mobility. The classical and enduring explanations of migration argued in the literature on mobility are framed by neoclassical economics and macro models of different stages of development (Lawson 1998, p. 41). These models are associated with push–pull factors of labour movement across regions, implying an unproblematic notion of place. As Silvey and Lawson (1999) argue, within this developmentalist perspective, migration is largely assumed to occur for economic reasons, reflecting a Western modernization trajectory. The narrow developmentalist focus and increasingly untenable assumption — that origins, destinations, and migrants themselves including their gender, race, and class are unproblematic parts of migration — leaves the other reasons for migration unquestioned (Silvey and Lawson 1999, pp. 122–123). Migration of women from rural to urban areas, in this narrow perspective, is a part of the problem of surplus labour in the rural agricultural sector and the growing demand for labour in industrial sectors in urban areas. Otherwise women relocate as a part of a broader family movement in search of better economic and social opportunities. This limited style of gender analysis has in effect marginalized women's mobility (Bilsborrow and United Nations Secretariat 1993).

In Indonesia, women's mobility in relation to social and economic changes "is complex and little understood" (Hugo 1997, p. 68). With some notable exceptions, such as migration studies by Robinson (1991, 2000*a*); Silvey (2000, 2001); and Wolf (1992), most research is concerned with the demography of women's migration or permanent movement, which is only the tip of the iceberg in the context of the total movement (Hugo 1997, p. 71). Very few studies have covered Indonesian women's travel and their ambivalent position in relation to space. Limited data in Indonesia inhibits study on other types of travel, leaving women's variety of travel as somewhat of a mystery. My concerns about women's identity in relation to changing space cut across a range of travels including migration.

Theoretically, a narrow focus on women's migration as part of a modernization trajectory limits the understanding of the potential multiplicity of identities of the women travelling. Using the dominant perspective the ways in which migrant subjects (and in a broader sense travellers) are conceptualized has remained unexamined (Silvey and Lawson 1999; Silvey 2001). In the context of Indonesia, women's agency in relation to mobility is under-theorized, as it is assumed to be a product of their structural class position and the forces of globalization, thus the women's voice, identity and meanings of mobility are commonly missing in migration research (Silvey and Lawson 1999, p. 126). Within the discipline of geography, Silvey (2000) was among the first to include women's agency in the research agenda on gender and mobility in Indonesia, incorporating not only determinants of structure in the historiography of locality but also individual action in a theorization of gender and mobility.

Feminist and cultural studies extend our knowledge of places and mobility by asking questions about the interpretations of places and how we might rethink the ideology of Self and Other (Bondi and Domosh 1998; Clifford 1988, 1997; Domosh 1991; Said 1979). These studies employ similar methods and data sources to Western historical geography, such as the examination of temporal practices of creating diaries, letters, books, music, documentaries, and various other cultural expressions to produce knowledge on and of mobility (Thrift 1993, p. 97). In geography, as in literary studies, much of the work on travel has been firmly established through analysis of textual materials, particularly analyses of travel writers of the past centuries who went to developing countries (see, for example, Barlow 1995; Bastin 1995; Blunt 1994*b*, 1999*a*, 1999*b*; Bondi and Domosh 1998; Frederick and McLeod 1993; Ghose 1998; Gullick 1995*b*; Morgan 1996). A substantial amount of work on women's travel writing has questioned the relationship between women and the private sphere along the public/private divide in the West (Mills 1991, p. 28). Much of this literature uses public/private divide and colonial/imperial discourse analysis. In this study, I analyse the experiences of contemporary women from Indonesia and write an ethnography of travel drawing on their own travel stories. My emphasis here is on the interconnections between women and the space of travel — the way women realign their identities and the fluidity of their relations with others while travelling

(McDowell 1999, p. 205) — which intersects with works on travel writing. My aim is to retrieve the voices of Eastern Indonesian women as they themselves articulate versions of their geographic imaginations (Kaplan 1996, p. 144).

Within the textual approach, studies on women's travel writing analyse links between gendered space and social relations through a representation of place or local ethnography. Feminist theorists have analysed the gendering of travel particularly in the context of colonialism (Blunt 1994*b*, 1999*a*, 1999*b*; Mills 1991; Pratt 1992). The documentation of women's travels in nineteenth century Southeast Asia has mostly been dominated by Western women's own accounts of their journeys (Gullick 1995*a*). The wider context of this travel was, for the most part, that of the colonial power managing the colonized. The reasons given for the women's travel included: accompanying their husbands and therefore supporting their careers; a religious mission; an escape from their area of origin, and the pleasure of discovering exotic places (Gullick 1995*a*). For example, Sophia Raffles travelled extensively in Southeast Asia (1817–1818) accompanying her famous husband, Thomas Stamford Raffles (Bastin 1995). Harriette McDougall's travel started in 1848 when she arrived in Sarawak with a religious mission (Saunders 1995), whereas Emily Inness came in 1875 as the wife of a colonial administrator (Gullick 1995*b*). Anna Leonowens became a teacher in the household of King Mongkut of Siam in 1862 (Smithies 1995). Anna Keith went to Java in 1882 to marry a naturalist, Henry Forbes and accompanied him, travelling by sea, around Indonesia and in particular Timor for one and half years (Barlow 1995; see also Gullick 1995*b*, p. vii). The range of such travels stays within the privilege associated with the social class and race of the women. More recently, studies of women's travel writing informed by feminist and post-colonial theories problematize the representation of place. Since travel is historically rooted in a distinctly masculine tradition of moving beyond home (Blunt 1994*b*, p. 18), women's independent travel is associated with transgressing boundaries of gendered spaces (Kaplan 1996).

Other interpretations of works of individual women travellers informed by recent feminist theory question the implicit assumptions of bounded space and woman's place at home (McDowell 1999, p. 206). These studies are mostly still based on the upper class Western women's experience, resulting in a gap in the literature where the travels of lower income women of colour might be represented. There were very few written accounts by Asian women travellers themselves in the last centuries (Gullick 1995*a*). The limited material concerning Thai women in the seventeenth-century Siam, for instance, mentions a woman trader, Oesoet Pegua, of Mon ethnic background, who became an intermediary between the Dutch company and the Siamese court (Andaya 2000, p. 21). She used her influence in both camps to negotiate lucrative international trading arrangements and became a successful trader by the early 1640s (Pombejra 2000, p. 202). Women's travel is thus still represented as a privilege of social class. Some analyses employing structural and post-structural frameworks, propose colonial relations as only a partial explanation of women's spatial movement. Such studies informed by feminist and post-colonial theories analyse textual material on women travellers of imperial times, paying attention to the ways space and subject are represented in the text (Mills 1991; Blunt 1994*b*) and are concerned with the relationship of space, gender and gendering of travel (Pile and Thrift 1995*b*), which is also my main line of reasoning.

The feminist geography literature offers some insights into understanding the complexities of women's travel in the form of women's ambivalent subject positions in relation to spatial movements (Blunt 1994*a*; Blunt 1994*b*). Feminist and post-colonial theorists problematize migrant identities and their ways of negotiating and inhabiting multiple subject positions (Kofman and England 1997). Within this wide range of approaches, recent works ascertain the importance of power relations in the constructed differences of gender, ethnicity, and class in shaping the experiences of women travellers. Critical ethnography on women's mobility has the theoretical potential to address the complex questions about women's identity and subjectivity in relation to multiple sites (Lawson 2000). Such work acknowledges that places are interpreted differently between gender, so decisions on mobility are also gendered (Lawson 2000; Silvey and Lawson 1999, p. 123). In this study I employ a critical ethnography of contemporary Eastern Indonesian women's travel to highlight the interplay of space, subjects, and subjectivities.

Taking into account subject and subjectivity

What happens when women step outside their home to travel, and thus encounter and engage with Others? The space of travel fits a notion of a liminal space that allows ambiguity and change. This transitory stage affords one leeway to transcend boundaries of spaces. In order to belong or to be included in a particular space with clear marked boundaries of norms of behaviour, an individual is compelled to stay within the boundaries. By contrast, conceptually, it is possible to stay on the temporal margin and to occupy ambivalent positions in the in-betweenness of spaces. The process of travel may be used as a liminal, in-between space with blurred norms, opening to contestation of relations between space and identities — hence the critical link between travel, liminal space, and going beyond boundaries.

The following classic story is about a woman who travels, crosses boundaries, and changes her position and identity in order to belong, as re-told by Pollock (1994, p. 70):

> ...a family driven by the terrible famine in their own land to seek food and survival in neighbouring country. A mother, her husband and their two sons travel around a land-locked sea to the mountainous regions they have watched from afar. Disaster, however soon befalls the family. The father dies. The two sons marry local women, going against the deeply held prohibition in their home culture to mingle with the women of their adopted land. They pay a price and die. The relics of this sad tale are thus the three women: a bereaved widow, and two childless daughters-in-law. The widow decides to go home and bids her two daughters-in-law to return to their own mothers, to their blood kin. Eventually after protest, one does. But the younger refuses to abandon her mother-in-law. She then says: "Do not urge me to leave you, to turn back and not to follow you. For wherever you go, I will go. Wherever you live, I will live. Your people shall be my people. Your God shall be my God. Where you die, I will die and there I will be buried."

This well-known story of Ruth and Naomi from the Book of Ruth (Christian Bible) illustrates a typical relationship between subject and subjectivity in connection to space. Ruth's changed relations accompanying her spatial movement from the country of her birth to the adopted country of Naomi's birth results in her shifting cultural identity (Pollock 1994, p. 71). This phenomenon of what happens to women's self-understanding when they move — women's subjectivity — and how women take on new subject positions following a spatial movement, is my interest. Women's travel, their related subjectivity and changing spaces in the context of a developing country have remained mostly unexamined, so it is here I hope to extend our understanding.

Exploring subject and subject position

I intend to examine women's experiences that reflect ways in which women as subjects understand their travel, paying attention to their experience as a repositioning of self (Pile and Thrift 1995*b*, pp. 20–21). Rather than objectify women, viewing them as migrants from peripheral areas and in terms of their social class position, I explore the ways women construct and re-construct their identities through the process of mobility (Silvey and Lawson 1999, p. 124) and their changing network of relations. The current research focusing on an analysis of women who move has shifted "from identifying the location on the continuum between structural and personal determination to looking at ways in which subjectivity is reproduced through time and space" in order to capture the fluidity, the ambivalence, the opacity and depth of the subject (Pile and Thrift 1995*b*, p. 5). Through the dualism — structure/agency — the body and the self in relation to structured determinations and meanings can be located, and frequent debates in feminist geography concern the ways in which gender, ethnicity, and class influence identity (Silvey and Lawson 1999, p. 125) and how to map these into the subject. The structure/agency dualism fails to interrogate everyday life as simultaneously real, imaginary, and symbolic (Thrift 1983, p. 1). This dualism has simultaneously characterized debates on the complication of mapping the subject, particularly on "the problem of subject formation in relation to, on one side, social rules, sanctions and prohibitions and, on the other side, the individual's feelings, thoughts and actions" (Pile and Thrift 1995*a*, p. 2). Recognizing such complication, I conceptualize a traveller as an agency constantly negotiating positions in the social structure to achieve personal goals:

> Through the processes of socialisation, the extent of physical environment, and so on, individuals draw upon social structure. But at each moment they do this they must also reconstitute that structure through the production or the reproduction of the condition of production and reproduction. They therefore have the possibility, as, in some sense, capable and knowing agents, of reconstituting or even transforming that structure. (Thrift 1983, p. 29)

I argue that moving physically in space provides subjects an opportunity to imaginatively redefine themselves into new and wider subject positions. Travel stimulates "the self-conscious recognition" of one's position and the potential to move beyond it (Blunt 1994*b*, p. 16). A woman at home who is a daughter, sister, aunt, niece, student, and family worker, may choose a new subject position as a professional, confidante, waged worker, colleague, fiancée, consumer or many other roles. The process of experiencing multiple spaces potentially affects women's subjectivity by moving through a range of relations, and I explore this at the level of everyday experience by attending to the specificity of the local relations and spaces of East Nusa Tenggara in the second half of this chapter. Particularly I pay attention to the naturalized space of women — home — and explore the gender division of space in the institutional structure of societies (McDowell 1999, p. 32). Women's space is socially constructed as a result of webs of power relations (Sarup 1994, p. 96). The local relations constitute women's gendered subjectivity at home, and uphold social wisdom that "clips their wings" (Lips 1994, p. 89). Women's travel then symbolizes a struggle for more power reflected in their decisions on mobility. Travel represents women's critical choice of space and time that drives them "to transgress society's 'naturalised' notions of gendered roles, identities and space" (Huang and Yeoh 1996, p. 107), which in turn affects women's subjectivity. Women have used travel as one of the regular practices of contestation of the meanings of space, where a social construction of space separates the space between women and men (Blunt and Rose 1994, p. 3).

The importance of gender, class, and race as determinants of women's mobility is shown by an expanding set of theoretical and empirical works on gender and mobility (see, for example, Pratt 1992; Yeoh and Huang 1999*a*). Women's physical movement opens new possibilities and represents a process of creating a space at the margin of their humdrum daily routines (Yeoh and Huang 1999*b*). The body of work on gender and migration, however, contains little information about contemporary Indonesian women's mobility, with the exception of some studies in the context of overseas and inter- and intra-provincial migration (see, for example, Heyzer and Wee 1994; Hugo 2000; Robinson 2000*a*; Silvey 2000, 2001; Wolf 1990).

This study of Eastern Indonesian women's travel can extend our understanding of the relationship between women, mobility and subjectivity. Part Two links women's travel to their notion of place and subjectivity, and I argue that women's travel as a production of the subjective space of power in the local context. The cultural meanings of space in everyday life reflect social relations in the islands, which are constantly negotiated through decisions on mobility. Women's travel thus embodies the dynamics of local culture and relations, in which there is no fixity of the notion of place, and thus travel may simultaneously represent transience, escape, and encounter (Clifford 1992, p. 105). This study focuses on subjects repositioning and negotiating the boundaries of marginality in relation to local practices and discourses with the emphasis on the constructions of gendered subjectivity in the analysis of travel (Blunt 1994*b*).

Harnessing travel

I have had to limit the materiality of travel in this study to allow me to focus on a certain range of travel practices among Eastern Indonesian women. Travel is not a static or constant action across time and space, but rather a fluid and dynamic concept, subject to continual change. The wide spectrum of the materiality of travel spans through "historical continuum from exploration to travel to tourism" (Blunt 1994*b*, p. 19). By exploring the specificities of Eastern Indonesian women's location and position, I am able to access some of their histories and identities, so theorizing these women's travel needs to be based on their spatialized histories (Kaplan 1996; Mohanty 1987).

In this context, I refer to women's travel as a spatial movement in a range of historical and geographical constructs, such as work migration, travel for education, travel for health services and for visiting friends and relatives (Rojek 1994; Frisby 1985). These type of travels, as will be shown, contain moods of "restlessness, circulation, fragmentation, and unfinished relations" (Baudelaire 1962) that raise issues of moving between social boundaries. In my field research, I have found that for Eastern Indonesian women, diverse travel practices are grounded in local everyday life and history, and are intertwined with competing discourses on women's identities and femininity.

Travel in a wider sense provides a link between the movement of the body and the dynamic relationship between subjectivity and space. The term and trope of travel in the literature is often associated with the "individualized often elite circumstances" of movement, particularly related to commercial and leisure activities in contemporary culture, despite the diverse modern experience of both the forced and voluntary flow of people (Kaplan 1996, p. 4). Yet only a small number of Eastern Indonesian women's travels fits this travel-for-leisure description. Thus more diverse articulations of third world women's travel and their politics of location are required (Mohanty 1987). Travel can perhaps be imagined as an axis staging various encounters and interactions, a temporal space offering an open process for alignment of identity (Kaplan 1996), and the space of travel is, like any space,

> constructed through sets of complex, intersecting social relation-
> ships that operate at a variety of levels and which are affected
> by beliefs and attitudes, images and symbols that are themselves
> increasingly variable and complex. (McDowell 1999, p. 30)

Travel, thus, is a constructed space and comprises a range of spatial practices offering a critical distance and a different perspective. The new perspective that arises from "the orientation and disorientation of travel relate[s] to both seeing and knowing" (Blunt 1994*b*, p. 17). Further,

> travel is bounded by points of departure and destination but in an
> arbitrary, retrospective way defined by perceptions of "home" that
> can themselves arise only with critical distance (ibid.).

The perceptions of home differ in the context of each culture as networks of socially negotiated meanings (Marcus and Fisher 1986). As a point of departure for the women, home, both physically and metaphorically, possesses rich and often contested meanings and influences on subjectivity. Discourses of home reflecting the nuanced arguments of home and the family have been well debated (hooks 1990; Sarup 1994; Minh-ha 1994; Webster 1998; Dwyer 1999; McDowell 1999). Home is theorized as a metaphysical location (Kaplan 1996) — a mixture site, not only of personal fulfilment, through relationships with the members of the family, but at times also a site of oppressive social relations and hard domestic labour for women (McDowell 1999, pp. 92–93).

Cultural and gendered meanings of home in association with women's mobility in some societies do not promote women's travel (Guest 1993). For instance, in North Tapanuli (Sumatra, Indonesia) and Peninsular Malaysia the local communities are reluctant to allow unattached women to move away from the protection of the family because their virtue needs to be preserved in order for them to play their future roles as wives and mothers (Bauer 1984; Khoo and Pirie 1984; Rodenburg 1997; Shah 1984). In contrast, young Malays and North Tapanuli men play an economic role and are therefore encouraged to *pergi merantau*, or to undertake a long journey in order to find better economic opportunities (Khoo and Pirie 1984; Rodenburg 1997). Although increasingly contested in many parts

of Indonesia, travel has traditionally been a man's discourse, whilst home
has been a woman's discourse.

Constructions of the gender division assign women's place to home.
Home in this sense emerges not only as a strongly gendered space, but
also as a constantly changing space constructed by specific power relations. Nevertheless, women's mobility is viewed differently depending on
their stage in the life cycle. This results in the age selectivity of women
on the move (Rodenburg 1997). Thus some groups of women can be,
and in some places are, perceived as out of place on the road outside
their home (McDowell 1999, p. 263). Notions of home are expanded by
black feminist scholars, including bell hooks who argues that home has
long been a site of resistance from the oppressive relations of the racist
society (hooks 1990, p. 42).

In contrast to the Western view, some other cultures recognize that
they can make places "travel" too (Strathern 1991, p. 117). In the Western view, people acquire identity from the places they are at: "Places
stay, persons move ... Classes are fixed, individuals mobile" (ibid.).
The alternative view is that people move together with notions of place
(Werbner 1999, p. 25), including notions of home. As I found in my field
research, people's notions of home change with their travel.

For Eastern Indonesians, women's travel may represent a reworking
of the notion of home. Home is closely linked to a house or dwelling which
serves as a basic unit of social organization, as for instance shown in a
representation of the house in Central Flores, where it is equivalent to the
identity of kin groups (Tule 2004; Howell 1995; Molnar 2000). It involves
a source of origin, such as in an ancestral house in Central Flores, which
is related to a family genealogy or source of blood (Tule 2004), and so a
home is strongly connected to both personal and collective identity. Thus
travel for many of my informants involves defamiliarization, a break, a
separation, and a critical distance from the familiar or domestic, and yet
simultaneously it becomes "the domestication of the unfamiliar" (Blunt
1994*b*, p. 17).

Spatiality and boundary

The spatiality of place or the ways East Nusa Tenggaran socially produced space/place can be explored by reviewing historical and socio-
cultural representations of place in the context of travel. As such it is

critical to emphasize how space is socially constructed and experienced. Claiming a space then involves drawing a boundary to exclude others. So how do women position themselves in the spatiality of space or play their politics of place? This interrelationship becomes the ethnographic frame within which my empirical study is nested. The field research itself reflected this frame, necessarily involving both observing context and experiencing everyday relations and also examining non-local forces that affect gender relations at various scales. I situate women travellers by layering ethnographic methods with the historical and cultural materiality that shapes their lives (Staeheli and Lawson 1994).

Consideration of multiple scales of power relations is critical to understand women's politics of place and in particular their politics of scale (Herod and Wright 2002). Through the practice of mobility women create their politics of scale. This means they not only cruise but most importantly also constitute social practices across spatial divides (Herod and Wright 2002, p. 11), whilst repositioning themselves in the network of relations. Geometries of power that constitute various forms of political, economic, and cultural relations, including the internal structure of domination and subordination, stretch out to women's lives through household, local community, state and globalization (Massey 1993). Women's various perspectives and practices of mobilities are potentially insightful for gaining an understanding of the politics of scale that are woven into their experience of place (Herod and Wright 2002, p. 13). So understanding a variety of women's travels requires problematizing and unpacking of different scales of relations beyond the mere physical movements.

As women attempt to reposition themselves in the power structure, the notion that travel provides in-between, liminal space to align their positions and identities raises interesting issues on boundaries and the associated inclusion/exclusion. Boundaries mark various relations at different scales. They are crucial in providing a sense of place and in establishing membership of a group. The politics of claiming to be "inside the boundary" often means the politics of claiming power (Massey and Jess 1995, pp. 116, 162). It is, therefore, useful to conceptualize women's mobility as creating an ambiguous in-between space with no clear boundaries, which is potentially quite liberating for the women. When fitted into women's experience of place, the notion of the in-between/liminal space in the context of gender mobility and subjectivity (Mitchell 1997) is helpful in illuminating the women's politics of place.

The experiences and metaphors of travel conveyed by my informants are mixed, but they vividly reflect a notion of negotiating cultural meanings or boundaries that are limited by gender. This position of limit corresponds with feminist and post-colonial critiques which suggest that:

> metaphors of travel are inseparable from those positions and constructions of marginality that give rise to the time-and place-specific subjectivity of the traveller. (Blunt 1994*b*, p. 19)

The constructions of marginality in relation to travel point to the underlying power structures that underpin identity. The idea of limits within the position of marginality at a specific time and place leads to the notion of boundary. At some level, somewhere, women travellers are in a liminal space, implying that they must negotiate varying degrees and types of difference, since they are neither included nor excluded in a particular socially constructed categorizing phenomenon (Newman and Paasi 1998; Tirtosudarmo 2002). A boundary then may be viewed as a contested cultural and symbolic manifestation of territoriality (Newman and Paasi 1998). Facing and negotiating differences in liminal space of travel opens up a mobile subjectivity.

Women who travel embody both:

> the self that moves physically...and the self that embarks on undetermined journeying practice, having constantly to negotiate between... a here, a there and an elsewhere. (Minh-ha 1994, p. 9)

Informants' travel stories, appearances and overt behaviours while travelling suggest these women are negotiating boundaries of positions of marginality. The social construction of boundaries is always an issue of power relations, whether one is being included or excluded:

> Places are made through power relations which construct the rules which define boundaries. These boundaries are both social and spatial — they define who belongs to a place and who may be excluded, as well as the location or site of the experience. (McDowell 1999, p. 4)

The local daily life of women provides rich data on the production of social boundaries. In the region, when women voyage they are not only physically crossing the open sea but they are also imaginatively negotiating and redefining boundaries or cultural meanings for themselves.

One of the implications of boundary is the exclusion of others from a socially constructed space or an Othering process. In considering the multiplicity of boundaries crossed or negotiated by women travellers, I start from the biophysical boundary. The Wallace line, which separates the east from the west of Indonesia, is the most obvious and yet taken-for-granted boundary based on the distinction between two different types of natural habitat (Chauvel 1996). The line becomes "a site of exceptional faunal disjunction", where crossing it to the west has traditionally implied going up and forwards through spatial hierarchy and time, to arrive at a more "sophisticated evolutionary stage of beings" (Instone 1999, p. 175). The Wallace line also represents a cultural boundary defining who belongs to the western part of Indonesia, the majority of whom are Javanese, and who does not, such as the Florense. Yet the line also marks further ethnic divisions, emphasizing the unstable socio-ethnic (*suku bangsa*) boundary.

An embodied ethnicity reflected in the physical characteristics of the eastern and western identification is a part of being on one or the other side of the line. Some of my informants would rather be identified with more power, as embodied in certain physical characteristics that are popularly stereotyped Javanese. In Java, some Eastern Indonesian women I know, paid hairdressers to straighten their curly hair. They conceded that straight hair and fairer skin, typical characteristics associated with the Javanese, were superior to the curly hair and dark skin characteristic of the Flores and Timor ethnic groups. Anthropologists who study these images and perceptions argue that this preference reflects the embodiment of ideology and a process of subjection. In some societies a pale complexion signified social standing. For example, in many parts of Asia women apply face powder and sometimes use caustic chemicals to achieve depigmentation to conform to local standards of beauty and purity (Nitchter and Nichter 1991). Some women from Flores with whom I talked, regarded their darker skin as not as attractive, as *jelek*, meaning bad. This embodiment of the idea of *jelek* indicates an internalized boundary of exclusion at the collective and personal bodily level. While originally a biological representation of place, the Wallace line, has evolved across time into a discourse or "social geometry of relation" (Instone 1999, p. 175) between the western and the eastern regions.

The local discourse on the relational identity to the centre (Java) hints at the same geometry of power and is also evident in oral folklore. The wealth of far-off Java as a source of economic inequality for the locals in East Nusa Tenggara is succinctly captured in the Central Flores legend *Ana Kola* (The Orphans), still told by elders in Lopijo in

Bajawa (Hamilton 1994, p. 108). This tale tells the story of a magic tree "where all manner of wealth grew from the branches". When an incident occurred with the orphans, the villagers chopped down the tree to get the wealth, but "the tree fell, [and] the tips of its branches reached all the way to Java. All the gold and other forms of wealth were lost to Java" (Hamilton 1994, p. 108). The significance of the threshold of sea that separates the two regions is also obvious, because it divides wealth from lack. The boundary separating Javanese from the non-Javanese reveals a geometry of power that operates at a larger, regional scale, and results in a feeling of being marginalized among the people, including my informants from East Nusa Tenggara.

The notion of crossing the exclusionary boundary of the sea is powerfully captured in the local term *langgar laut* (crossing the threshold of the ocean) as used by the women. The experience of an ocean crossing implies increased social and personal power at home, the place of departure. The women's travel stories as told in the following chapters suggest that the construction of space, with its often contested boundaries such as "Eastern Indonesia" that define the region, influences the way a subject located in the specificity of place interprets and experiences mobility.

The contemporary "Eastern Indonesia" boundaries shift according to the discourse, practices, and policies of the government of the day. Nevertheless these boundaries are significant as sites of production of categories, orders and meanings. The state discourse defines the region as physically consisting of a collection of provinces in the eastern part of the country. In one definition Kawasan Timur Indonesia (KTI), or the eastern region, comprises thirteen provinces (in Kalimantan, Sulawesi, the Nusa Tenggaras, Maluku and West Papua, also known as Irian Jaya). Other determinants of boundary are used to define eastern Indonesia, each with their own contexts, purposes and meanings, such as Indonesia Bagian Timur (IBT) (Indonesian eastern region), which was first coined in 1980 in East Nusa Tenggara and gained currency when President Soeharto later used it (Chauvel 1996, p. 63). Other influential socio-economic eastern Indonesia boundaries (Indonesia Timur) are used by the National Development Planning Agency BAPPENAS and other state institutions such as the Central Bureau of Statistics and the Department of Transport and Communications. These classifications of the eastern provinces comprise different combinations of areas. Notably, East Nusa Tenggara, which is the setting of my ethnographic work, is featured prominently within all these sets of Eastern Indonesian boundaries. This regional identity of East Nusa Tenggara as a part of the "lagging regions" has become naturalized in government policies, statistics, transport connections and other everyday practices. The region in this way is conceptualized as an explicit tool of governance of an area with a "problem", emphasizing the identification of abnormality or lack in the particular space that is the object of governance (Gibson 2001). Thus the collective identification of East Nusa Tenggara as a "lacking" identity has been internalized by many of my informants. The state's influence in homogenizing and creating normalized values and ideas was a political strategy. The New Order regime had expanded the state apparatus and ideological education of Pancasila (five prime principles), which is the "sole basis of Indonesian national identity", emphasizing order (Berger 2001, p. 202). These state political strategies are characterized by imposing conformity across regions and people, adopting Pancasila as a source of moral code and marking its power and influences in many areas of life. Such strategies often have moral form and contain conceptions of the authority at the time (Rose 1999, p. 26).

Since the 1950s the state's efforts to strengthen the centre's hold on control of the archipelago have resulted in the extension and consolidation of state power. Within this context, the eastern region has been viewed, in the widest sense, as posing social as well as major economic developmental challenges. This is evident from the practices and special policies enacted by the central state to "correct" imbalances in Eastern Indonesia. For example, in the 1990 presidential budget speech, President Soeharto formalized the intention to assist Eastern Indonesia's poor communications and "isolated communities" (Chauvel 1996, pp. 61–62).

The discourses of "differences" across boundaries between the regions has also materialized in debates about economic growth. The state has viewed the socio-economic diversity in Indonesia as a threat to national security, so minimizing imbalances and differences is also a political strategy in governmentality to avoid regional separatism (Chauvel 1996). For example the Broad Outline of State Policy (GBHN) has been the source of government policies and practices. By 1975, the New Order regime's priority had become overwhelmingly economic (Berger 2001, p. 202). In this regard, economic indicators show that East Nusa Tenggara is the poorest province in the country. The province has limited natural resources, slower economic growth, and is located away from the major commercial centres, with the gross regional product (income) per capita

being less than 40 per cent of the national average (excluding income
from oil) (Hill 1996, p. 226). Thus the economic boundaries of Eastern
Indonesia are characterized with explicit terms and attributes of being
tertinggal or backward (Barlow, Gondowarsito, Birowo, and Jayasuriya
1990, p. 5; Barlow and Hardjono 1996; Chauvel 1996; Hill 1989; Sayogyo
1994).

By extension, the spatial strategy of Wawasan Nusantara, a discourse
of national integration for political and strategic security control, has
privileged transport infrastructure development as a high national priority goal (Departemen Perhubungan 1996). At the same time, the distance
away from the centre of power is enacted in other policies and practices.
As the least connected region in terms of its transport links with the rest
of the country (Rutz 1976; Williams 1999), Eastern Indonesia's isolation
is materialized through the state discourse and vocabulary of the policy
of the National Transport System (Sistem Transportasi Nasional):

> ...the function of the National Transport System is to provide ef-
> fective transport to open isolated regions, to serve remote areas
> and islands, to accelerate the growth of *backward* regions and *lag-*
> *ging* villages, particularly in Eastern Indonesia... (Departemen Per-
> hubungan 1996, p. 10) (my translation and emphasize)

The vocabulary of "isolated, remote, and backward" permeates official
attitudes towards Eastern Indonesia, legitimizing its regional identity as
marginalized and on the periphery. Once again, the geometry of power
between the centre and the region reflects the regional subjection, which
is mutually reconstituted with interactions. Until the fall of Soeharto,
there had been very few serious public debates in Indonesia concerning
relations among regions and between regions and the state. The political transformation following the collapse of the New Order regime has
provided a space for public debates in the context of decentralization,
resulting in pressures for political and administrative reforms of the relations between the state/centre and the regions and wider opportunity for
East Nusa Tenggara. Yet many of my informants still seem to internalize
this regional boundary of marginality.

In contrast to these externally imposed social categories or boundaries, there are indigenous boundaries reflecting other realities of local
people's lives. For instance, in Kéo, Central Flores, people's attachment
to land has been crucial in their everyday social, cultural, and economic
practices. This relationship with the land is an important source of a

social and cultural boundary between "the children of the land" (*ana tana*) and "new comers/migrants" (*ata demba mai*) (Tule 2004, p. 30). The children of the land, following this category, become groups with a centre of power which then develops into clan identity with certain privileges. Thus, the migrants form the groups with lagging power, which is linked to lack of knowledge of places and intimate relation to the land (Tule 2004, p. 30). There are other similar boundaries within East Nusa Tenggara, but this example indicates how a different reality can exist alongside the main discourse of being a "lagging" region and having an identity of "lacking" development or appropriate social and cultural attributes.

Mapping women in travel involves describing the ways women negotiate a range of boundaries, including hierarchies and categories. Recently, post-colonial and feminist theorists have placed emphasis on travellers as gendered subjects in research incorporating power relations resulting from the intersections of the class, race, ethnic, and gender dimension of their identities (Blunt and Rose 1994; Blunt 1994*b*; Mills 1991; Morin 1999). Here, I particularly emphasize the importance of gender in shaping women's mobility patterns and experience, as suggested by Silvey and Lawson (1999, p. 127).

Travel as part of women's relation to space in the local context is a structured cultural form. Space, spatial orientation, spatial order, and direction categories are embedded in social and cosmological aspects of societies, containing both material and symbolic meanings (Forth 1991*b*, p. 138). For instance, the cosmological references to the spatial orientation of the sun, the land and directions such as seaward, the rivers and other topographical features of the locations are common references among various societies in Eastern Indonesia (Kedang, Timor, Roti, Nage and others, see Tule 2004, pp. 95–96; for detailed discussions of various localities, see also Barnes 1974, pp. 78–88; Cunningham 1964, p. 36; Forth 1991*a*; Fox 1997; Hamilton 1994). In local East Nusa Tenggaran cultures, the people, land, sea, ancestral spirits and the universe are closely linked in space, embodying a process and a desire to live harmoniously with the macrocosmos. For example in West Timor, McWilliam (1997) points out a continuum in cultural conventions for mapping both the body and the landscape, a convention where "body symbolism is used for compass direction" and the directional references represent a cognitive map where:

people situate themselves in the land, accord significance to places
in that landscape, and affiliate themselves within complex social
and political networks across territory.(p. 103)

This example shows how bodies, minds and spirits, communities, land,
landscape, and ancestral spirits are intimately linked and constitute space
in East Nusa Tenggara. Enacting harmony for an Eastern Indonesian
implies a mixing of belief systems, that is monotheistic religion with
local beliefs and culture. In this way the divinity, the land and ancestral
spirits are and remain directly connected with the people (Fernandez
1990; Tule 2004).

Within this framework, a range of boundaries positioning women in
social relations may be understood in terms of the socio-spatial organization. As Bubandt (1997, p. 132) suggests in his study of the Buli people
of Halmahera in northeast Indonesia, conventions for space "function to
posit both individual subjectivity and cultural identity" of the people.
More recent ethnographic works on Eastern Indonesia provide detailed
analyses of the diverse cultures of the people (Aoki 1997; Barnes 1974;
Forth 1981, 1991*a*, 1991*b*, 1998; Fox 1980; 1997; 1999; Graham 1991;
Lewis 1988; Tule 2004), and extend knowledge of spatial conventions
that help in situating women in local social relations.

Bodies, in the local context, are always moving but increasingly looking to be harmonized, both internally and externally, with other entities
in space, including the community and the ancestral spirits. Boundaries
in this way are imagined and relative. Spatial markers are relative, as
Bubandt (1997, p. 136) explains, "as one's position in space moves, so too
do the possibilities for assigning features in the landscape to act as reference points." A person is situated relative to others and other realms
and things, which are always changing. In travel, a woman's position
in space moves, so while the movement disrupts one level of harmony
in her household and kin relations, it may also be a journey creating
new reference points for wider connections, producing a different kind of
balance.

In the eastern Kéo and Ende areas of Central Flores, the notion of
space is expressed in the relative opposition of landward–seaward, upper–
below, above–beneath, and sunrise–sunset, which do not necessarily coin-
cide with the compass/physical orientation of the location. For instance,
places far across the sea are referred to as *dau* or *rhau* meaning seaward,
which is generally referred to as south but which however can be located
in any direction (Tule 2004, p. 96). The Kéo women travelling to Java,

for instance, often say *dau demma*, or "go south", but in effect they go towards the west. There are many other ways of referring to a person's physical location and orientations in space. In Eastern Indonesia, women's travel contains tensions and contradictions as bodies and selves move in space searching for harmony in their cosmological connections. Simultaneously, their travels may be associated with creating a space, crossing scales of power relations, or disrupting a boundary at another level, such as one established within family and kin groups.

At one particular scale of relations Tule (2004) points out that the geographical imagination of boundaries refers to belonging to different social and political alliances. People from a particular social group create alliances to strengthen their positions in social relations. The hierarchical boundaries of a class system in stratified communities are demonstrated by the upper/important lineages maintaining special houses which serve as ceremonial places. The position of this physical "source house" in Kéo (*sa'o pu'u*) or "large house" (*sa'o mére*) reflects the importance of the lineage head, which is transmitted patrilineally, and thus implies the stronger power of a male sibling as hamlet leader "to face the dark and evil spirits" (deJong 2000, p. 267; Tule 2004). Boundaries of alliance, which are marked by their belonging to the "source house", are inscribed and enforced to enhance a group's power in local relations.

The notion of occupying a space refers to both physical and social location, therefore a house location in the hamlet, for instance, represents a significant social marking of individual or group identity (Tule 2004, p. 105). Descent categories (*suku*) determine different class memberships in the community usually automated by birth (deJong 2000, p. 267). To go beyond the boundary of class is possible by upward social mobility, such as achieving a significant economic success or marrying a person of a high social status. Hamlet leaders, commoners, and the lower class live together in the village "within the clan framework, bound together by mutual obligation" (Hamilton 1994, p. 28). Physical houses in the spatial organization of the village become symbolic of people's location in the local social organization. Particularly for women, their designated space in the house provides cues to their location in their social relations, revealing that gendered spaces are constructed through hierarchical boundaries created not just by gender but also by class, descent, and ethnicity.

The gendered space of Central Flores is illuminated by the spatial microcosmos of the home, where a socio-spatial boundary is exposed in "dual-division of house parts", implying "the precedence of male over female ... and male jobs over female jobs" (Tule 2004, p. 129). The home, like other parts of life, is saturated with the beliefs and influences of maintaining harmonious arrangements with the macrocosmos (Fernandez 1990; Lubis 1987, p. 32), thus members of the family are obliged to accept the cultural gender precedence. There is a designated male area in the house, associated with important activities such as receiving honourable guests, while a female area is associated with mundane activities such as weaving baskets and food preparation (Tule 2004, p. 130).

These negotiated meanings of the gendered space of Central Flores leads me to the notion of boundary as offered by Ong and Peletz (1995), which includes boundaries as constructions of propriety and maintenance of space where restriction and exclusion are imposed and reproduced in everyday practices. Boundaries represent inscriptions of power through various ways by which the society maps rules onto bodies (Ong and Peletz 1995, p. 6). Discursive constructions of bodies plot different categories of women in certain bounded spaces as a way of maintaining social hierarchy. In this way, women's bodies "straying across borders" are constructed as going against propriety or being "deviant" (Ong and Peletz 1995, p. 6; Stallybrass and White 1986, p. 10). Women's bodies moving in travel — that shift positions in social relations and cross boundaries — thus represent "ideological images of transgression and deviance" (Ong and Peletz 1995, p. 6).

In my field research in many parts of Flores, I observed clearly gendered boundaries in the spaces of homes and in the divisions of labour in the household. For instance, women did the cooking, weaving, taking care of children, fetching water, and other women's task; while men did tasks, such as working on the land, constructing houses, tapping the palm wines, and performing traditional rituals. Men are head of the household as institutionalized in *adat* (customary law) through the kinship system. They are able to control the labour of women and children both in the spaces of homes and in public. *Adat* governs the rights and duties in family affairs, as deJong's study of Nggela in Ende shows, where "wives hold power inside the household, the husbands outside the household" (deJong 2000, p. 266). Women have some designated space at and around the home, as confirmed by other ethnographic works on Flores (see, for example, Forth 1981, 1991b, 1998; Tule 2004; Vatter 1932) where women's ventures beyond the household context are viewed with suspicion. The increasing presence of women in the public space — just as Bondi and Domosh (1998, p. 270) suggest in their study on Victorian women in

Western cities in the late 1800s — creates a social anxiety because it evokes a feeling in the observer of "women going against propriety and transgressing the boundaries that define the centre".

Space to manoeuvre: between notions and practices of femininity

The increasing presence of working women outside the home in Indonesia in public space is an aspect of the development of the labour market. In East Nusa Tenggara, more than half of the numbers of women of the total working age population were recorded as working or looking for work in the 2000 Census. The significant increase in employment opportunities in formal sectors such as health and education in urban areas has attracted women's participation. These jobs provide a justification for travel and, as I show in Chapter 5, also create a space for women to manoeuvre within the notions and conventions of gendered behaviour in their home villages. This economic shift neccessarily involving travel, has created new spaces in which women experiment with different practices of femininity within the prevailing notions of propriety.

The influence of the state ideology on women's social function has been pervasive (Raharjo 1997; Suryakusuma 1996). The gender ideology of the New Order regime constituted and reconstituted prescriptions and prohibitions concerning the family and women in particular (Koning, Nolten, Rodenburg, and Saptari 2000, p. xii). The emphasis of the state's discourse was on the homogenizing of women's identities, which suppressed differences and hid the ways gender intersects with other axes of power, such as class and spiritual potency (Robinson 2000*b*, p. 146; Robinson and Bessel 2002, p. 8; see also Stoler 1977; and Errington 1990). Women's *peran ganda*, or dual roles, both as waged workers and, most importantly, as family carers and educators, was used as a model of femininity. The emphasis on women's domestic activities officially puts the burden of household responsibilities for caring for the family on women (Aripurnami 2000, p. 59; *Suara Pembaruan* (Indonesian daily newspaper) 1999).

It follows, then, that a woman's role in contemporary Indonesia is formally that of a nurturer, preserving and continuing cultural values, in line with the GBHN on women's primary role (Aripurnami 2000, p. 58; Raharjo 1997, p. 168). Later, this role has expanded to include an economic role to support the family (Robinson 2000*b*). The strong influence of state discourse on women's roles has created a notion of femininity which has firmly grounded women in the home. This discourse has also emphasized a narrow range of "feminine jobs" as appropriate, despite women's increased access to a variety of education and to vocational and professional training. In turn, the gendered space of the labour market reproduces and naturalizes the feminine jobs.

Thus two major forces intertwine and influence women's choices in life. The discourse of the state ideology of femininity as exemplified in the notion of the "state *Ibu*-ism", as "procreators of the nation, as mothers and educators of children" (Suryakusuma 1996, p. 101) is accompanied by a discourse of traditional culture as encapsulated in kinship-based institutions (Koning, Nolten, Rodenburg, and Saptari 2000, p. xii). These discourses mutually constitute "propriety" for a woman. Propriety entails remaining within circumscribed boundaries or prescribed limits for behaviour. As a result, these limits that defined propriety circumscribe women's spatial mobility.

The local tradition expects that a woman carries out her roles and duties with love and devotion. Particularly for Lio (Flores) women, the self-sacrifice model is magnified in the legend of the Rice Maiden (*Ine Mbu*) who is physically prepared to die for the benefit of others. The legend tells that she is afterwards transformed into food for the advantage of her people (Orinbao 1992*b*, p. 98). Indeed this self-sacrificing image is expected and naturalized in women's everyday domestic tasks around the home. Such tasks, mobility patterns and behaviours are reinforced by the fear of public disapproval that would result from transgressing the circumscribed gender boundaries.

The local notion of propriety requires a woman to seek the consent of the male head of the household to travel beyond any everyday business requirements. In spite of increasing female mobility to urban areas to study and work, travel is quietly regulated and decided on by people other than the women themselves. A male head of kin continues to exercise authority regarding women's mobility, as shown later in the case studies. Wolf's study on decision making in Java suggests that the decision makers in the family reveal their powerful position in the kin hierarchy (1990, p. 61). In many parts of Flores, the male head of the household takes on the role as decision maker for the rest of the family.

Many of these family decisions are about spaces and places women can occupy and when. Thus fathers, brothers, and uncles in Flores are traditionally able to contain the mobility of their female kin, keeping women within the particular boundaries they have determined. For example, in Ende a simple leisurely stroll to a movie after dusk for a woman is considered improper. In Indonesian terms, a woman on an errand alone at night is known as *kupu-kupu malam*, which literally means "a night butterfly", a term for a sex worker. One of my informants explained her reluctance to offend her father by going out at night because this would transgress the boundaries delimiting "a good woman". Such control over daughters' movement is a way to rule women's body and sexuality and is commonly found in other places in Indonesia.

> Fathers and brothers protect and do their best to control a young woman's sexuality until she marries; at that time, her husband becomes her guardian. A young woman must, in the end adhere to a father's or older brother's decisions. (Wolf 1992, p. 61)

A woman's sexuality, reputation and her marriage prospects are the business of her kin. In East Nusa Tenggara, as in Java, there is a stigma attached to a woman who remains single. Women have little choice about whether they want to marry or remain single (Wolf 1992, p. 61; Koning 2000, p. 194). The failure of parents to marry off their daughter can imply that she has committed "an impropriety" (*kelakuannya tidak baik*) (Koning 2000, p. 194). Except if a woman becomes a Catholic nun, requiring a single status and celibacy, she is expected to marry. In Sikka, Flores, a single woman's life is considered unfulfilled and incomplete unless she marries (Fernandez 1990, p. 215). Any impropriety or transgression committed by a young woman reflects badly on the father as her guardian, so fathers take control over daughters' mobility.

Travel in the context of contributing to the family income does fit with the local notion of femininity. In effect, it also serves to loosen the grip of male kin's control over women's sexuality, and many women from East Nusa Tenggara travel to work in the urban sectors. Women frame their travel around the need to feed and educate the family, which fits with the expected femininity. Particularly in the period following the 1997 financial crisis, women's paid jobs allowed them to contribute significantly to easing the problems of decreasing real household income because of the general price hikes. Women are now more likely to exploit opportunities to work including in poorly paid jobs or in work which may involve travel, and have the opportunity to widen their subject positions away from home.

Women at home

Domestic symbols: water, firewood and looms

For women, crossing the ocean(*langgar laut*) contains a strong image of leaving the security of the familiar home, and central to understanding women's interpretation and sense of place is that of the spaces of homes as a place of departure. Indeed their understanding of home often emerged because of the distance from it. Women's everyday practices at home as structured by notions of femininity include rituals of marriage and its institution which illuminate their sense of place and relations. Some of the tensions arising from my informants' mobility, for instance, are connected to their social instinct to remain within the gendered spaces.

The following analysis of domestic life concerns women from rural and semi-rural areas in three of the five poorest regencies (*kabupaten*), namely Flores Timur, Sikka, and Ende. The commonalities in the women's socio-economic backgrounds and their similar socialization in the local gendered space meant that there were few variations in their daily practices/routines and chores.

The strongly gendered division of labour at the household and community levels is exemplified in the women's daily experience, as a mother, a wife, a daughter, a sister, and a member of the clan/community, and only secondly as a worker and income earner. These primary and secondary roles materialize in women's domestic tasks, with small variations among localities. Typically, women, with the rest of the family, are involved in subsistence farming and dry land planting of corn, and cassava, but also more recently in cultivating cash crops such as coconut, candle nut, chocolate, cashew nut, and coffee.

The women's subsistence activities are affected by the system of agricultural land ownership in Flores. Land is distributed in small parcels between a half hectare to two hectares, representing nearly 60 per cent of the assets of households. In the *kabupaten* of Ende more than 21 per cent of the households had no land or less than a half hectare of land to work on. Sitorus and Weka (1994) report that many households in Ende consume their own produce, mainly cassava followed by corn and, occasionally, rice. In my field observations during the monetary crisis, in semi-rural areas I found people mixed rice and thinly grated cassava as their daily staple.

Families often find that their garden has not provided enough subsistence food and that they need an additional income. To supplement household income women are often involved in micro-enterprises such as manual processing of coconut oil and, most importantly, textile weaving using hand looms (deJong 2000; Sitorus and Weka 1994, p. 43). The community and everyday life are regulated around clan obligations and rituals, showing distinct gendered activities which have changed very little since Vatter (1932) noted:

> At noon when most men work in the field or hunt, the women and girls are busy in the village. They work and do various tasks in front of the houses. When there is a special task to do, they work together on the wooden bench inside or outside the house. All the female tasks have something to do with the household and kitchen: to fetch water, to prepare the food such as to take off corn from the cobs, to pound and clean the rice and finally to cook. The women cook in a particular place in the house. On top of that, women also weave baskets, spin and dye the cotton and weave using a hand loom. (p. 65) (my translation)

The women's pattern of movement is, therefore, mostly related to their domestic roles in the household. In my field research I found women of Kedang (Lembata Island) spent a significant time walking a considerable distance twice daily to fetch water from springs. I also observed the labour-intensive activities of preparing food for the family, lighting the fire first thing in the morning using firewood, and manually pounding a few corn kernels at a time for corn flakes *(jagung titi)*. Then I was impressed by women's long hours and hard physical labour in producing elaborate hand loom textiles. Three strong material symbols — water, firewood and looms — stand out among others to represent femininity in which women's tasks are reproduced and naturalized in their domestic activities. These activities are tightly governed by notions of propriety for women in their gendered spaces of family and kinship system. Water and firewood signify women's work to provide food and other services for household reproduction, whilst the loom signifies women's role within the clan or community in upholding obligations to *adat* (customary law). Hand-woven textiles, *tenun ikat*, involve a very labour-intensive process with the finest products used mainly for ceremonial purposes. *Tenun ikat* incorporates elements that can be viewed as both domestic and market oriented, and thus represents women's activities both in private and public space. This textile plays a significant and somewhat ambiguous role in both ritual and everyday life (Cooper 1994, p. 72).

The prevalence of subsistence farming in the region also requires rural women to work outside the home. Women work the land with other family members, doing female jobs such as planting, weeding, and harvesting. At harvest time they carry the excess produce of the garden to sell at the market. Women go to local markets using public transport or else walk with baskets of fruits and vegetables on their heads to the nearest market to sell their goods to supplement the household income. This pattern of movement is connected to their care for the family so it falls within the boundary of local notions of propriety.

Figure 3.1: Hand weaving.

Women are responsible for keeping a supply of water in the house, thus fetching water from springs, rivers, or community wells is a part of their daily movement. In 2000, the majority of households in East Nusa Tenggara (82 per cent) had no access to piped water or pumps. Most rely on spring, river, and rain water as their source of drinking water. So women walk to collect drinking water either first thing at dusk or after bathing in the community spring at dawn.

Scarcity heightens the significance of water in people's lives, and is reflected by the many places whose names are related to water (McWilliam 1997, p. 104). The preoccupation by water for example in the local (West Timor) Meto language many places have the affix "oe" meaning water such as *Oe Ekam* or Pandanus Water; *Oe Nunuh* or Banyan Water; *Oe Aiyo* or Casuarina Water (ibid.). Women's instrumental role in bringing water, as I observed in Lembata island, fits the earlier description of Vatter (1932) of the scarcity of water in his ethnography of the island:

> The closest water spring in Leloba is an hour walking towards the ocean. Women and young girls go to fetch water by carrying it in a marrow container on their heads twice daily (early at dawn and at dusk). They walk through a narrow rocky path to the beach [where the spring is]. In the dry season, water is very scarce and therefore so precious. It is understandable that water is used only for drinking and cooking and not for profane activities such as to wash oneself. Women and girls have a bath in the spring or at the beach in the ocean. Men do the same, they usually have a bath before going home from work in the garden. However for the

children, particularly the really young ones, they may not touch any drop of water for weeks so they are very dirty. If rain falls, they stand under the gutter below the roof of the house and clean themselves. (p.47) (my translation)

Clearly, women's domestic work is naturalized in the everyday routine of local gendered space. Rural girls are trained from the early age of nine or their early teens to carry out the domestic tasks including bringing water inside the house (see Figure 3.2) and collecting firewood from the closest wilderness.

Figure 3.2: Carrying water from the spring.

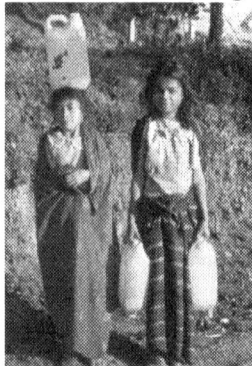

Women's movements around the garden, the market and their travels on public transport are domestic necessities. Yet travelling even within the same route and place but at a different time and context — for instance a woman going to the market to have a date with a man at night — is considered improper. The expectation of certain behaviours associated with places represents a boundary which is evident when it is transgressed (Cresswell 1996). Thus women's activities and movements beyond the boundary of femininity imply a disruption of the status quo in local relations. This carries an implicit social warning of being marked as "loose". A woman's status and that of her family is often connected to her "proper" mobility in the context of her femininity. While some travels, as already discussed, conform to the ascribed feminine identity and are accepted and naturalized in everyday life, however other travels, such as for self-realization, are more problematic because these practices are not within the discourses of the local notion of femininity.

A local notion of femininity is embodied in an image of a virtuous woman dressed in a traditional costume of hand-woven textiles, *tenun ikat,* as the basic item (Hamilton 1994, p. 41). The *tenun ikat* worn as a sarong or a shoulder cloth provides a material symbol of identity of its wearer. Across localities the significance of *tenun ikat* represents the structural conceptions of local gender ideology that reflect social relations in East Nusa Tenggara. Despite the regional similarity of the form of traditional garments, Hamilton (1994, p. 42) records distinct differences in the Sikka region in decorative technique, design and motif, providing cues about the wearer's individual ethnic identity, social status/class, and occasionally marital status, particularly for ceremonial occasions:

> married women weave sarongs with motifs learned from their mothers, but arrange those motifs within the design format associated with the household of their husbands. The finished sarong thus carries a visible expression of the relationship between the two kin groups. (Hamilton 1994, p. 44)

Behind the beautiful pieces of cloth, the femininity of the women materializes in their subject position as daughter, wife and craftswoman or weaver. As a weaver, a woman is able to exert control over her own labour products and, to some extent, over the other members of the household. The high economic value of *tenun ikat* in turn strengthens the position of local women in household power relations because of their role as *tenun ikat* producers in generating significant income (deJong 2000, p. 274).

Figure 3.3: Ritual dancing: The finest ikat for adat purposes.

Tenun ikat also serve as "markers of special events or objects" in which major ceremonial events and religious rites require participants and leaders to wear the finest garments which are decorated with the clan's heirloom ornaments (see Figure 3.3). Wearing the traditional costume at the investiture of a new priest is one of the Catholic Church's adaptation to local custom (Hamilton 1994, p. 42). On the occasion of an investiture of a new priest in Sikka, I could identify people of different clan groups in the area by the *tenun ikat* they were wearing at this important ritual.

Tenun ikat thus represents a material symbol of a woman's creativity and is a metaphor for her refined cultural knowledge (Orinbao 1992*a*). There is a large variation within Flores and Timor in women's physical skills, detailed routines of *tenun ikat*, and in quality and designs. The more intricate the design and the more time consuming and complicated the task, the better is the final product, representing a high artistic performance and a signifier of femininity. Women of the *kabupaten* Ende usually learn hand weaving when they are early teenagers. However, not all women of the region have the skill as a result of the historical prohibition of women from certain regions weaving, such as in particular regions of Lio. The local belief gives strong customary *adat* sanction against the prohibited groups who weave as this used to be viewed as a source of community disaster (Orinbao 1992a).

In general, to weave a piece of cloth using a hand loom requires strong dedication and perseverance and involves hard physical labour. A weaver needs to coordinate her limbs, hands, and eyes, and she also needs good concentration. The heavy loom is secured on the woman's hip, feet, and other parts of the body. The woman's limbs, hands, neck, and eyes are fully dedicated and focused only to the one task of hand weaving. The physical hardship is described in the Sikka dialect (Orinbao 1992a, p. 82) in a local oral narrative:

> how much a woman suffers
> suffers the self sacrifice
> self sacrifice causing sorrows
> your hip feels as if it is broken
> (my translation).

The back-stage process of weaving, and in turn, on-stage performance of wearing the *tenun ikat* is an integrated enactment of femininity. The silent suffering involved in *tenun* represents the idealized femininity, a process of becoming a virtuous woman. In most parts of Flores women learn how to weave, as the skill is a measure of their femininity (Orinbao 1992a). A young woman who wears her own beautifully made *tenun ikat* "properly" represents a girl coming of age and blooming to full womanhood (Orinbao 1992a). Beauty, then, is based on the pinnacle of femininity, requiring conformity. *Tenun ikat* materializes women's ability to suffer physical hardships, symbolizes a total family dedication, and is an evidence of femininity, embodying a high degree of perseverance (Orinbao 1992a, pp. 84–85). Women growing up in a family in East Nusa Tenggara are subjected to the "ideal" notion of femininity and so are expected to attain this feminine quality in order to be deserving of men's approval.

This notion of femininity is related to women's propriety of behaviour, including their mobility. Some forms of travel are out of bounds, controlled by the head of household's authority. Denial of permission for travel by a woman's male kinsfolk is often based on the fear of people's negative perception of the woman transgressing this femininity and, by extension, the kin group's good status. This social control of women's mobility is evoked through the fear of being the subject of gossip. Women's travel in this context reflects negotiations of this naturalized gendered space, where social construction of femininity constitutes women's space and propriety, and where women's position in their household, kin, and community is reflected in attitudes to marriage and its institution.

Marriage and bridewealth

Many of the young women whose travel stories encompass Java and abroad rehearsed a similar maiden's dream when asked what they wanted in life. Despite their travel, the women's wish "to get married and have a family" (*berumah tangga*) remains a significant personal goal. Marriage in Indonesia is one of the most important events in the family and personal life (Koning 2000, p. 193), and is the lens through which a woman's position in her kin and community can be gauged. Throughout my encounters and engagement with local women I became aware of the importance of the marriage institution and rituals, particularly that of bridewealth. Ethnographic work in Eastern Indonesia acknowledges that marriage is one of the most significant rituals in the local social relation, particularly with regard to clan relations (Barnes 1974, p. 242; Tule 2004). Through this relation of clans "people establish their link to place", both as a place of origin in terms of a source of family/blood connection and as a place of dwelling (Graham 1991, p. 83). Thus a woman's identities in this context are closely related to her place in marriage and clan relations as well as the materiality of space and relations surround her.

The attitude towards marriage and bridewealth varied among my informants, pointing to differences in their stages of life, outlook, status, and position. Liana, one young informant, had a shy smile on her lit-up face when she told me of her "good fortune" that she was engaged to be married in the near future. Her boyfriend's kin had started bringing parts of the bridewealth (*belis*). In contrast, Martha, a widow, showed her aversion towards *belis*, which had brought calamity in her life. Martha's story, told in Chapter 4, indicated that her life had already been "paid for" by the late husband's clan. She suffered physical abuse from the clan of her dead husband, such as being kicked in the stomach. Kicking Martha was considered the same as kicking the horse, a part of her bridewealth. *Belis* in this way is argued as a trade-in, in which a husband exchanges horses, pigs, cattle, and other things for his wife and thus he is able to treat her as he pleases (Purnama 2001, p. 42), which has been a contested position. Bulbeck (1998) in her study on the relationship between brideprice/bridewealth and domestic violence asserts:

> But wives who attract a brideprice may also experience unhappy domestic relations, their husbands perhaps arguing they "own" them and therefore have the right to beat them. (p. 121)

The above examples show a possible spectrum of women's experience as wives and, in spite of ethnic differences in marriage practices throughout Flores, the concept of bridewealth exists with few variations (Hamilton 1994, p. 44).

Women's position in social relations is reflected and negotiated in marriage practices and rituals (see Barnes 1974; and Hicks 1990 for detailed marriage alliances of specific areas of Flores, and for further analysis on social organization, see Fox 1980) . Marriage alliance provides an important clue to the structural principles of the society:

> Marriages were arranged asymmetrically, meaning that brothers married women from one set of lineages, while their sisters could marry men only from a different set of lineages. This marriage pattern created relationships among groups that anthropologists have called "wife-givers" and "wife-takers." Groups allied in this manner were committed to meet reciprocal obligations. At marriage rites and funerals, they exchanged food, textiles, and other valuable goods, a practice that is still of great importance today. The social idea was to perpetuate these relationships generation after generation through first-cousin marriage. (Hamilton 1994, p. 28)

A marriage alliance provides kinship frameworks of birth family and in-laws, which are the main source of reference for individuals. However because of the Catholic Church's opposition to arranged first-cousin marriages and to the young people's desire for more freedom of choice of partner, new alliances are now being formed and are traditionally formalized through bridewealth (Hamilton 1994, pp. 37-38).

Marriage rituals themselves reflect the women's place in the clan. Although there are differences in terms of the actual physical rituals across Flores and Timor, there are shared social categories and meanings. For instance there is a similarity in the meanings of marriage by which the women obtain an important status and are viewed as "the bringer of life" (Barnes 1974; Hicks 1990, p. 5). Before marriage, the position of a girl in the family is reflected in her clan membership, which is one of lower status than that of a male sibling. A significant feature of the local social organization emphasizes the difference between having a daughter and a son. Like many other places in Flores, descent in Manggarai, for example, follows a patrilineal pattern in that only a son belongs to his father's descent:

> At birth the expression of *ata one* ("inside person," that is, one who remains within the clan) announces the birth of a boy, while the expression *ata pe'ang* ("outside person," or one who leaves the clan) signifies the birth of a girl. Parents consider a girl a temporary ward, a child to be clothed, fed, and worked until she marries. (Gordon 1980, p. 49)

Parents' goals are to have a daughter married to a man of the same or higher social standing. Thus marriage which involves bridewealth is associated with the concerns of clan groups to enhance social status. The preferred matrilineal cross-cousin marriage typically aims to preserve or increase the social status of the family and also to carry out and fulfil ritual obligations to the ancestors' spirits.

In some areas in Flores, including parts of Flores Timur (Lamaholot), tradition dictates that whoever marries into the prohibited lineage suffers the sanction of social exclusion. My informant, a widow from Lembata island, told of her relationship with a man from a prohibited lineage and how she suffered negative consequences. Once her bridewealth was paid by the clan of the husband, even after he died she was still bound to his clan and unable to make a unilateral decision about her future marriage.

The intricate relations of clans reflected in a marriage arrangement imply that marriage is not merely the bride and groom's personal business but, more importantly, the business of both clans as for instance in Central Flores:

> Marriage is not an individual matter but a social institution which involves various social units. Marriage is a social affair which calls for active participation of two main categories: the wife-taking group (*ana weta*) and the wife-giving group (*embu mame*). The wife-giving group (*embu mame*) is also metaphorically termed the upper rank (*ape wawo*) or the waiting side (*papa kére*). The wife-taking group (*ana weta*) is termed the lower rank (*ape wena*) or the coming side (*papa demba*). By and large marriage calls for total

participation from the lowest social unit (a nuclear family) up to the highest unit of all kin groups. (Tule 2004, p. 169)

A woman does not usually have authority over her marriage affairs; for instance she does not directly have any part in the decision over the amount or the allocation of the bridewealth (*belis*). The normal marriage process starts with a proposal ceremony. Although this varies in name throughout Flores and Timor, it similarly encompasses the following stages: deciding the bridewealth, accumulating the bridewealth — animals, gold, elephant tusks, hand-loomed textile/cloth (*tenun ikat*); formal proposal; and, lastly, paying the bridewealth.

Belis, the bridewealth, is significant in the life of the family which entrenches it in the traditional ritual of marriage. The value of *belis* reflects the family position in the kinship system and its status in the local community and relations. Typically, the bride's family negotiates the *belis*, which traditionally symbolizes a groom's acknowledgement of the bride's willingness to leave her own parents, to change her identity by giving up her maiden name as well as residence, and as a sign of her new connection/relationship with the man's family. In particular, *belis* supposedly symbolizes the groom's acknowledgement to the bride's family who has taken care of the girl so far. If the groom is unable to pay the bridewealth fully, he may have to stay and work for the bride's family until he pays off the *belis* completely.

There is an inherent contradiction between a daughter's status and autonomy in the family. On the one hand she is valued highly for her qualities — physical appearance, femininity, education and other skills — which is materialized in *belis*, and in the marriage ritual, as "the bringer of life" (Barnes 1974; Hicks 1990, p. 5; Tule 2004). On the other hand she has little autonomy to decide the direction of the arrangement for her marriage. The woman's status and autonomy do not go hand in hand because high status does not necessarily mean high personal autonomy. This structure of gender, in which achieving a high status for women may mean conforming to the boundaries of propriety implicated in daily non-autonomous lives, remains problematic (Jackson 2002, p. 501).

The marriage rituals involving various stages which culminate in gift exchanges are a sign of strengthened clan relations between two parties. Anthropologists working in Eastern Indonesia explain that a marriage involves a series of exchanging of gifts between the clans of the bride and groom. Such exchanges are used to strengthen ties and maintain peace

between groups (Barnes 1980; Tule 2004, p. 195). The local Kéo termi-
nology for bridewealth, *wedi*, contains a notion of "trading the bride", but
Tule (2004, p. 179) argues that these are reciprocal gifts made to build
and maintain relationships between the bride and the groom's clans. The
responsibility of paying the bridewealth does not reside with the groom
alone but rather with the clan as a whole. Similarly, the bride's clan
receives bridewealth as an entity and the schedule of payment of *belis*
may take decades to complete, which implies that a clan holds in common all outstanding debts and obligations (Barnes 1974: pp. 282–294;
Barnes 1980: p. 78). However once the bridewealth has been received,
an agreement on a woman's position in both clans is sealed.

A woman faces stricter boundaries of proper behaviour once she is
engaged to a man, because she is accountable for her behaviour to both
clans. A bride-to-be is largely bounded by both parties' agreement, thus
she can not come and go as she pleases, which affects her spatial movement. Once a bride's family accepts a part of the agreed *belis*, it is a
sign of the girl getting engaged. Once the *belis* obligation is paid, the
marriage relationship is sealed by the *adat* and it is often followed by
a church ceremony. Only then does authority and responsibility for the
bride shift from her parents to the husband.

An unmarried daughter living at home is under the paternal protection for her well-being and purity. The strong Catholic Church influences
in Flores have glorified a young unmarried woman's purity, signified by
her virginity. In my travels in East Nusa Tenggara I often observed
young girls travelling together, but occasionally I met a girl travelling
alone. Girls travelling alone to urban areas for study or work live outside the kin's control and protection. In my field research I learnt about
cases of girls falling pregnant before marriage. In the local context, an
unmarried pregnant woman is considered to be transgressing the boundary of propriety. Some local men whom I spoke to were very clear about
the "ideal" woman to marry, who needs to be a virgin. This phenomenon
was pointed out to me by a young priest, who said that men are "obsessed
about hymen" (*gila selaput dara*). This term implies the society's double
standard, where men are often obsessed by women's physical virginity,
but on the other hand, men and society in general do not care about
men's social and physical purity. Women's embodied purity is viewed as
increasing men's status, because men consider themselves able to control
women's sexuality.

These days some argue that the social prescription for a woman to remain a virgin before marriage is not as strictly observed. Others think that virginity is not an issue, for instance, in some parts of Flores there is a practice of a man marrying the widow of his late brother. Young couples having sexual relationships resulting in pregnancy outside marriage is an increasingly common occurrence. If the couple is not formally engaged, the man will be fined to redeem the unfortunate "shame" of the girl's family, which is regulated by the customary law (*adat*). Nevertheless in some parts of East Nusa Tenggara, people show strong concerns about virginity, reflecting the influence of Christianity. The boundaries of propriety, sexual purity, and mobility are often challenged by women's travel, creating tensions for the individual women and the families.

There has been a range of perceptions in Flores and West Timor regarding the sexuality of unmarried women, but premarital sex is usually discouraged (Hicks 1990, p. 39). In Lamaholot tradition in Flores Timur, some believe that an important requirement of a girl to be married is her virginity. Her purity is connected to the family's reputation and social status. Once the girl loses her virginity, particularly if she falls pregnant, she is considered as having lost her virtue and, by extension, the family's social status suffers. In the local context, the sexually active single girl is considered to be going beyond the boundary of propriety within the *adat*. Her hymen embodies a spatial boundary of propriety for an unmarried woman. As a sanction against her later, if she is finally able to marry, her marriage may not be celebrated with the usual wedding feast. In Dawan tradition in Timor, the virginity of a girl before marriage is revered. This gendered practice of bodily boundary of propriety for an unmarried woman is controlled and reproduced in rituals. On the wedding night there used to be a designated person to guard the bedroom of the newly weds (*penjaga tempat tidur*) to see the proof and confirm the virginity of the bride (Djeki 1977).

The femininity of a bride, embodied in the intactness of the hymen as a physical symbol of virginity, reflects the notion of propriety of body. This boundary is institutionalized, among other ways, in the forms of the *belis*. The higher the girl's perceived purity, the greater the *belis*. A daughter's position is mutually constituted by the family's social standing and by its efforts in protecting and educating her. The non-autonomous position of the woman relates to the link or connection she had with both sides of the clan/family — the bride's family as the receiver of the bridewealth and the groom's family as the one who pays it.

Some daughters by-pass this purity issue with an elopement. This kind of mobility to some extent also offers a chance for a woman to marry a man of her choice within the *adat*. If a daughter decides to marry against the family's wish, she can leave the family home and follow a tradition of eloping. In Dawan tradition, in Timor, a woman who elopes is expected to leave a few symbols such as silver coin, one sarong (*tenun ikat*), and betel nuts (*sirih pinang*) at her home as a sign of elopement with her man. Both the bride and the groom are supposed to come out of their hiding place outside the village no later than three days after eloping and to fulfil the *adat* obligation to the bride's family. The groom will have to pay some material fines. So in East Nusa Tenggara in the last few decades while parents continue to play a significant role over the children's choice of spouse yet increasingly the children insist on their own choices (Hicks 1990, p. 38).

Women negotiating mobility: tracing the folk narratives

The implications of increased mobility for women are tensions within the community, clan and family, and also within women's internal harmony. Some women I met actively engaged in negotiations around their mobility to reach their own balance of harmony. This is shown in their travel stories recorded in later chapters and also in a number of folk narratives which emphasize women's agency in negotiating the boundary of structural gendered space.

Folk stories and legends that embody local thoughts and perceptions pass between generations through a range of forms of oral tradition. In the broad sense, stories, songs, and proverbs are the most common orally transmitted traditions (Finnegan 1992, p. 11). The folk stories by themselves are not my main interest here and I am aware of the problems of interpretation because oral expression takes many different forms and functions, including myth and aesthetic performance for its own sake (Finnegan 1992, p. 48). My interest is in exploring a folk tale as one of the many possible avenues to uncover local meanings of the women's experience of mobility in their gendered space.

The contexts of women's travel are extremely varied, and only some are captured in the informants' stories. The study of society through oral sources is well established and rigorously used alongside examination of documentary sources, especially in researching experiences of the "voiceless" such as rural women (Finnegan 1992, p. 47). With regard to women's mobility, I am interested in unpacking the unstated cultural assumptions embedded in folktale. Some folktales relating to women's mobility in a wider sense are selected here to provide a window through which we can view women's lives and resourcefulness in relation to mobility and social change.

The common setting for women to tell folk tales and legends, for example in So'a in Flores, is by moonlight and while eating new season corn. The stories frequently tell of everyday lives, to provide insights into the local social relations which structure the women's lives (Mommersteeg and Dirkzwager 1999, p. 7). Barnes, an anthropologist who did extensive ethnographic work in Kedang in Lembata island in the early 1970s, documented the following story of Bota Ili and Wata Rian. These mythological names have honorific connotations. *Bota* is a woman's name, and *ili* means mountain, so a woman is associated with the stationary mountain. *Wata* means beach, and *rian* means great, so a man is associated with the great, dynamic ocean (Barnes 1974, p. 40).

Bota Ili and Wata Rian

Bota Ili lived at the top of the mountain. Her body was covered with long hair, and she had extremely long fingernails and toe nails. The hair on top of her head was a large tangled pile. She ate snakes, lizards, geckos and iguanas. In order to light a fire to cook these animals, she would strike her arse on a rock. Before long the fire would begin to glow and she would cook the animals to eat them.

Wata Rian lived at the beach.

In the mornings he looked up at the top of the mountain and saw smoke from a fire. One morning he thought that the smoke in the mountain must mean that a human lived there.

Therefore he decided, "I must climb the mountain and see who is there."

In preparation, he went fishing and got several fish; then he tapped a little palm wine. Then one morning, quite early, he set out to climb the mountain. He climbed and climbed until — precisely at noon — he finally arrived. There he saw a place where a human lived and a hearth. However, no one was there because Bota Ili had gone hunting and had not yet returned. He waited and waited, but she did not soon return. Therefore taking his dog with him, he climbed a tree and sat waiting in the branches. He waited and waited, until finally he saw that Bota Ili had come back. She was bent over carrying on her shoulder snakes, lizards, geckos, and iguanas. She tossed off her heavy load and rested a little. When she had finished resting, she struck her arse again and again on a rock to get fire; but the fire would not light; so she stopped and thought, 'Who can be here?' She looked here and looked there. Suddenly she saw Wata Rian sitting in the branches of the tree. Then she got very angry.

'Hey, you there kept my fire from lighting,' she said. 'Come down so I can bite you to tatters.'

Wata Rian replied, 'Don't make trouble. If you do, I'll let my dog loose and it will bite you.'

Bota Ili then said, 'Just come down. I won't do anything, if you don't let your dog bite me. Climb down so we can cook the animals and eat.'

Wata Rian climbed down.

When he was down, Bota Ili tried to start the fire and the fire lit. They built the fire and cooked the animals along with the fish Wata Rian had brought. When the food was ready they sat down and ate. Wata Rian had brought a bamboo of palm wine so they could drink the palm wine with their meal; however, he did not drink much himself, but poured a lot for Bota Ili.

Down, down, Bota Ili fell down drunk. She fell so fast asleep that she was no longer aware of her body. After a while, Wata Rian took a knife and shaved her from head to foot. When he was through he saw that Bota Ili was a woman.

Afterwards they lived together and married.

(pp.40-41)

This story conveys a sense of origin of civilization which is equated to a man. A woman is associated with uncivilized nature which is symbolized by her hairy body. She needs to be shaved, tamed and domesticated in a marriage. This representation offers a simple notion of power as domination, where the man is able to take power from the woman, dictate his will and change her body appearance. After she has been shaved and has married Wata Rian, she followed his way. Culture is associated with men and is seen as coming from the shore (Barnes 1974).

The association of woman with a mountain and man with the ocean is likely to be an underlying cultural assumption which contains a strong message of the different patterns of mobility between genders. A man generally is more mobile where the wide open ocean is the only limitation; while a woman stays on top of the mountain self-sufficiently involved in her domestic tasks. Men are seen as more powerful as they are free to explore the world, *pergi merantau*. The metaphor for men's mobility as dynamics of the sea and the term of a wave in rough sea which is *"raja"*, the king or the powerful (Barnes 1974, p. 246) assumes gendered mobility. Mobility is equated only with men's power, while women are grounded at home in the local notion of femininity. Thus being a female subject situated in local gender relations, a woman faces structural barriers against her mobility. A woman mostly occupies domestic subject positions as she gathers her food, lights the fire and cooks the food. The folk tale also presents the woman as an uncivilized being, whose body is covered with hair; and on the other hand it presents the man as endowed with the power of civilization and ready to domesticate the woman. This is a simplistic representation of power, but it is enough to indicate a crucial dimension of the local gender relations. The simplistic opposition between the mountain and the sea indicates a general dichotomy followed in many aspects of local life (Barnes 1974, pp. 40, 80), with static and mundane domestic roles strongly linked with femininity whilst the dynamic and adventurous is associated with masculinity.

Women nevertheless do negotiate the local gendered space and their stories indicate a shifting between various subject positions. Some women initiate mobility, shift subjectivities, and lead dynamic lives. In contrast to the previous folktale, another dimension of power as fluid and fractured in multiple positions can be read from a folktale of a young woman who is about to be married to a man from a different village in So'a. The families of both parties had agreed to the engagement, but the girl atypically refuses the offer of marriage.

Leda, a girl from Bhela clan

Leda, a girl from the Bhela clan, was getting married to Wae, a young man from Rawe clan.

When he started bringing *sirih pinang* [betel nut] to the family of the bride-to-be, Leda did not approve of him. But the mother and father and her brothers approved of him.

At the hunting season, all the family conducted a ceremony to bring the bridewealth and they also brought firewood.

Wae brought some gold and put it on the mat. He also brought ten buffaloes and ten horses in addition to ten goats and lambs.

After that the young man came to work [in the field of the bride's family] but the girl avoided him. Every time the man came, Leda went somewhere else. But the man worked as usual. He worked until the rainy season and he cleared the weeds.

He worked in the western plot of land with the brothers and mother and father [of the bride], whilst Leda the girl of Bhela weeded on the eastern part of the plot of land.

Then one day when the rain dropped heavily at midday, the mother, father and brothers sought protection from the rain in a hut. Wae, the young man from Rawe, and Leda, the girl of Bhela, also sought protection from the rain.

When it was still raining, Leda the girl of Bhela drew up her sarong and wore it like a man, took out a machete and started to provoke the lightning and thunder.

Leda, the girl of Bhela, came out in front of the hut and danced with the direction of east to west and with her machete moved fast and said: 'Ooh I am Leda, a lightning girl, please strike Wae, the man from Rawe.' Then Wae replied: "Leda, if you don't want me, I will go." Wae thought about it, then left. Before leaving, he told her brothers: "I want to leave because Leda doesn't want me. Don't stop me otherwise the lightning will strike me." So Wae left.

When he arrived in the village of Rawe, he told his mother and father: "I don't have any wife. She may have tempted me and I may die. Let's go and ask back for our *belis* to be returned." The mother and father answered: "Ooh son, don't worry about it, otherwise we may be killed in So'a." The bridewealth was never returned and has stayed with Leda's family until now.

Leda is the girl of a village of Lade of Bhela clan. Up till now in Lade there is Bhela clan.

(Mommersteeg and Dirkzwager 1999, pp. 158-160) [my translation].

The position of an unmarried girl, as previously discussed, is commonly subordinate in the family hierarchy. The girl in this folktale had to act unusually in refusing to conform with the local notions of propriety for her behaviour. She had to change her identity, performing as a man — the way she dressed, behaved, and danced — to position herself as an equal in the local gender relations. This folk narrative emphasizes a female negotiating the boundaries of what it is to be woman, which is signified in dress, deportment, and movement. Women's travel outside the domestic context is also a movement which usually belongs to the men's domain. Women's travel in this way negotiates various scales of boundary. Similar to the folktale, with their mobility, women transform themselves, change subject positions and enact changes.

Once Leda's *belis* is paid, the engagement with the man officially means she is attached to the man's clan. Nevertheless there is an interesting twist to the story when Leda transgresses the boundary of propriety and challenges Wae, her fiancé. She has to create a metaphysical space and calls upon the transcendental power of lightning to win the authority to say "no" to their union. This episode, similar to other local So'a folk tales, tells of a woman challenging a structural boundary and reclaiming power. It also tells a story of a woman's decentred and shifting subjectivity, performing different identities to gain her power.

Analysing such folk narratives enables me to see how within the gendered space of East Nusa Tenggara, the structure of power in its many elements influences women's strategies in everyday life and routine. The collective thoughts represented in the plots of the stories show a possibility of multiplicities of positions and relations of power of women. Women perform this possibility in mobility by imaginatively moving between different subject positions, allowing them to produce a space that constitutes power.

The spatiality of mobility confronts discursive boundaries of propriety which tend to structurally position women's identity in the local gendered spaces as marginalized and fixed. Women's travel represents not only a physical movement but also a negotiation of a range of boundaries of marginality at different scales. Travel is a contradictory space, where women are still expected to follow certain notions of propriety and yet the distance from home may offer a space for new practices and identities. Isolated from the context of home, women are likely to negotiate their own boundaries of behaviour and social positioning.

Women's travel in this way becomes a source of critical tensions within individual women and in their social relations, as some examples discussed in later chapters show. In this context I am interested in travel as a physical movement as well as a metaphorical journey of the way subjects recreate identities despite the hegemonic power of dominant discourses and practices (Gibson 2001, p. 641). Women travellers move against, as well as with, ideas of propriety, reflecting some access to power. Through the spatiality of mobility, women contest and negotiate their positions of affiliation and exclusion in social relations in the contexts of household, clan, community and work.

Part Two

Journeys

Through unpacking travel stories and being myself a fellow traveller on voyages, I trace the complexities and diversity of travelling identities of Eastern Indonesian women. Paying attention to the local context of social relations opens a space for articulating the physical as well the metaphorical journeys of crossing the ocean. Individuals inhabited different subject positions in various nodes of relations. Travellers move in and out of a wider range of subject positions allowing new subjectivities to emerge. I ground the empirical evidence of travel on three basic sea routes, namely travel inter-islands, travel to urban centres, and travel to overseas destinations. Travellers' tales provide clues to the creation of contested and liminal spaces where new identities are imagined.

CHAPTER 4

Inter-island Travel: Women Negotiating Boundaries of Propriety

At the end of July 1999 on one of my visits to Flores Timur, I travelled to Kedang on the island of Lembata. Like many women from the region, I took the ferry between islands because this was the most economical and practical way to circulate in the region. That day there was hardly any drama competing with other passengers to get seats on the ferry. When we were halfway into the journey, I climbed the upper deck of the ferry and thought I would take a few photographs of the view.

Even in that short four-hour inter-island trip there was a sense of surprise waiting around the corner. In an effort to extend my network I approached a group of women travelling together to attend a traditional village celebration. They were quite amicable. Apparently, my camera had signified me as a tourist — separating me as a different kind of traveller. Eventually, the four women cheerfully posed on the deck for a photograph. However, as I was about to take that shot with the beautiful background view, a man who had watched us from a distance, approached us and bluntly stopped me: "do not take their photograph!" There was confusion and tension among us women. The man was protective of the local women travellers. These women's association with me while on the voyage aroused this man's anxiety. Why?

Circulating: going with and against propriety

nter-island movements of East Nusa Tenggaran women are characterized by temporary, short-distance and sometimes repetitive trips. Women in the region have travelled as part of the family for a long time, yet this vignette indicates independent women circulating between islands can still create a sense of social unease. An implied cultural assumption that women are stationary at home underlies the problematic empirical evidence of women circulating in travel.

Historically, men's domain of mobility, for instance in pre-colonial trade and other localized interactions including migration, were conducted through the inter-island routes, as Graham (1999, p. 72) illustrates:

> The ancestral migrations and early exchanges of goods and know-how are memorialised in mythic form by many people of Flores, who regard knowing and respecting their origins as crucial to their contemporary survival. Such myths and historical accounts often depict Flores not as a bounded entity, but in relations with various "outsiders".

Through mythical representation in the form of folk narratives, locals think of themselves in terms of their relationship with the Other. Travel has been a way of encountering the Other but it now has the added dynamic of women being included as both traveller and Other. Contemporary women now follow their male ancestral trails by sailing inter-island, to forge connections with other coasts. Rather than just waiting for their men to come home, women also circulate, engaging in their own politics of mobility. Thus circulating for women can be viewed as stepping into a contested space of ambiguity.

During my inter-island travel in the region I could sense, and experienced, many different ways in which the social anxiety about the propriety of women's movement manifested itself. In one ferry trip in Flores, I avoided a man who inquisitively wanted to know about my background. He was also a fellow passenger and he noticed me constantly engaging with women throughout our voyage. Obviously he knew that I was not a local, so he wanted to know why I was so interested in local women. When I walked towards the rear of the ferry to stretch my legs, he followed me. The man began the conversation with: *"Sendiri?"* or "Are you alone?" To which my answer was a positive "yes". From his disparaging reaction, there was a sense of a woman being reckless for travelling alone, *"berani ya?"* or "brave aren't you?", indicating the impropriety of my movement. I felt abashed and confused, "a woman out of place" as experienced by Tsing (1993) in her field research among the Dayaks in Kalimantan. Both of our experiences in the field confirmed this view that "a travelling woman is a disorderly woman" (Tsing 1993, p. 219).

Most likely the man was suspicious of the "impropriety" of my mobility, since he gave me a strange look and asked what I was doing with the women. I was there alone, a free-floating female traveller with no local connection. He could not situate me in any ordinary context of the trip, because I did not have local relatives or friends, I was neither a government employee nor did I have a job there, and I did not look like a nun or a trader either. He might have perceived me as someone who did not fit in any local framework of a "good" woman, evidenced as by my sole mobility. I suspected the man then warned the women about my "misfit" position and impropriety, because I soon noticed a change in demeanour of the women. Right there on the ferry the man had excluded me from the safe space inside the boundaries of propriety. He took the trouble to investigate my background and halted my interactions with other women. Not surprisingly a cold sweat appeared on my forehead in the hot tropical day. Emotionally I felt disturbed by the man's authority and the anxiety he caused the women. A similar experience to that of Ong (1990) while conducting fieldwork in a Malaysian village confirms an extension of a man's role as a protector of all village women's moral status. The way my interaction with the women and the man intersected at that particular time on the boat pointed to my being a woman "out of place".

Clearly women travelling alone with no proper reason were viewed as "disorderly". The need for male protection while travelling, implied women were "weak". This man acted in accordance with the local cultural norm. In the absence of a young woman's guardian while away from home, he felt responsible. It is with the benefit of hindsight that it became clear that the man was indeed the one with authority. As a young local priest in civilian dress who rightly thought I was an outsider, he was obligated to be a "protector" of women travellers. I did not realize it then, but soon learnt about the web of gender relations and particularly the authority and power of religious leaders (priests and brothers) in a mainly Catholic region such as Flores. In subsequent chance interactions while on the island and in my role as a church-goer, I introduced myself and my research to this same priest. He turned out to be quite supportive of my project and became a catalyst for meeting with some local women. In contrast to our first encounter on the ferry, his authority was used then to assure the women's trust in my research project. So an initial chance meeting on the ferry, however unpleasant, had created an opportunity in the island for "proper" engagements with local women, this notion of "proper" implying conformity to certain norms and authorities, which often means male approval.

Women's faces among the crowd

Behind the seemingly mundane nature of inter-island travel, the most modest in terms of financial outlay and process, lies the powerful local concept of *langgar laut*. This term is equally significant for both men and women. The year before the economic crisis of 1997-98, there were over 1.35 million passenger trips between the islands of East Nusa Tenggara province (Passenger Survey 1996). The financial and political crises imposed significant structural changes in Indonesia and the social impact of the crises has generated considerable debate. However the extent of the impact on women's temporary movement has been hard to ascertain as data on passengers' movement by gender, particularly since the financial crisis, has been scarce. Here, I am interested in the broader meaning of the women's travel resulting from local interactions rather than as a specific response to the crisis. Within this broad framework I intend to go beyond the commonplace reasons derived from transport surveys to excavate the underlying meanings of women's inter-island travel.

Women travel through routes from Flores to the surrounding islands of Adonara, Lembata, Alor, Timor, Rote, Savu, and Sumba. Their travels are served by private and state owned ferries and in some cases by PELNI ships as parts of long haul journeys (Figure 2.5). Larantuka, Kalabahi and Kupang were the busiest local hubs with the biggest number of passenger movements. The PELNI ships *Awu* and *Pangrango* ships, for instance, call at East Nusa Tenggara ports fortnightly. As parts of inter-island travel, the journey by ship may involve an overnight or longer journey. Each ferry journey has its sailing schedule and route. The frequency of the ferry varies between daily and weekly. Depending on the distance, the trips may take up to twelve hours (see Figure 4.1).

Figure 4.1: Travel time, selected ferry routes.

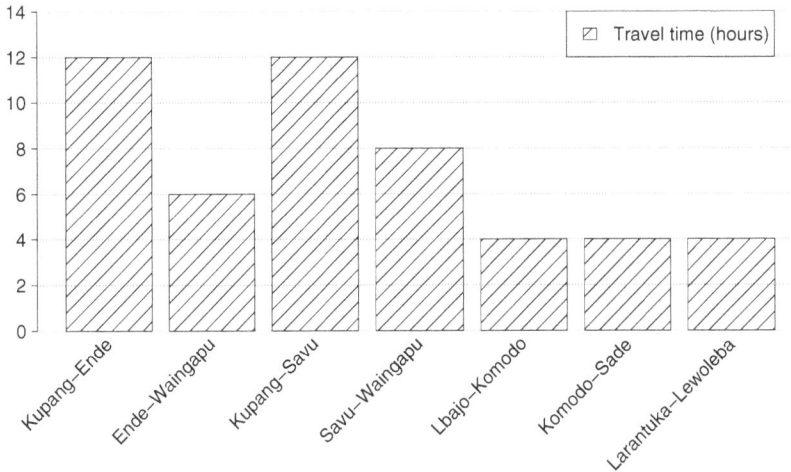

Source: Fieldnotes and Bureau of Transport Economics (1999).

As anticipated, the ferry trips were physically easier to handle because of their shorter duration. In terms of travel logistics, there was less competition for space with other passengers on the smaller ferries, which made the trip easier to manage. Typically, a small ferry carries around 100 passengers in addition to motor vehicles, bicycles, bulky goods, notably cash crops and household goods, and occasionally live goats and chickens, both for personal consumption and sale.

Observations in the field showed that ships and ferries operated at full capacity and often over their capacities in carrying passengers to their inter-island destinations. At the same time, little is known about the travel of the increasing number of women circulating inter-island or about the reasons for their journeys as there has not been detailed survey of the passenger by gender. Even less is known about how these trips have affected the lives of the women. So my research was targetted to fill this gap, initially by exploring the women's own travel stories.

As shown in Table 4.1, twenty women were interviewed for this study, either on ferries/ships, in transit or in their homes, mainly on Flores.

Table 4.1: Inter-island travellers.

Name	Origin	Marital Status	Job	Religion	Age	Edu Level	Reason	Travel Alone
Ade	Flores Timur	Married	Housewife	Catholic	46	1	VRF	yes
Betani	Flores Timur	Married	Housewife	Catholic	42	1	VRF	yes
Clara	Sumba	Married	Housewife	Protestant	50	2	VRF	no
Dominika	Manggarai	Married	Housewife	Catholic	47	1	VRF	no
Rika	Manggarai	Married	Housewife	Catholic	28	2	VRF	yes
Ela	Ngada	Married	Housewife	Catholic	40	1	VRF	no
Siska	Ngada	Married	Housewife	Catholic	32	1	VRF	no
Farida	Ende	Widow	Self-employed	Muslim	52	2	VRF	no
Adelina	Sikka	Single	Self-employed	Catholic	50	2	VRF	no
Mita	Kupang	Married	Self-employed	Catholic	35	1	VRF	yes*
Martha	Flores Timur	Widow	Self-employed	Catholic	39	1	VRF	yes
Ela	Ngada	Married	Self-employed	Catholic	40	1	VRF	yes
Irma	Ende	Single	Student	Catholic	20	2	Edu	no
Tina	Ende	Single	Student	Catholic	19	2	Edu	no
Sima	Ende	Single	Student	Catholic	21	2	Edu	yes
Eva	Ende	Single	Student	Catholic	23	3	Edu	yes
Vivi	Ende	Single	Student	Catholic	20	2	Edu	yes
Marieta	Sikka	Single	Professional	Catholic	35	3	Work	yes
Yani	Sikka	Single	Professional	Catholic	25	2	Work	yes
Mina	Ende	Single	Professional	Catholic	28	3	Work	yes

Note: * with a child. VRF (Visiting Relatives and Friends). Edu (Education) 1 = Primary; 2 = Secondary; 3 = Tertiary

Source: Fieldwork.

They were a mixed group of a range of ages and marital status, with nine being single, nine married, and two widows. Of the nine married women travellers, seven were housewives mainly visiting relatives and friends (VRF). The median age of the married women was 42 years, the oldest being 50 years and the youngest 28. The inter-island movements of these women indicated a stage of their life cycle with less childcare responsibility. Both the widows interviewed were self-employed and, together with three single professionals travelling for work, pointed out a relationship between their mobility and financial independence. Out of the nine single women, five of them were students aged between 19 and 23 years, travelling for education (Edu). Before examining their specific journeys to demonstrate that the trip itself has wider connotations, I recount first my own trip to expose the flavour of the inter-island travel.

Impropriety and being reckless

The inter-island trip is becoming increasingly common among women from East Nusa Tenggara in line with long-term declining costs and easier access to transport. Nevertheless some sections in the community still suspiciously regard a woman traveller with no obvious purpose as *nekat* or reckless, as my own experience in the field indicated. Inter-island travel for women is not customarily a simple and loosely autonomous trip, rather it is situated and nested in a rich-textured institutional setting of family, clan and local connections.

Like other travel stories that I have heard, my inter-island trips provided an opportunity to establish and attach to a different network of relations by creating a distance from an ordinary everyday routine. My own travel reflected an entrance to an ambiguous space of uncertainty and unfamiliarity. The voyage held the surprise of meeting new contacts, and at times opened new avenues for my research. Many other passengers also networked, such as with housewives travelling to visit relatives and friends.

One of my inter-island travels culminated at my destination on one dark midnight when the ship I was on slowly moored at the port of Ende on Flores. On the upper deck I prepared myself to struggle off the ship with my suitcase in hand and a green baseball cap on my head. People — mainly younger men and traders — impatiently pushed forward, closing in on the main doors of the ship. They were tussling to rush off the MV *Pangrango* which had sailed from Surabaya. This PELNI ship had been scheduled to arrive two hours earlier to complete its three-day voyage, but rough seas encountered after reaching Labuan Bajo in north-west Flores had forced it to slow down. Similar turbulent waves were described by Bickmore (1868, p. 111), a fellow of the Royal Geographical Society of London passing along this very same route:

> ... as we came into the Indian Ocean, we experienced a strong breeze from the southeast. The current, which had been with us and against the wind, was met off the southwest promontory of Floris by a current with the wind from the east, and at once the sea rose up into pyramidal masses, or formed waves that rolled over and broke against the wind, like those from the windward quarter of a ship which is sailing "on a wind."

This delay resulting from strong waves, in addition to sea sickness, overcrowding, and an anxiety to reach their destination, only served to further annoy the already agitated passengers. The fully loaded ship was now highly charged with emotions. Men waited and blocked the path to the main door.

The MV *Pangrango* was a three-year-old ship at the time, 74 by 15.2 metres, with a cruising speed of 14 knots (as indicated by the PELNI 1999 timetable). The ship was overloaded with more than 50 per cent above its formal capacity of 500 passengers. People were everywhere, in the corridor, on the outside decks, in front of the administrative office, in front of the kitchen, and on the stair landings. One could hardly find space inside the lower decks to rest a weary body. Among the 800 or so passengers most were crammed in the economy class (lower decks). They were restless and agitated, being compressed in such hot and confining conditions.

More than one-quarter of the total passengers on the ship were women as shown in the ship manifest. They often travelled in pairs, in small groups, or with the family. There were also twelve women in cabins who shared one-third of the total 34 berth private cabins. The remainder travelled in economy class (also referred to as deck class). Many passengers appeared to have little concern for their own privacy while travelling, possibly because they were used to living in overcrowded dwellings. Nevertheless, most people were showing restraint in a stuffy and confined compartment.

Passengers interacted during the longer voyage and, at times, even formed groups based not only on physical proximity within the ship, but also on common interests and personal understanding. The "members" were fiercely loyal to these fluid groups and protected their "territory" or seats until the end of a member's voyage. I found myself circulating between two groups of completely different ages, a younger group for company, and a more mature group for security and patronage. They became familiar with one another by sharing conversation and sometimes food. Commonly, the women took care of each other when queueing for food and the bathroom/toilet, and also, in some instances, through sharing childcare. One woman from Flores told me that she always looked around for a Catholic nun. A nun stands out by her uniform (headdress and habit) and, being a Catholic, this traveller felt safe in her company. Most women preferred to travel with friends or male relatives, reinforcing their propriety as being under male protection.

Some young women travel by sea alone. However, they are still regarded as "unusual". The way my fellow passengers inquisitively asked about my voyage indicated my unconventional behaviour. In one mature-aged woman's words: *"Kenapa nekat betul, pergi naik kapal sendiri"* or "Why were you so reckless as to travel by ship alone?" By breaking the rule of propriety, I realized what was socially acceptable. The experiences of other young women who had to travel alone in the past also confirmed this common perception. Nonetheless, self-supporting women were often more mobile because of their economic resources allowing more autonomy in their travels.

Travellers had no choice but to put up with one another whilst on journeys. Inside the stuffy lower deck of the ship, which was grossly lacking in proper ventilation, the strong pungent smell of cigarette smoke mixed with people's perspiration was overwhelming. The lower decks of the ship were supposed to be air-conditioned but the system rarely worked. The prominent no-smoking signs were ignored and the smoke was a considerable inconvenience to women and children. They had to endure the situation. Emotional aspects such as the feeling of a loss of control over what was happening on the ship also have spatial consequences. To avoid feeling fear, women would avoid places that triggered the negative feeling. Spatial exclusion is one way of overcoming fear, which reflects gender power relations (Koskela 1999). On the ship, however, the women had to put up with men smoking as there was nowhere else to go.

Young women travelling by themselves — myself included — were approached by men flirting, perhaps to overcome boredom at sea. Men circulated within the ship searching for such an opportunity. However, overcrowding frequently limited movement. Within the confines of the lower decks I participated in activities and conversations to build an understanding of the journeys of other women. The often chaotic and cramped situation of the ship worsened each time it stopped at a port to take on more passengers. The longer the distance the harder the physical challenge, particularly for a relatively new traveller like myself. After hours of sitting on a hard wooden bench my bottom was feeling numb. In most parts of this journey through Badas–Labuan Bajo–Waingapu and Ende, my whole body ached, especially my head, perhaps because of the constrained space, the stale air and dehydration compounded by seasickness. Purposefully I limited my food and fluid intake to avoid queueing at the inadequate toilet, which was an everyday reality for many. Sleeping in an upright sitting position was common, as space quickly ran out as more people boarded at various ports. The physical difficulties of reaching one's destination can be quite overwhelming.

Most passengers for Ende eagerly anticipated the approaching destination. Their faces lifted. Some women combed their hair and a girl nearby powdered her nose. It was pleasing, finally, to see from afar the lights of Port Ende in the pitch black night. There I stood on the outside upstairs deck, hanging on to the gate rail. Suddenly I heard the crush of people swarming onto the top deck. I found myself in the front row of those wanting to disembark. Unexpectedly, a ship official had decided that, rather than going out through the usual main door, passengers should go through the gate rail in front of where I stood. Being pushed from behind, inevitably I was one of the first passengers to disembark. Meanwhile people behind me surged forward like a wave. I felt anxious and nervous walking down the ramp towards the pier because everything was new and unfamiliar. Other passengers, mainly men, rushed and screamed and jostled with their luggage to get ahead of others. Finally we arrived at our destination, each with a different purpose. Feeling run down, I walked towards the front gate of the port clutching my bag. There I was on a new shore and in a new field site. At the end of the journey I found myself full of a strange anticipation of something new and better.

A sense of unfamiliarity is a feeling that agonizes women as they initially cross the shore to unknown places. At that time I had never been to Ende and I knew no one there. However, I had hoped that a friend had made arrangements for someone to meet me at the port with the identification of my green baseball cap. But what a futile plan. In the dark port no one would be able to see the green cap, let alone my unfamiliar face. At that moment I truly felt alone in a strange place. Yet, so many women had travelled this very same route for various reasons. Despite the difficulties involved in sea travel, the voyages of contemporary Eastern Indonesian women reflect the conceptual appeal of movement of reaching a new shore.

My own travels have made me appreciate some of the physical and emotional challenges that women of the region experience in inter-island travel. In particular it was interesting to observe and learn how, within our seemingly similar physical mobilities, our experience of place and space indeed does vary. The following sections present others' travel stories, which are necessarily compressed, jumping from one to the next story rather quickly. My main aim is to capture the nuances and dynamics of interactions in the gendered space of the voyage and beyond. Situating travellers in a range of dynamic routes, I explore how the diversity of motives of travel surfaces when women are mapped with respect to their different subject positions within a particular institutionalized mechanism, whether the family, community, church or the state. So far, women have been included in or excluded from social institutions based on socially constructed categories (Kobayashi 1997, p. 4), which both prevent and result in movement. Three broad motives of inter-island travel are considered — social trips, school trips, and work trips — each with more complex underlying personal motives. Visiting families and friends, at a glance, simply seems like leisure travel but it may contain more complex reasons and consequences.

Social trips: flight of fancy

Women who travelled inter-island reported a feeling of excitement especially on their first journey. The imagined rather than the physical journey of *langgar laut*, I argue, is related to women successfully negotiating scale and position of propriety. This is evident in the experiences of two housewives, Rika and Mita. Their inter-island travels reflect the dynamics of their travel in going beyond the boundary of propriety to produce a different scale and network of social relations. Rika was a housewife in her late twenties, originally from Flores, who was travelling from her home in Badas in West Flores to Kupang by the MV *Pangrango*.

She had travelled this route many times before. Her simple expression "going sightseeing" (*pesiar*) as her motive for travel captures the spirit of her leisurely travel to enjoy the surprises of an imaginative journey. Her agenda, which later became apparent, went beyond the conspicuously simple reason of visiting her sister who had just given birth to a baby girl. On the other hand, Mita was a housewife in her thirties travelling with a three-year-old daughter, Imelda, in economy class on the PELNI ship *Awu*, from Kupang to Ende. They were visiting her familial home near Wolowaru in Flores. The mother and child seemed to be comfortable, sharing a hired thin, vinyl-covered mattress, in a corner of the outside upper deck of the ship. On the airy deck, Imelda was happily playing with her toys under the watchful eyes of other female passengers. This was a better option than being on the inside lower decks, full of men smoking the pungent *kretek* or clove cigarettes. Mita seemed content on the journey, as I observed her following some of her domestic routines in caring for her child. On the ship, the availability of hot water on tap enabled her to bath her little girl, even if this was done in the cramped hand basin. The voyage was in this respect, in contrast with my own experience, a temporary luxury for Mita, when compared to her everyday living with no piped water. The variety of these women's narratives exposes the diversity of women's experience of space in the simplest material form of being on the ship.

Relieving social and economic pressures: Mita

Mita came from a modest socio-economic background. She had left school aged 11 and worked as a labourer prior to getting married and her subsequent migration to Kupang. While taking care of her husband and family at home, she supplemented the family income by selling snacks in her *kampung*. The recent price hikes as a result of the economic crisis, particularly in food costs, forced her to shut down her small business. It had become increasingly difficult to maintain the selling price while the cost of production doubled. The timing of her journey was interesting, because of her difficult financial situation and the fact that she had not been back to Flores for a couple of years.

When asked what she would do there, it was simply *"kunjung bapa-mama"* or "visiting dad and mum" and when pressed further, *"kerja kebun"* or "some gardening". Her tentative answer did not provide more specific information on the purpose of her travel. In particular she also planned to stay indefinitely in Wolowaru, her village in Ende Regency: "Not sure yet when [I] will be back. I will have to wait and see how it is in the village." The real reason for Mita's voyage was not actually revealed, even though she mentioned visiting the family as the prime purpose for travel. Why would she suddenly return home after years of absence? Perhaps the Indonesian economic crisis had driven people out of the cities in desperation and back to their rural roots. Not knowing her undisclosed agenda for retreating to her home base, I could only speculate. It might possibly be a marriage problem. Equally, it might be that it was a combination of marital, work and money problems.

One thing was certain, families were finding it

Figure 4.2: Voyaging with a child.

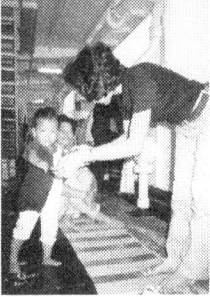

hard to survive as urban employment shrank during the crisis. Mita did mention doing some gardening. Subsistence farming or gardening in her rural place of birth seemed a reasonable option in the period of economic uncertainty. Structural change in the economy has triggered movement of men and women who lost their employment in the formal sectors. The crisis has forced people to move from the formal to informal sectors and from urban to rural areas. The sharp reduction in real wages and the doubling of the general level of prices has resulted in families being obliged to send women and children to work to supplement their income (Hendytio, Moelyarto, Gaduh, and Feridhanusetyawan 1999, p. 6). If the family still owns a piece of rural land, choosing subsistence farming would seem an attractive option.

Besides, returning home is associated with an expectation of being accepted and trusted. There was also an opportunity to relive the sensual feeling of childhood — eating familiar food and smelling familiar smells (Ganguly 1992). It was evident from her reason to travel — to come home to her parents — that Mita expected her travel to bring a sense of comfort. This journey could either be the real first step towards a change to the gruelling reality of life or an imaginary temporary comfort. Possibly, she had to travel inter-island and leave her husband and household in Kupang to take charge of her life again. Faced with household and economic challenges, Mita negotiated the boundaries of propriety as a housewife staying in her own home and chose to relocate herself and her daughter at least temporarily.

An interlude on the ship: Rika

Rika, in contrast, showed signs that she was a seasoned traveller and enjoyed being on the move. Going on voyages was in her view like an adventure. She came on board prepared. Her clothes looked comfortable and her preparations included a plastic basket full of food and a supply of bottled water and other necessities for the trip. The food she carried seemed to be equal in volume to her luggage. One possible reason, as explained by Frederick and McLeod (1993, p. 12), who refer to Victorian women travellers, could equally be applicable here:

> The female travellers' clothing and domestic objects provided an
> official identity and facade behind which the women could develop
> not only their publicly condoned feminine role, but also their in-
> nermost human dimensions.

Even though Rika travelled alone, she looked in charge among the crowds. On the ship's lower decks Rika looked well groomed, her made-up face accentuated with crimson lipstick and her slender build complemented by a fashionable suit, comprising a pair of black slacks and a red top. Within no time she had gained a travelling companion of another young woman whom she met on the decks. They sat close together, watching the hustle and bustle of many other travellers. Passengers around the same decks were quite pleasant to the two women, lending them magazines to read and offering tidbits. In return, Rika offered dry biscuits and other snacks from her well-stocked food basket.

A few hours into the voyage, most passengers seemed to have calmed down after initially feeling tense while trying to find a space. All tried to make themselves comfortable in the lower decks. Rika started her move to be more comfortable because she knew one of the ship's crew (*Anak Buah Kapal or ABK*), so discreetly she asked other crew members for him. Unfortunately, he was off duty (on-shore), so one of the crew volunteered to look after her. Thus, if Rika needed anything, she could get in touch with the crew member.

When night fell, Rika disappeared from the decks. She admitted to me later, with giggles, of spending the night in a crew bedroom, which was described as being much more comfortable than her cramped space on our lower decks. Boastfully, she also told me that it would have cost more than Rp100,000 (A$20) to have the privilege of staying in a crew room that night. In her case, it was free. Rika seemed pleased to be successfully negotiating the boundaries of propriety in her travel by staying the night at the crew's room.

Looking groomed and refreshed the next morning — her hair still wet after showering, presumably using the crew's facility — she reappeared on the lower decks. Holding a dish of fried rice for her breakfast, she explained that the crew had much better food than passengers like us in the economy class. We had the common staple breakfast of boiled rice and eggs that morning, while the crew apparently had meat and fried rice.

Figure 4.3: Ship crew providing information.

Rika's twinkling eyes gave away her excitement about being on the ship. Travelling alone, she was free to go beyond the boundaries of proper behaviour and to explore a new space of her travel, offering a range of possibilities. With her charming smile, she had attracted several of the ship's crew. Intermittently, she sat and chatted with them on the lower decks in between the crew's shifts. She liked travelling on the ship because of the prospects of new adventures: *"Saya senang naik kapal, karena siapa tahu kita ketemu kenalan baru"* or "I like travelling on the ship because who knows we may meet someone new." Rika's casual answer to my question of what she liked best about her travel highlights the boat as space of in-between with uncertain rules of propriety and hence the possibility of rendezvous.

In creating an in-between space of travel, Rika was able to exercise a new scale of relations and power. This was a different experience from her humdrum everyday role as a housewife in the household. In the fleeting space of the voyage she was able to enjoy being a feminine young woman. The ship represents material liminal space and thus a space of adventure. The borrowing of a crew room — with or without payment — is quite prevalent on PELNI ships, as I found out from other passengers. I was offered one myself on another voyage. For Rika though, who admitted enjoying travel as a means of finding new encounters, her connections with the ship's crew was a bonus. Quite evidently she was pleased to obtain a free berth for sleeping. Only a selected few were able to gain access to this privilege. This often depends as much on a woman's network among the ship's crew as her social skills and experience. Obtaining this space on a ship is not necessarily a straight-forward negotiation. As it allowed sexual relations to occur, it also became a negotiation of a space of adventure for all parties involved. Materially, the cost of a room for private encounters was sometimes deliberately kept blurred.

Rika's brief sojourn on the ship was immersed with the joy of discovery of a new encounter and charged with the delight of doing what was considered improper for a married woman at home. The unexpected excitement of a serendipitous moment of encounter created by this ambiguous space of her voyage was apparent. On the ship at that moment Rika seemed to transgress norms of propriety as she pursued a new and interesting encounter through the temporal space of travel.

Invariably the uncertain boundaries of proper behaviour in this in-between space raises the issue of sexuality in travel. The ambiguity of this space in-between is evident from a newspaper article which reports a case of sexual harassment involving a housewife travelling from Sumbawa to Kupang and a crew member of a PELNI ship.

A housewife almost raped on a ship

On Thursday (8/7/99) Mrs B, accompanied by her husband reported SH, a crew member of the Ship *Pangrango*, to the police in Kupang. SH almost raped her on the voyage from Sumbawa to Kupang on last Thursday (24/6/99). According to Mrs B, while in the ship on the way to visit her husband who works in Kupang, she felt sea-sick. At the time the crew member who admitted already noticing her after she boarded the ship, offered his crew room, so that she could have a rest. "I was offered to sleep in a crew room and also he offered to give my shoulder some massages. However, soon after that he closed the door and locked it from the inside, he forcefully attempted to take off the lower part of my clothes. He imposed himself upon me but I refused and also I talked him out of it," said Mrs B.

Nevertheless, once he realised that he was unsuccessful in carrying out his bad plan, according to Mrs B, he still persisted, and a few times made advances towards her. When she shifted to Deck Four, SH looked for her and tried to approach her by giving her some food and persuade her to come back and sleep in his crew room again. As the ship approached the port of Tenau, Kupang, according to Mrs B, she was again almost raped in the toilet but managed to get out of the situation.

"I went to the toilet and suddenly he followed me and then locked the door from the inside and demanded I go along with his plan even if it was only for a minute," said Mrs B. According to Mrs

B, when she went off board the ship and was met by her husband, she kept it quiet. However since then, every night she was tortured because she kept the incident secret from her husband. "Two days ago I just told my husband about the incident and I asked to report it to the police in Kupang," she said.

(*Pos Kupang*, 9 July 1999) (my translation).

This article may be viewed as exposing impropriety of a woman travelling alone and offering a warning sign to other women — a sanction against going beyond the boundaries. Such ideological restrictions on women's movements reflects and reinforces notions of a woman's place (Huang and Yeoh 1996, p. 107), where going beyond this context is viewed as improper.

As women travel, leaving their homes and showing an increasing presence in public places, "the feminine within the masculine sphere" is unavoidable and results in a sense of social anxiety (Bondi and Domosh 1998, p. 270). Amongst Indonesian women, a warning sign which evokes a feeling of fear is cultivated as a means of control. Particularly in Java, from childhood, fear is taught to control behaviour, including to control one's spatial movement. Similarly if a woman does not "behave" and does not stick to a certain "propriety", she is taught that something wrong will happen to her (Berninghausen and Kerstan 1992, p. 73).

The newspaper article places a woman within the boundary of propriety behaviour, in a certain gender relation with her husband, where she is supposed to be weak and thus in need of protection (Lawrence 1994, p. 38). The article evokes a woman's fear of being harassed while travelling alone. One way to overcome this fear is by travelling with a friend whenever possible. Yet increasingly women from the region are able to negotiate the boundary, as will be explored in Martha's story.

Impropriety and escape: Martha

More intense than the previous pattern of social visits for maintaining contacts, the trip discussed next contains the notion of social exclusion. Indeed some women were locally excommunicated and had little choice but to leave. The "forced trip" resulted from impropriety of behaviour in the local gendered space and relations, causing a spatial exclusion. Distance created by mobility produces different scales of relations and perspectives, and this shift of perspective marked Martha's first travel.

Martha was a 39-year-old village widow from Kedang, on Lembata Island in Flores, who felt compelled to leave Flores. She had to escape from the community "curse" resulting from a "forbidden relationship" with a man, and her travel outside the island was her first. The daughter of a modest farmer with a family of eight girls, she did not finish primary school. Like the rest of the family she was illiterate, and eventually was married to a local farmer. Both husband and wife struggled to make a living. Some years into the marriage, her husband decided to voyage to Malaysia to improve their economic situation. Unfortunately he came back very sick. They had three children before her husband died in 1991 as a result of the sickness acquired while working on a plantation in Malaysia.

Until 1995 Martha had lived a quiet life as a widow with her three children in the village under the protection of her late husband's *suku* or clan. They managed to survive with produce from her subsistence garden, but "life was hard as a widow in the village," (*susah hidup jadi janda di kampung*). That same year a 48-year-old man named Darius, a distant relation, wanted to have intimate relations with her. He was already married and had seven boys. However he said that he desired to have a daughter with Martha. Despite Martha's initial refusal, his insistence and assistance weakened her resolve. After several encounters, Martha became pregnant with Darius' baby.

In the eyes of Martha's kin, community, and the Catholic church, she made a grave mistake in her extramarital relationship with a "prohibited" man. Prohibited relationships between men and women are identified through local genealogies. Such relationships are viewed seriously as incest which brings disharmony to the island's cosmology. As described by Forth (1998), there are parts of Flores with rituals aimed at "neutralizing sexual transgression". People involved in incestuous relationships are required to undergo "a rite of banishment". One such rite involves the practice of scattering rice and other grains as a sign of effecting separation to reclaim the notion of harmony of local space (Forth 1998, p. 221). According to local beliefs a destitute woman who disturbs the village's harmony, such as Martha, was a source of bad luck, possibly causing drought in the village. As this scandal caused an uproar in the clan of her late husband, Martha was pressured to leave the island.

Martha felt so ashamed when going into her third month of pregnancy that she left her village. Following several local people on the move, she left Flores, tracing the inter-island routes, and eventually became stranded in East Kalimantan. She had previously never contemplated travelling outside Lembata because of her domestic responsibilities and limited resources. As a mother of three young children she had been house-bound. Through her own efforts, she managed to pay for a sea passage and left in a hurry to escape the unbearable shame.

Even though Martha was a Catholic and thus, according to church rules, was able to marry again after her husband died, the local cultural tradition did not necessarily allow this. After marriage, when a woman's kin receives her bridewealth, she belongs to the husband's clan group (*suku*). If she remarried, it would have meant she would divorce her late husband's *suku* and so would have to pay back the bridewealth, which apparently was a very complicated matter and hardly ever happened where she lived. The perception of a wife belonging to the husband's whole clan because she has already been paid for through her bridewealth represents a boundary that a woman has to remain within.

Paradoxically, Martha's *langgar laut* and banishment from the island, instead of giving punishment, brought mobility and new social relations. Following her inter-island travel, Martha was able to tap even further into a mobility network as an undocumented migrant to East Malaysia. Her children stayed behind with their grandmother. Joining a group of her local villagers who worked in a plantation, she helped with cooking for the workers and was paid a small wage, *uang sabun* or, literally, money to buy soap. Outside Flores, strangely, Martha felt safe staying with others from the same origins who protected her from other males.

Figure 4.4: Collecting water.

When Martha later came back to the village, her late husband's clan reacted violently towards her and her illegitimate child. Martha was physically abused, being beaten by Didi, the younger brother of her late husband, who was still single. Didi felt that he was fully justified in controlling her. Martha had to formally ask for the clan's forgiveness for her transgression and was then allowed to stay with her baby in the *kampung* as part of the husband's clan. Eventually, the unwanted baby died, aged seven months.

Since then, Martha lived under the protection of Didi, who was single and who moved in with her because he did not possess his own house. They lived as husband and wife which resulted in Martha becoming pregnant again. In the context of the Catholic church's influence in Flores and the government policy, contraception is available only for married couples under family planning provisions, hence the unwanted pregnancy resulting from the unavailability of birth control devices. A month before Martha was due to give birth, Didi disappeared from the village. Reportedly, he sailed to Malaysia as an undocumented migrant to escape his responsibility to Martha and the child. So Martha's struggles continued with her recent baby now aged five months.

Martha found that being away from home for a while was a liberating experience, because as she said, *"bisa bebas"* (she could do what she liked). When Martha *langgar laut*, she escaped from the local boundaries of propriety. From Martha's point of view, then, her main reason for travel was to escape the local villagers' hostile response to her prohibited relationship. Interestingly, in the in-between space of her travel, the boundary dissolved and she dislodged from a particular way of being and seeing.

In the past, the social and ritual importance of her kinship group was paramount in creating boundaries that limited her and that led to engagement in burdensome community work, such as providing for *adat* rituals. Martha realized that, at home, she was inevitably involved in all community, kinship and traditions. Kin obligations within her circle of social relations demanded much of her time, energy and resources. Martha described to me how she changed. Before travel, her everyday life was based and grounded in the locality and she remained within the local boundaries of propriety without qualms. Unless one's behaviour was inside these boundaries, one would not be accepted as a full member of the kin groups and community. After her travels, her life was rather isolated from her kin group, but she had gained access to a wider circle of social connections. There were tensions within herself and with others as a result of the new insights she had gained while travelling. These tensions continued as she struggled to make sense of the social distance she felt and the associated emotions that had affected her. At the same time, the struggles and tensions create growth and strength. Martha's story reflects the ways in which her travel was used as a negotiation of gendered space, where crossing the physical threshold of home in effect produced space for the emergence of different identities.

The stories of Rika, Mita, and Martha show that through travels, women contested the boundaries of propriety. Their stories provide examples of travel as the means through which women go beyond the familiar circle to access different scales of social relations and power. The seemingly ordinary inter-island travels of the women encapsulated their desire to negotiate rules and norms in order to create a space to enact changes.

School trips: a class privilege

In Eastern Indonesia, higher education is positively correlated to mobility. In general, education is relatively expensive when it is connected to accessibility. Few parents from rural backgrounds can afford secondary and tertiary education for their children because these services are normally available only in cities (Tirtosudarmo 1996, p. 147). Parents who send children inter-island to towns to go to school are perceived as being of strong economic and, in turn, high social standing.

Figure 4.5: Percentage of population 10 years old and above by gender and educational attainment, 2000.

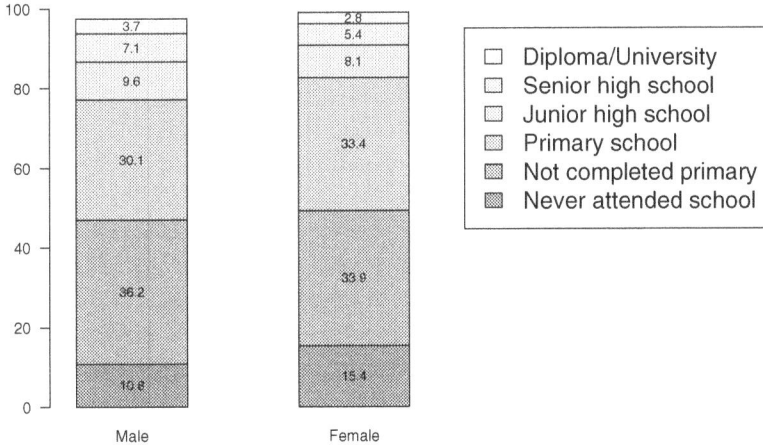

Source: Badan Pusat Statistik Propinsi NTT (2001).

Moreover, stereotypical socialization patterns differ between social roles for daughters and sons. In the past, though slowly changing today, daughters had been prepared for mainly domestic activities requiring less formal education. Nevertheless, as Oey-Gardiner (1997, p. 147) argues, in Indonesia parents are increasingly prepared to invest in education for both boys and girls. As shown in Figure 4.5, in East Nusa Tenggara a larger proportion of men (20.4 per cent) have secondary and tertiary education than women (16.3 per cent) according to the National Socio-Economic Survey, 2000. Only 5.4 per cent of women ten years and above in the province had the privilege of senior high school education, and an even smaller proportion, 2.8 per cent, have tertiary education. Parents' social and economic status determines daughters' access to education in the cities. To maintain the status of the family, young women related their mobility for education to an increase in their responsibility to remain within the boundaries of propriety.

For girls from rural Flores such as Eva, to travel to study at tertiary level in Kupang was not regarded as a right; it was a rare chance. With the consent of her family, Eva, a young woman in her early 20s, went to study in Kupang, buoyed by the dream of getting a highly paid job. What Eva still clearly remembers of her first trip on a PELNI ship from Larantuka was her strong emotions about that voyage: *"Saya begitu bangga, pergi untuk mencapai cita-cita saya"* or "I was so proud to be on my way to reach my goal." Going on her first inter-island trip was crossing the threshold of local relations to begin a personal quest. *Langgar laut*, or crossing the ocean, was a special experience because she believed it was reserved for the privileged class only. She conveyed her feeling of *bangga* or pride tempered a little only by travel sickness on the ship, from which she quickly recovered. Eva recognized that this privilege *mencari ilmu*, to acquire knowledge, gave her a further responsibility to maintain or even enhance the family status (*menjaga nama baik keluarga*).

From Eva's parents' viewpoint, sending a daughter to gain an education outside Flores was a highly beneficial investment in many ways. Generally, highly skilled women have a chance of better employment and salary. In addition, educated girls may command higher bridewealth. More importantly, sending children away to study also demonstrates the household social status. As Eva said: *Kalau bisa menyekolahkan anaknya di kota, orang tuanya dipandang hebat,* or "if one can send the children to study in the city, the parents are considered to be of privilege class."

Eva's responsibility to uphold her parents' status by following the boundaries set at her home village continued in the distant Kupang. There she performed different roles as a student and a single woman living away from home. Through these she admitted that she gained intellectual and emotional maturity. She described the ways she related to her kin, peers and others in the new place of living, all carefully handled so that she would not overstep proper behaviour (*salah langkah*). At the beginning of her move, Eva viewed her inter-island travel as a challenge to her self-identity as a village girl (*anak desa*). Now residing in a boarding house within a middle-class area in a more urbanized environment than her village, she reflected how she negotiated her identities and kept the boundaries of propriety:

> When I arrived, I was a very innocent and simple girl who didn't have many friends. I might have looked such a modest girl, as my dresses were unsophisticated from the village. I looked at my friends, some of them enjoying the new freedom of being away from home. Then I said to myself that I didn't want to be like some of them. (Fieldwork)

Eva recognized the possibilities of a new space that *langgar laut* provides, and her travel represents complex negotiations between class/social privilege, gender, and a naive quality of rurality. She chose to remain within her familiar boundaries. She resisted some new lifestyle changes and confidently kept her image of naivete (*polos*). Eva was careful not to behave too freely (*bebas*), often implying sexual freedom. While some of her friends were busy exploring the new space, she took comfort in the familiar routine of doing domestic chores at the boarding house to cut costs.

In the construction of her own space of travel and at the transitional stage to her adulthood, Eva observed how some other young women from the same place of origin experimented with different identities. Eva admitted to being puzzled by other women's transformation following their travel to the city. The absence of family supervision while away from home enabled them to transgress the proper behaviour at home and more freely experiment with different identities and relations. The wide range of attitudes in maintaining "proper behaviour" shown by Eva and her friends highlights the new possibilities of their travel.

Certainly the realization of sexual freedom is well known in the history of travel. Scholars such as Lawrence (1994) discuss links between "movement and straying from the path" in the history of travel. A traveller is opposed to a pilgrim with "a purposeful quest", and a female traveller is linked to promiscuity (Lawrence 1994, p. 16). Through mobility women have the opportunity to forge a path to overcome some of the constraints of propriety on their access to power and knowledge

(Laws 1997). Travel affords women a temporal space of experimenta-
tion with significant material and cultural differences, in the ways of
dressing, behaving, and thinking. Women's bodily performances and the
transitional space of travel are thus mutually constituted (Women and
Geography Study Group of the IBG 1997, p. 196).

Travel, in this case, is regarded as an intersecting space of independence and becoming, although some of my informants perceived it as
being fraught with horrors and hazards. Eva's anxiety and fears of overstepping the boundaries in this highly contested space resurfaced in a
suggestion to me that I should write a book warning girls about risks
involved in travelling away from home. Her intention to uphold the
"proper" behaviour for herself and for other women was sincere. In response, I explained frankly that I could not promise such a book. Rather
I promised I would write about her stories, views and thoughts as well
as those of others. On the last opportunity I had to say farewell, I was
greatly touched by her friendly gesture of giving me her hand-woven
scarf, *tenun ikat*, with motifs from her place of origin. This small token
of intimacy heightened a sense of journey in my own research, making
me as an extension of the women's voices in the context of their politics
of mobility. Within the similar motive of gaining education, these young
women's travels reflect a wide spectrum of experiences in contesting and
producing the in-between space of travel.

Work trips: a maiden's dream

Women from all over East Nusa Tenggara travel to the city of Kupang
to work. The provincial capital, Kupang, is a place of opportunities,
not only for education but also for employment, as reflected in the large
number of formally employed women there. In terms of the job market,
the Kupang urban areas offers more high salary jobs for women than any
other part of East Nusa Tenggara, as evident from the Intercensal Population Survey (SUPAS 1995). The problems of finding jobs in other areas
of East Nusa Tenggara were illustrated by a survey of 800 high school
graduates in Timor who completed the high school exam in 1996. This
showed that many young people were unsure about their future careers
because of the increasing competition in the job market and difficulties
in continuing their education or securing local jobs (Najib 1997, p. 3).

Employment in East Nusa Tenggara has so far been dominated by the agricultural sector with its limited employment growth. Some informants who had previously been job hunting and then decided to migrate had first tried to find local jobs without success. The reasons for their failure might include a lack of experience as well as the limited availability of local employment as these women are situated in East Nusa Tenggaran regional labour markets with limited local employment opportunities. This necessitates their inter-island travel to find better jobs. Lina from Flores is an example of an increasing number of young women who refuse to work on the land. She expressed her discomfort in the hard labour of subsistence farming and monotony at home:

> In the island of Flores, I could not see my future after finishing high school, what sort of job I could get. I was also feeling uncomfortable at home, the same thing over and over again. I then tried to talk to my father, to make him understand and ask for a permission to work [away from home]. (Fieldwork)

Lina's increasing feeling of discomfort stemmed from the monotony of home and not having enough authority over her own life. The promised future income outside Flores was an incentive to leave home. However other personal reasons have proved to be as important in the decision of other women leaving home.

Contemporary urban East Nusa Tenggara is characterized by a mixture of modern influences and traditional ways of life. Simultaneously, these places of employment and opportunity for women from Flores were regarded suspiciously as a source of "impurity", as indicated in many media reports of "sexual transgressions" in Kupang. Rural cultural traditions in the islands impose strict boundaries of propriety on the movement of women beyond their local domain without a male protector. This is illustrated by practices in Flores which prevent single women from going out alone in public places after dusk.

Women travelling inter-island alone represents both negotiations of the boundary and re-creating a new space. Mina, aged 28 years, embraced her opportunity to travel to Kupang for work as a chance for upward social mobility. She works in a well-paid job as a middle manager in the active retail trade in Kupang.

As a typical professional single woman travelling alone between Kupang and Ende, Mina used the same sea route at least twice a year in a routine journey between home and work. She travelled with great panache, her hair neatly tied up in a bun, a look-alike designer handbag on her shoulder, perfect make-up and red nail polish on her neatly manicured fingers. In the middle of the weary passengers struggling to find space on the ship, she elegantly navigated herself through the clutter on board. Mina stood out. Everything seemed to fall into the right place for Mina. Even the luggage was just the right amount that she could handle by herself if she wished. Apparently, Mina was used to travelling alone. This explained her calmness and composure in the crowded ship. In addition, she had a berth in second class, a four-person female only cabin, which at the time she shared with three others.

Mina had sufficient means to support herself and thus she made her own decisions about travelling. Since she was a teenager, she has been used to travelling between the islands of Timor and Flores, either accompanied by her family or alone. I suspected that her father's military background facilitated her success in securing a berth in a private cabin. My own experience shows that it is not a simple matter for a woman to buy a cabin ticket from a PELNI office. Because there are more men than women travelling, its allocation of berth by gender facilitates selling a ticket to men. Without any help, I had difficulties obtaining a PELNI cabin ticket. Particularly in school or public holiday seasons, the ship was typically very full. Obviously, the presence of someone in a military uniform accompanying Mina when boarding the ship had helped considerably to smooth the process of embarkation. The ship crew seemed friendly to her. I

Figure 4.6: Subsistence gardening is too demanding for some.

noticed at the beginning of the voyage that someone had brought her cabin key to her with a smile, while others had to push into a crowded jumble of people supposedly queueing in front of the information booth on the ship. Mina's higher social status made the physical aspect of voyaging to her destination less demanding than for most women. As a financially independent professional equipped with her tertiary degree and the right social connections, Mina had the necessary resources to travel in style and comfort.

Mina, in her role as daughter, conformed to perfect norms of propriety as demonstrated by her regular journeys between Flores and Timor. She described her trips as necessary for her career as well as her domestic obligations of visiting her family's home:

> I miss home and my family terribly and I also miss the big open space, which I can't find in the place where I work. As much as I can, I go home to see my family. But I also enjoy my work and life there. So it is necessary that I go back and forth [between home and work] as far as my finances allow it. (Fieldwork)

Her successful negotiation of propriety is shown by her family's acceptance of her following a professional career in Kupang. Her voyages allow her to maintain a presence in both home and work domains, and she would be considered as both a "good" daughter and a professional. Mina's resources and social networks allowed her to travel inter-island with ease. Despite her career in management, Mina spoke of her future dreams of setting up a home with a husband, *"berumah tangga"*. These very words, meaning to have a family, rehearsed many of the domestic dreams of maiden voyages: eventually, to be a good mother and wife. The norms of propriety at home imposed over women, prescribing futures which include *"berumah tangga"*, evidently constituted Mina's identities.

The stories of women's travel for work show how they contain a dichotomy between home and career. When both domains are separated by a distance, this embodies tensions for the travellers, such as in Mina's case. Leaving home is often associated with independence, which breaks the nexus between the Self and domestic tasks and identities. On the other hand, the social expectation of women's main role, as the homemaker and having a family, creates a desire for domestic roles among women. Tensions embedded in this type of travel indicate on one hand the conceptual appeal of travel so that women can achieve a better position in circuits of relations, and on the other hand, it may be going too far against the dream of being a homemaker.

Dynamics of inter-island routes

In examining the link between women, mobility, and the boundaries of propriety, I demonstrate in this chapter through the inter-island travel stories how travel reflects and reproduces gendered space in East Nusa Tenggara. This research problematizes feminine codes of behaviour prescribed in the local gendered propriety. Drawing on the multi-dimensional purposes and various narratives of travel I explore the emerging different identities as women travel. Much of the travel stories, such as Rika's and Martha's, contain a notion of travel as a space for negotiating boundaries in the sense of going beyond the local scale of social categories and hierarchies. Creating different scale of relations and power, Rika's marital status did not stop her availability to other men and Martha's social exclusion brought her an economic independence. The analytical focus has been on how material and emotional distance can release the hegemonic hold of boundaries of local proprieties.

The critical attention to women's everyday activities and their negotiating strategies as they travel provides an insight into their politics of place (and scale) that stretch beyond localities. Within the limits and marginality of their previous positions in social relations, including within the household and the community, they are able to reposition themselves in a different scale of network of social relations. I examine the production of gendered subjectivity at home and away, and how women do align their femininities in reference to space. In the liminal space of travel, a concept which is expanded in the next chapter, certain boundaries, including norms of behaviour, are negotiated. I suggest that this liminal space is viewed with a more nuanced approach, in which women go with and against boundaries to play their politics of place. The women's stories capture different dynamics of travel, either transgressing the boundaries of propriety or going with it in order to be included in a particular social network. Liminal space of travel is effectively used in their politics of place. Women use travel as a space to contest the norms of propriety and also as a strategy to circulate, to enter a wider set and a better position in networks of relations.

The stories presented here illustrate travel for visiting relatives, education, and for work, and show women's strategic moves in re-evaluating their positions through travel. I unpack the heterogeneity of their travel to reveal the ambivalence of subject positions the travellers occupy (Blunt 1994*b*). The women's stories reveal complex tensions in negotiating boundaries of propriety in their inter-island travel. While *langgar laut* in this instance is a seemingly trivial short-distance journey, it is a highly significant step in which women undermine the local status quo relations of power by spatially creating a distance between themselves and their kin and community. Despite the risk of impropriety inherent in women's travel, absence from the family home provides a space of opportunity for new insights and roles in different contexts of social relations.

CHAPTER 5

Travel to Urban Centres: Nurses and Teachers Mobilizing Selves

My association with a female teacher, *ibu guru*, started when, sailing to Flores, I literary bumped into Dami, the teacher's nephew. Later, I was invited to Dami's village to celebrate *misa sulung*, the First Mass, of a newly ordained Catholic priest and was asked to stay with the *ibu guru*. The teacher's family welcomed me into their house — a neat three-bedroom brick house equipped with its own bathroom and kitchen at the back, an above-average facility in the area.

The next day, after the great celebration of the First Mass, the teacher took me around to talk to the local women who had gone *langgar laut*, like herself. Before leaving, she changed her Western style dress to a *sarung* (sarong), and lent me one to wear as well. Reluctant to offend my kind hostess, I did not ask the reason but just followed her example. And she smiled approvingly when I reappeared in the living room walking rather awkwardly in the *sarung* matched with a plain blouse. "Oh you look proper, (*pantas*), just like one of us," she said as every one including some men in the room agreed. The teacher saw it as important for us to dress in the *sarung*, to visit local women in their homes, doing things "their way" to achieve our aims.

Performing multiple femininities

In the local gendered space of Flores, our bodily appearance — the material space — and social relations are formed and negotiated as a strategy to achieve a specified aim, as the previous vignette illustrates. Travel to the city in the local context, as suggested by the women's stories in this chapter, involves aligning their body, gender, and sexual behaviours. Why? In the local context, similar to the early twentieth century cities in Europe, women's presence in the cities might be seen as a problem because it symbolized the promise of sexual adventure, "a problem of order" (Wilson 1991, pp. 5–6). In Indonesia, sexual adventure, excessive ambition, and assertiveness for women is seen as a deviation (Hatley 1997, p. 94). Cities represent disorder and ambiguity as far as women's sexuality is concerned, but at the same time they also offer wealth and opportunity, promising liberation (Wilson 1991, p. 6). The women's travel stories in this chapter illustrate precisely this contrast, reflecting deeper experiences of strategically locating themselves in a polarized opposite position between conforming and transgressing the local notion of femininity.

During my field research, I noticed how women chose to present their travels to the city with reasons surrounding their function as professional carers as nurses and teachers. Although many are carers, I exclude Catholic nuns in my analysis because of the significant difference in freedom of movement for this smaller group of specialized travellers. To a certain extent, they follow orders from their superiors, whilst generally teachers and nurses may choose the place they work. These professions fall well within the appropriate femininity. The women's ambivalence to urban spaces points to their associating these spaces with ambiguity. Particular representations of urban space as hazardous for women play a crucial role in production (and contestation) of specific discourses about appropriate gender roles and behaviours (Bondi and Domosh 1998; England 1991; Hubbard 1998; Wilson 1991).

In their travel to urban areas, I found the women seemingly conformed to the dominant discourse of their gender roles in choosing their feminine jobs. Analysing their travels further, however, shows that taking up their feminine professions actually also generates power. Women have more space to practise different kind of femininities and identities through travel. My informants' travels to the cities to be professionals demonstrate the process of change in traveller subject positions and subjectivity. Their stories show how women partly sustained the local status quo of power, "doing things in their (local) way", in order to move beyond local relations into the more ambiguous space of urban areas. This shift leads me to think of their travel as fitting the notion of liminal space — a transient, fleeting, and ambiguous space — which is full of uncertainties. I argue that women can exploit the fluidity and multiplicity of roles and identities in the liminal space of travel, enabling their shifting subjectivities.

The analysis of travel of these professional women — nurses and teachers — as they work in the city attempts to tease out the emerging and changing constitution of travelling subjects. To do so, I trace the ways they imagine and take up different identities. First, I examine the elevation of these feminine professions, which is traced back to the state's ideology and the local discourse of femininity. This discourse is reproduced and used by the women as a justification for their travel to the city. Then, I present the stories of Detti, Evita, and Ima, which not only provide the observable material condition of the women's move to the city, but also sketch their imaginative journeys of identity through exploring their practices of femininities. Examining the ways women construct and practise feminine identities while travelling to the city enables me to explore women's shifting subjectivities in the local contexts. Lastly, I explore how in the liminal space of travel, women attempt to balance social expectations with their own strategies to be "oneself", (*menjadi diri sendiri*) — to gain autonomy and independence.

Jobs in urban centres

Early in my reconnaissance trip, I became aware of many women of East Nusa Tenggara travelling to cities such as Makassar and Surabaya. I observed the women's presence in public places such as hospitals, schools, and churches, through recognizing their distinctive physical features. Women's travel to these cities has been supported by the fast-growing sectors of education and health services, providing sources of mass employment (Oey-Gardiner 1997, p. 135; Manning 1998, p. 100). For instance, teaching jobs in cities have grown rapidly with an ongoing expansion of national education, with total annual costs of Rp21.7 billion. This expenditure on education comprises 5 per cent of the GNP. Recent figures show that more than 42 million students are enrolled in more than 227,000 institutions, which employ more than 2 million teachers, offering an opportunity for secure employment (Purwadi and Muljoatmojo 2000, p. 92). Eastern Indonesian women have been part of this migration to take up these feminine jobs. My field observations of this group of migrant professionals led me to focus on teachers and nurses in the traditionally feminine jobs.

By taking up careers such as teaching and nursing, women perform the femininity which is "socially, historically and geographically constituted" (Laurie, Dwyer, Holloway, and Smith 1999, p. 4). The embedded femininity within the caring professions is an historical social process, as explored in Chapter 3 (the notions and practices of femininity). My informants evidently performed the dominant femininity in their travel to loosen the tight grip of the local cultural constraints, as revealed later in their stories . The elevation of teaching and nursing professions as a "Divine calling" produces a unique mission that necessitates travel for women as part of their "vocation". This connection between women's movement to the city and the practice of "caring" rests upon the common theme of a romanticised representation of femininity in the professional occupations of caring for others.

The history of romantic travels within the West — begun in the late eighteenth century and lasting through to the end of the nineteenth century — repeats itself within journeys of contemporary Eastern Indonesian women travelling for *panggilan* or vocation. One of the central goals of romantic travel is to be immersed in cultural difference (Duncan and Gregory 1999, p. 8) — and this resonates with the Eastern Indonesian women's wish to travel to urban centres. They too seek an experience of difference from their rural or semi-rural origin, and this curiosity is framed through a romanticizing of their motives as being those of caring for others.

Figure 5.1: A woman's role is to nurture.

The availability of teaching and nursing jobs in the cities facilitates the flow. However, woman's agency is as important as the economic structure in directing a woman towards these feminized occupations (Bozzoli 1991). As discussed in Chapter 3, the dominant approach to the study of migration emphasizes the economic structure of the flow of rural-urban migration. This approach ignores the subject because it focuses on the economic factors of unequal distribution of resources as the main reasons for young people to move to the cities. In describing the patterns of economic flows, such an approach does not reveal the importance of the subject and subjectivity of women. Indeed, within a labour market system, women who move to work in the city are seen as labour power only, excluding the migrant subjects, subjectivities, identities and desires from the analysis (Lawson 2000; Pile and Thrift 1995*a*; Silvey and Lawson 1999). Therefore such an approach precludes attention to the interplay between the structural factors and young women's personal desires and decisions to move to urban areas. I address the question of subject and subjectivity by analysing the travels of nurses and teachers to the city and offering a critical ethnography of their experiences of migration.

Virtuous women and sacred professions

A professional path as a teacher or a health worker in the context of East Nusa Tenggara commands high respect from the community. Both professions contain a "sacred" connotation, *pekerjaan mulia*, meaning honourable job. *Ibu guru* is a reverent title for a female teacher, meaning madam teacher. In the villages I visited in Flores, a headmaster is one among the highest in social status. This is followed, among others, by a *mantri* or a health worker. The status of these professions reflects possession of both knowledge and power in the local community. The elevation of these feminized professions relates to the dominant discourses of femininity, as previously discussed in Chapter 3. The naturalized gender roles provide a strong basis for local women's decisions to engage in the socially acceptable professions as the carer and nurturer. Moreover, both nurses and teachers are in a position of knowing and acting as a source of information, which thus translates into power.

It is a source of pride for a local family to have a daughter become a teacher or a health worker. As a teacher or a nurse, a woman maintains the gender role of caring but transfers this to the public sphere, in schools or hospitals. Given this community pressure to conform to propriety within the dominant discourse of femininity, these professions raise an issue of the extent of freedom of choice for women entering these feminized occupations. I support Bozzoli (1991) who argues that the reason for entering these occupations coincides with the women's initiative in creating the most of the available opportunities by travelling away from home. A woman's following of such a profession highlights her travel as a strategy, not as merely a result of labour market opportunity. The advantages of choosing such occupations include women's internalized training in domestic responsibilities as a part of their upbringing, better pay than working on the farm, and an increased prospect of marriage

(Bozzoli 1991, p. 96).

Women's choice of a "safe" (implying socially acceptable) occupation of carers in contemporary Indonesia under State *ibu*-ism becomes a perfect frame for their travel to achieve other personal goals. My field research shows that in their *kampung* (hamlets), not only do people respect women in these sacred professions but they also perceive them as virtuous women, despite their travel. Thus women who were teachers or nurses could remain within the boundaries of the gendered space and at the same time they can travel to the city for their own personal reasons.

Vocation: a representation of caring jobs

The language used for professions indicates the significance of the jobs — sacred professions, *pekerjaan mulia*. Some women felt strongly that they were being "called", *terpanggil* — the way the Catholic religious (priests or nuns) were called to serve God — to take on the responsibilities of caring. When asked to tell their stories, my informants echoed similar concerns and mostly chose a virtuous representation of rescuing the young, sick, or poor. This representation fits with Wilkes' description of the romantic construction of a caring career:

> The world was a place in which wrongs could be righted, tears mended, and the proper order restored. These were the points in the narratives when speakers' accounts became quite vivid, and the women spoke with forthright passion and conviction. (Wilkes 1995, p. 242)

As women "restoring order", how could they be "out of order" themselves? The nurses and teachers whom I interviewed were similarly passionate in describing their *panggilan* or vocation rather than referring to it merely as a profession. And this *panggilan* necessitated and justified travel. Romantic narratives of the caring profession often begin with solitary dreams or ambitions in early life (Wilkes 1995, p. 239). The romantic form of my informants' description of their *panggilan* was, however, contingent upon the context and sequence of the stories. Behind each travel story there is a shared theme of how the individual is strategically distancing herself from home and the family to create a liminal space for mobilizing self.

I interviewed fifteen informants from East Nusa Tenggara, seven teachers and eight nurses, who work in Surabaya and Makassar (see Table 5.1). Most nominated an altruistic motive of "being able to help

Table 5.1: Nurses and teachers working in urban centres.

Name	Origin	Marital Status	Job	Religion	Age	Edu	Work Place
Evita	Sikka	Married	Nurse	Catholic	29	3	Surabaya
Roswita	Sikka	Married	Nurse	Catholic	29	3	Surabaya
Henrica	Lembata	Married	Nurse	Catholic	27	3	Makassar
Anastasia	Sikka	Married	Nurse	Catholic	30	3	Surabaya
Detti	Timor	Single	Nurse	Catholic	32	3	Surabaya
Tin	Ende	Single	Nurse	Catholic	25	3	Makassar
Fatima	Ende	Single	Nurse	Muslim	32	3	Makassar
Livi	Sikka	Single	Nurse	Catholic	24	3	Surabaya
Emi	Ende	Single	Teacher	Catholic	22	3	Surabaya
Maria	Sikka	Single	Teacher	Catholic	35	2	Makassar
Bibiana	Sumba	Single	Teacher	Protestant	27	3	East Java
Ima	Sikka	Single	Teacher	Catholic	35	3	Makassar
Greta	Ende	Single	Teacher	Catholic	29	2	Makassar
Eliana	Ngada	Single	Teacher	Catholic	26	2	Makassar
Wati	Timor	Single	Teacher	Catholic	25	2	Surabaya

Note: Edu (Education) 1 = Primary; 2 = Secondary; 3 = Tertiary
Source: Fieldwork.

people" as they moved to take up teaching and nursing. They presented themselves in a predictable way in their reliance on the idealized image of femininity, which also bears the footprints of the state's dominant gender ideology. This view drew heavily on the expected behaviour of "knowing one's place", a woman's place is to nurture. Even though this woman's place is an increasingly unstable and contested space in national debates.

Nursing, caring in public and in private: Detti

Detti was a single, soft-spoken nurse in her early thirties, who I met in a hospital in Surabaya. As the youngest in a family of seven children of whom all, except her, had married and left home, Detti was the last in the family's hierarchy. As an unmarried daughter and a youngest sister, she was under the protection and authority of her family. This relationship reflected the hierarchical gender and kinship structure of the local community in Timor Barat. However Detti turned her life around, starting with her travel to the city. Her justification for leaving the village was that she was "called" to care for others. This line of reasoning was too noble for the family to dismiss, although her decision to independently pursue this profession evidently challenged her typically subordinate relationship within her family.

Detti arrived in Surabaya ten years ago to study to become a nurse. Her most recent trip back to her home in a district of Kefamenanu in Timor Barat was the first in the past three years. Vaguely, she mentioned some pressures and resentment from the family regarding her rare visits home. The few travels back home were the product of her rational decision, where the cost of transport and other problems associated with going home, including *oleh-oleh*, meaning gifts from travel, was expensive in relation to her income. However, she herself did not mind being away from her family for a prolonged time. Detti displays a sense of autonomy in her relations with the family in her home village.

One weekend I unexpectedly stayed with Detti overnight in her tiny one-bedroom rented house in a small alley in Surabaya. It was six o'clock in the evening and beginning to get dark and torrential rain poured down. The area was severely flooded, so I was stranded there. I offered to buy our dinner in a nearby flooded small food stall, and went there by *beca* (trishaw). Kindly, Detti later invited me to share her single bed in a cramped two-by-two metre room, which I gratefully accepted. While busy helping her empty the constantly filling buckets of water whooshing from the roof cracks, I shared a piece of Detti's everyday life routine, typical of living in the city by herself.

I had met Detti several times before and she impressed me as being independent and mobile. Detti knew the city well and was comfortable taking public transport alone in Surabaya at any time. When she was off-shift from nursing, she was busy attending social functions, such as church choir practices. She actively built social networks around her in Surabaya. Meanwhile, she stressed that although her family was important to her, she did not see any point in maintaining physical proximity in the village just for the sake of family. Her father had wanted her to follow in his footsteps as a local government officer, but she was not interested in staying in the region. She also expressed a strong intention to break with her mother's life path as a local housewife, as she imagined and preferred different identities. Her wish was to be an independent and professional woman. She achieved this through her movement to the city because there was no nursing school in her village.

Ironically, Detti having renegotiated her identities and turned her back on the subject position of "housewife", seemed to have located herself within the domestic role as a carer — as a motherly figure. She indicated that it was her vocation to be "there" in Surabaya and to care not only for the physically sick but also "to help anyone in need". Detti believed that it was her role to provide a meeting place for others from her region of origin. She not only provided food, sharing a traditional favourite corn dish, *jagung bose*, but also gave an emergency accommodation in her modest rented dwelling. Other references and remarks that she made showed her concern to present herself as being open to people who needed her. Not surprisingly, I witnessed her strong bond with some others from the region who often visited her rented house. Her identities as a single woman, a motherly figure for a small group of young students from East Nusa Tenggara, and a professional nurse were grounded in the local context of living in a *kampung* within Javanese neighbourhoods and working in a city's hospital.

In the city, where Detti performed the role as a caring motherly figure in the neighbourhood, she was accepted and respected. As the youngest daughter in the family she had always been obliged to follow the family's wish. However, unlike others who were compelled to travel home often, her strong sense of agency found a way to create a sense of home and familiarity there in Surabaya. There were rituals which she maintained to materially produce a home away from home. For example, food was an important part of creating a sense of home among the East Nusa Tenggaran people, often bringing them together. As a migrant subject living away from home, she had the choice of maintaining her Timorese identity through her choice of food. Being pragmatic, the occasional serving of her traditional food to acquaintances was a part of Detti's performance to reproduce a familiar space:

> If missing home, we would eat food that we normally prepare back home ... In everyday routine however, people are busy and don't have time to cook anything too elaborate, so just something very simple. I am like that and being single, I don't bother cooking very much, just eat simply. Often only instant noodles, it's cheap and nice. So if I cook *jagung bose*, our local specialty corn dish, I would call some friends and we would eat together. (Fieldwork)

Besides her cooking, Detti attracted the affection of the people for other good reasons. She was capable of competently solving problems by drawing on her wide social network. This was an asset for the community. While with her, I observed her reaction to an incident which unfolded before our eyes as she helped an elderly couple from her village of origin. They were on a mission from Timor to find their daughter's boyfriend in Surabaya. The young couple were students there, but the boy had disappeared after the girl confided that she was carrying his baby.

Competently, Detti made arrangements involving the confused family. As the youngest child, she would not usually command such authority in her own family. She took the elderly couple to her rented house, providing them with a place to stay, however crowded, and served them food. The couple were in obvious distress over the state of their daughter's affairs. Their daughter was perceived as "living in a state of sin" according to their Catholic faith. By extension the parents were "impure" and were denied holy communion by their local parish priest. Calmly, Detti managed to solve the problem. She arranged a party to search for the frightened boy. He was given a "lesson" and thus suffered bruises, but he agreed to marry the girl. By contacting the right people Detti helped to arrange for a private church marriage for the young couple. According to their local tradition there would be *adat* (customary law) to be taken care of and the young man's family would have to pay a fine in addition to the girl's bridewealth. The story of the young couple ended amicably, through Detti's intervention.

This incident displays the mutual constitution and performativity of both spaces and identities (Blunt 1999*b*, p. 423; Women and Geography Study Group of the IBG 1997, p. 196). In the liminal space that she created through her travel, Detti emerged not only as an autonomous capable woman but also as an authoritative figure with the right connections in the community and the local church. Her relocation enabled shifting subjectivities as she moved between various identities. She used a simplistic altruistic line to explain her romanticized move:

> It was my duty to help others. I travelled all the way here, there must be a purpose for this. There is some thing that I have to do, which is actually my "calling". (Fieldwork)

Void of an immediate responsibility for her own nuclear family, Detti's tiny rented house located in a narrow alley of a crowded neighbourhood was popularly frequented by young people from Flores and Timor, whom

she referred to as *adik-adik* (the younger siblings). She had accommo-
dated them and prepared to exchange her care with their acceptance.
Intermittently, they came from all over the city and nearby towns seeking a motherly figure. In between times of studying, these young people
visited her and took care of one another. Gracefully, Detti accepted their
help as there were never ending maintenance jobs to be done, such as
repairing leaking roofs, getting water from a neighbour (as there was
no piped water in the house) and other jobs around the place. In return, she provided a place to meet and food, creating a strong attraction
for the ever-hungry young students. Beneath the altruistic reason Detti
gave, there were many practical reasons for a single woman looking for
a network of social support to perform socially accepted feminine roles.

Detti's feminine caring identity seemed to be an integral part of
achieving her autonomy, which she contextualized in materially specific
ways to suit the space. First, by her voyage leaving Timor island and
then setting up a home by herself in Surabaya. Before travel, and being
the youngest in the family hierarchy, she had very few chances to exercise her authority. Detti strategically planned and executed the idealized
feminine identity of "nurse" so that she could achieve her mobility and
gain social recognition of her own agency. Practically, as a single woman
in the city, she was required to maintain social networks which provided
mutual support as well as involving obligations, thus her generosity in
providing food and accommodation. The multiple identities Detti occupies within the main discourse of femininity nevertheless situate her on
a firm footing as an autonomous subject within her circle in the city.

Detti's femininity away from home, both in the informal social group
as well as being a nurse in the hospital space, moved her through different scales of social relations and power. As her story indicates, the
private and public spheres of Detti's everyday life created norms and
practices that produce and reproduce gendered activities and social relations within them (Martin 1992, p. 208). Her decision to pursue her
profession in the city proves that her travel was a strategic move. The
practice of reproducing and reinforcing the idealized femininity in Detti's
story, however contingent, is also shared by the following travel story.

Mobility and purity: Evita

Evita's profile fits the image of a successful contemporary Flores woman
pursuing a professional nursing career in a city. A 29-year-old, attractive

and outgoing married nurse, Evita gained a reputation among her peers as an exemplary nurse. Originally from Lela, near Maumere she was the first child of seven children of a tightly knit family of a *suku* or clan of Sikka. Evita's travel started when she was 18 years old as she voyaged to enter the nursing school in Surabaya. However, her imaginary mobility started with a fantasy when she was barely seven years old and had wanted to go and study in Java:

> I had been wanting to be a nurse since I was a little girl. My mum was hospitalised once, when I was about seven years old and I had a direct experience of knowing the nurses who looked after her. They were lovely persons in white uniforms so I was very impressed. Although I didn't know much about a nurse's duties at the time. This left a lasting impression deep in my mind, that I would like to be like those nurses when I grew up. Ever since I could remember I had always wanted to be like them in white uniform and helping sick people...
>
> I also have an auntie who is a nurse. She meant the world to me and I wanted to be like her. She is nice, clever and moreover she is a nurse in a white uniform. I always remember what she said about a nurse, that you are directly involved with your patient in the day-to-day business of recovering, whilst a doctor only interacts with the patient from time to time. (Fieldwork)

Later, after completing her education, she secured a permanent job as a nurse in a reputable hospital in Surabaya. Ever since, she has travelled regularly between Surabaya and Flores. Evita's residence was in a two-floor brick house on the side of a busy road in a central area in Surabaya. Her husband worked in a private company, earning a very good income. The couple lived comfortably, as shown by their house and the modern household appliances in their home, including a big television and stereo sets. The lounge room was spacious, painted in off-white colour, three-by-four metres in size. On the wall there were two of her 1998 enlarged wedding photos in fancy frames. The lounge chairs were comfortable, made of carved mahogany wood with crimson velvet upholstery, an interior style commonly found in middle-class Javanese houses in urban areas. As we sat comfortably sipping a glass of iced tea which a maid had served us, she told me her story.

Her life, in her own words, was *penuh badai* (full of storm) and had its share of torments and troubles. An advantage of being away since such a young age was in her words, *"bisa menjadi diri sendiri"*, to be herself.

She was able to resist indirect kin and community pressure to remain at her home village until marriage. She was aware that her mobility to the city defied certain local norms of gendered propriety. Her frequent travels aroused gossip about the possibility of improper relations with men in other places.

Evita's solo travels to and within urban areas created a perception at home that she was "loose". This had negatively affected a relationship with a previous potential spouse. The time of her courtship with her (now) husband was plagued with arguments and his jealousy. He accused her of playing around, on the basis of her mobility. In this sense her mobility was equated with freedom of the road, including sexual freedom. The polarity of purity/impurity of her body in connection with her travel appeared several times throughout her stories.

Despite her personal and financial independence Evita still recognized the significance of her family and community's influence over her. Her subject position as a daughter and a member of the clan simultaneously created a dilemma between on one hand, her obedience to the family, who were concerned with the purity of her body, and on the other hand her choice of a different feminine identity as an autonomous and attractive woman. The resulting "daughter's obedience from a distance" approach taken by Evita was an indication of the strong family connections which are grounded in the local historical context.

Evita shared with me her internal tensions dealing with the external perception of her femininity, which is somewhat beyond her control. Her efforts in realigning her identities to suit a particular space and time indicate a strong sense of agency. Evita's frequent travels as a single girl had created her family's anxiety because she was rumoured to have had some male suitors in different places. However she was resolute in her decision to continue travelling. From her comments about her community I found that she was aware of the society's double standard applied to women's purity in relation to travel. This purity of the body is never an issue in men's travel.

In Evita's case, her resistance to the double standard on purity of the body related to her mobility manifested itself in a stance against the fiancé, which resulted in a tense relationship with him. He (now married to her) accused her of having an affair. There have recently been repeated cases of single Florenese girls who fell pregnant, known as "losing their virtues" after intimate relationships in the city. Evita was particularly hurt at being accused of *hilang kesuciannya*, or losing her virginity/virtue:

> I did not defend myself or any effort to that effect, just challenged
> him [the fiancé] to find another girl whom he was certain that she
> was a virgin... However he did not want to end the relationship
> and eventually we got married. At our wedding night he sobbed
> and asked for forgiveness for once doubting my virginity, as he then
> knew the truth. (Fieldwork)

Evita's frank story and reflections on her travels highlights direct confrontations in performing multiple femininities. The dominant femininity relates impurity of body and women's mobility. Within the local cultural historical context, Evita had little control over the way her mobility was perceived by others. People's perceptions of women's travel reflects the deeper intolerance of freedom of movement for women in urban areas, demonstrating dominant power relations to control women. Evita's past travels meant that she had to endure rumours of having a tainted reputation. People's perception of Evita's mobility, however, changed after her marriage because they were no longer preoccupied about her virginal and social purity.

As Evita's travel shows, women are able to perform multiple femininities through travel. They imagine and perform diverse identities which are mutually constituted through and with spaces. Travel to take up a caring occupation becomes an entry point for exercising one's own agency. To understand Evita's moving subject positions and shifting subjectivities, as a dependent, obedient daughter, to a mature, independent and attractive nurse, requires moving with the travelling subject in her multiple identities through different locations and changing contexts during her travel.

Teaching and becoming: Ima

Many contemporary Eastern Indonesian women choose to work as teachers — one among a range of social roles in urban centres in which women perform their feminine identity. Teaching jobs with security of tenure not only bring a reliable source of income but also local prestige. Women of the region have taken the opportunity of getting a teaching job in the city as a way to access knowledge and different scales of power, as the following story indicates.

Ima was a single, friendly teacher in her mid-thirties, originally from Palue island in Flores. She travelled to take up her teaching appointment in Makassar in 1991 and has since voyaged regularly between Makassar and Flores. She goes home at least once a year during the Christmas and New Year break. Her simple yet autonomous, independent lifestyle as a single professional was one aspect of her life she valued most. This dimension of power was possible from a distance — in a liminal space — she created between herself and the family. She was very passionate about her teaching job and viewed it as her life's mission, and I observed how she thrived and excelled in that feminine role.

Ima's gentle behaviour fitted the social expectation of femininity of the teaching profession. One word — compassionate — first came to my mind in an attempt to describe her character. Her very pleasant personality was obviously an asset in her teaching career and in her relations with others. Most of the time she enjoyed teaching in a Catholic high school in Makassar, which was managed by a Catholic congregation. Ima's sensitive style of teaching, however, sometimes led to clashes with the headmaster, a Catholic brother originally of Flores, who preferred the use of corporal punishment to discipline the teenage students. Apparently Ima was popular among her students and became their confidante, and the following story reflected her bond with her students. I was outside Ima's front veranda when she listened to one girl's anguish and anger of a broken heart and a pregnancy. Unfortunately, the headmaster had taken a hard line, scolding the girl and calling her *gadis murahan*, a term often associated with a prostitute, literally meaning "a cheap girl". The distraught girl disappeared from the school the next day. I saw later how devastated Ima was, reflecting her concern over her students. She was a committed teacher, deeply engrossed in her teaching responsibilities. In her words: "my calling is to teach." Such was her dedication to her students, she implied that she did not have time for a romantic relationship.

In the liminal space of her travel, Ima displayed a personal autonomy in making the decision about her future and remaining single. Distance from family, she commented, was essential to being *mandiri*, or independent. There was less family interference with her private life, or *"keluarga tidak banyak campur tangan"*. Being in this liminal space provided her with a necessary environment to move between a range of identities and roles in relation to space. She was able to make a unilateral decision of refusing an arranged marriage and stick by it. Gentle as Ima might have appeared, she had defied her extended family's wish for her as their daughter to get a husband of some social status.

In the local context, a single status for a woman was thought of as *tidak laku* or "nobody wants you" — making a woman's life "incomplete" and thus showing her to be of a lower status. The state's ideology of the dominant femininity projected an image of a fulfilled woman as "a supportive wife, a good mother and an impeccable housewife, and a worthy parent who raises good citizens for the benefit of the state" (Wolf 1992, p. 68). This ideology produces and reproduces a stigmatized identity for a single mature woman which is known as *perawan tua*, meaning an old maid, as observed in many parts of Indonesia. In Java, the social pressure for single eligible woman to marry is very strong:

> Once a woman has been accepted into the adult community, her sphere of activities broadens considerably, even if the marriage does not last. Compared with the societal devaluation of women who remain single, divorced or widowed women are stigmatized to a much lesser degree. However, women who live alone for whatever reason are especially subject to suspicion and destructive gossip on the part of others. (Berninghausen and Kerstan 1992, p. 116)

Unavoidably, Ima must have attracted a fair portion of the village's gossip. Particularly because of her attractive physical and feminine qualities, it was expected that she would not have any problem finding a potential husband. She was an average height, slim, sweet, dark-skinned lady with bright eyes, a dainty nose and pleasant smile. Her rather curly black hair which was grown to shoulder length graced her friendly face. With such physical assets and a good family background, in the local context she was expected to marry instead of remaining single. Daughters are valued among others for their potential of bringing a bridewealth to increase the family's social status.

In her village of origin, Ima transgressed the boundaries of "proper" femininity by remaining single well into her thirties. As far as Ima's family was concerned, her case was a lost opportunity for an alliance with a high-status family. The extended family was upset, and for a period of time they refused to talk to her. When she visited her grandmother who lived with her uncle, the family avoided and ignored her by going out to the garden to work. By distancing herself from the family and making her own decision, she was being excluded from the kin and family relations, or *"dikucilkan keluarga"*. Whatever her private reason for remaining single, Ima seemed pleased to live by her decision. Despite enduring negative treatment from her extended family for some time, she firmly believed that her vocation was to nurture as a teacher rather than as a mother.

Time and distance gradually healed the family tension and Ima's decision regarding her single status prevailed. At least her nuclear family has since respected her decision. For Ima, her teaching was, on one hand conforming to the dominant femininity in caring for the young, on the other hand, being single went against that same femininity. Watching Ima interacting compassionately with some of her students as I spent time with her, I appreciated the extent of her commitment to teaching and the long hours she devoted to the profession. The question remains, how does teaching in the city provide her with power to decide her life path?

Throughout her adult life, in the various gendered spaces of home and work, Ima performed the dominant femininity. However, the physical and emotional distance of travel, and its creation of the liminal space, allowed her to go against that very same femininity. By becoming a single professional, she defied her family authority. Being separated from the family provided her with a liminal space to constitute a shifting subjectivity, to create an identity of a single professional woman, because her personal desires were important for her. Here, the liminal space of her travel allows a process of becoming.

In presenting and analysing the stories of women's travels, I find, like Lawrence (1994), that the trope of travel "provides a particularly fertile imaginative field for narrative representations of women's historical and personal agency" (Lawrence 1994, p. 20). Travel provides a liminal space to manoeuvre around. Another informant, similar to Ima, demonstrated her agency in a desire to travel and be independent so as to change trajectories of her everyday life:

> I had enough of the monotony of home. Usually women wait at home to be married. But I want to extend my horizon and to be myself and not depend on anyone else. (Fieldwork)

Ima's story is similar to the previous stories highlighting the women's agency in creating the liminal space for themselves. This space mutually constitutes a wider range of identities and shifting roles. In creating the physical and emotional distance, women are able to make their own decisions, instead of relying on kin, parents, or a husband.

Travel constitutes a space of possibilities and uncertainties, enabling women's shifting subjectivity. The micro politics of women's strategic moves to the city, as Ima's story shows, underlies the economic reason of finding a teaching job in the urban areas. Other women found travelling provided a transient space of exploration of multiple feminine identities. The ship, in particular, became a contested liminal space of gender relations, as the following travel story demonstrates.

Contesting liminal space: Bibi

The physical process of travel itself creates an in-between space with blurred norms, opening to contestation of relations between space and identities. For Bibiana, the physical travel on a ship provided both distance and the space in-between, and was a dynamic and fleeting space mutually reconstituting changing identities.

Bibiana, or Bibi for short, was a cheerful 27-year-old teacher from Sumba, voyaging on a PELNI ship from Surabaya to Waingapu in Sumba. Her travel actually originated from Gresik in East Java, where she worked as a primary school teacher. Bibi had a mischievous smile with a pair of dimples on her face that created a youthful look. Her choice of trendy fashion — a pair of jeans and a sporty light blue polo top — completed the look. In the lower deck (economy class) of the ship, she joined a group of three young people boarding from the port of Perak (Surabaya) to their destinations in the Eastern islands.

The three-day journey offered many opportunities for interactions and making new acquaintances. As the voyage progressed, Bibi and her companions were quite jolly, treating the ship as a meeting place. I was on the periphery of this newly formed group of young people, not quite an outsider who watched from the sidelines, but I floated away at times too. We ate our rationed dinners, shared food and did a few other things together. The group sat close together, filled in crossword puzzles and told each other jokes. Bibi was definitely the star and centre of interaction as her bubbly personality outshone the others. In particular, she won the admiration of a good looking, tall young man in the group. When Bibi complained of a headache, he instantly fussed over her.

Getting intimate on a ship seemed natural. Being confined in the same place for a lengthy period encouraged people to pass the time by communicating with each other. Depending on the time of the day, the group would split and then came back together, such as at meal times and entertainment/movie time. On the first night, I noticed that Bibiana and the man walked hand-in-hand on the outside deck where the light was dim and there were fewer people. In the confines of the crowded ship, their physical closeness in the in-between space was almost unavoidable.

In this transient and fleeting space of her travel, Bibi initiated moves to closeness and the man responded positively. In the next afternoon, as we sat around in the lower deck getting rather bored, Bibiana cheerfully announced that she needed a hair trim. In no time she produced a pair of scissors from her luggage and asked the man whom she had been with to trim her hair. Rather hesitantly he obliged and trimmed her hair. Stroking Bibi's black hair with a comb he took his time brushing and tidying up her hair while we were watching them amusedly. The physical contact of the hair cut gave a further excuse for intimacy and seemed to legitimate the couple to get physically closer in front of other passengers.

The fleeting quality of this liminal space of the voyage might have given the couple a sense of equality in the relationship. They might have been aware that theirs was a transient intimacy, limited by the point of departure and the next place of destination. For reasons which I did not fully comprehend, they separately chose to confide in me, thus I was caught up in their relationship.

Bibi and this young man's encounter was apparently a one-off chance for flirting, or in Bibi's word *selingan*, meaning a change. Bibi privately admitted that she already had a boyfriend. She hastily added that she did not have a strong feeling towards her fiancé in the village, whom her parents approved of because of his financial security. She was undeniably flattered by the man's attention and I suspected that their attraction was mutual. It seems that the voyage created a space with blurred norms constituting some of the inward delight of being admired and pursued.

In the middle of other passengers and in their own space of temporary intimacy, the young couple gradually withdrew from the rest of the group. The young man was smitten and the relationship became more intense as time passed, with a great deal of physical intimacy — embracing and touching each other in the quiet of the outside deck. Out of the corner of my eye I saw him leaning over Bibi's shoulder to whisper something, and Bibi responded by putting her right hand around his waist.

The young man discreetly admitted to me later that he really liked Bibi, who was also a Christian like himself. However he had a Muslim girlfriend in East Java. He shared his dilemma with me one quiet evening while we stood on the outside deck — when Bibi was queueing for a shower — expecting sympathetic hearing in relation to his problem.

The disclosure of these intimate feelings came very unexpectedly as I sat on the ship's stern chatting to each on separate occasions. They obviously knew where to find me because I spent some time there alone, writing my ethnographic notes. I did not previously anticipate that we would engage in topics at such a personal level at such an early stage of meeting. In a way, it was quite disturbing to be involved as a middle person in their temporary encounter on the ship. Perhaps, as I appeared to be a mature person in the group, they wanted to tell it all to someone willing to listen to their confusion in this contested space. On this ship it seemed that most norms were blurred and new practices were produced. I was unsure how much Bibi knew about the young man's situation and reciprocally how much Bibi told him of her real situation, thus I had to walk on egg shells when talking to them. For that moment on the ship I recall mixed feelings — I felt anxiously uncertain about what might happen next, confounded by the physical exhaustion, yet I also felt a sense of power that people trusted me. Like Bibi and others on the ship, I also performed my own multiple identities in this liminal space.

The ship becomes a contested space of relations, reflecting the mutual performativity of the space and our range of identities. Away from the social pressure as a teacher, Bibi did not have to carry out her externally ascribed role of the dominant femininity. She seemed to be free in exploring her multiple identities, here, as a single woman travelling alone.

Liminal space: being away and a becoming

When I analyse these women's travel stories, they reveal the changes in the women's identities, subjectivities and desires. Their travel embedded changes from the status quo of local relations to wider connections and it reflected the women's desire to gain more power through personal autonomy and independence. Gaining control of their own lives might have been the women's primary, if concealed, goal in the first place. As I unpack their travel to the cities and look beyond the romance of the caring representations in relation to women's mobility, the notion of *langgar laut* for these women emerges as creating a liminal space to enact other identities. Women may imaginatively conform to the dominant discourses of femininity to care for others; however, simultaneously, they travel to perform other identities and access other networks of relations.

The travel stories in this chapter have demonstrated how women exploit both the state's construction of the dominant femininity and the local discourse on virtuous woman. At a theoretical level, this is how my concerns with the liminal space of travel and women's agency intersects with discourses of femininity. Women manoeuvred within the accepted femininities to launch themselves to the city in order to mobilize selves with wider possibilities to access knowledge and power. Their stories present the imaginative nature of women's travel as real, "both materially and performatively" (Duncan and Gregory 1999, p. 9).

The ways these teachers and nurses described their reasons for choosing the caring occupations are not a new insight. Contingent, micro, every day interactions strongly shape a woman's choice of sets of social roles. At the individual level of choosing a caring occupation, a woman is to some extent constrained by the dominant femininity. Their agency is crucial in the decision to pursue caring jobs in the cities, providing a justification for travel. Some informants were acutely aware of the reality of meagre salaries as nurses and teachers, whether working in the government or in private institutions, but the travel stories of Ima and Evita show how they used the liminal space of their travel to fulfil their personal desires and to recreate identities for themselves.

Once gaining mobility, the women are on the path of new possibility. The women similarly travel to be able to explore a sense of self, to be autonomous and independent (*mandiri*). This interpretation resonates with the experiences of other women travellers in different spaces and time. Biographies and interpretation of works of individual women travellers of the West in the nineteenth century confirm that, despite being confined to a woman's place "which was first and foremost at home", when a woman voyaged, her construction of femininity in its relation to the domestic sphere was altered (Lawrence 1994, p. x).

Women's romantic pursuits during a voyage illustrates the performativity of femininity in various spaces. Local inhibitions usually restrain a respectable female subject from expressing physical intimacy in public. However, while on the ship, a woman may perform a role of playful feminine identity, where she contests the local norms and creates new practices. On the ship, Bibi for instance exercised her sense of self as an autonomous individual — as an equal with man — allowing displays of physical intimacy. A secret liaison conducted on the ship on the windy outside deck is likely to be even more exciting because it transgresses the boundaries of propriety.

As women's travel to the cities shows, individuals manoeuvre within notions of femininity in whichever way provides advantages in a set of social relations. Caring jobs are one of the ways in which women both spatially and socially reposition themselves. Women's travel creates a liminal space opening up new possibilities for renegotiation of their roles and realigning their identities.

Throughout the various travel stories, there emerged a theme of women's shifting subjectivity in their localized relations. The plurality of the narratives of their mobility in relation to their feminized professions similarly indicates tensions between their ideal of their chosen professions with the reality of low salary. This reality points to their significant reason for their mobility, containing desires to gain personal autonomy. Through women's travel stories I have shown tensions resulting from the process of movement, the conflicting perceptions, thoughts, and feelings, so as to draw connections between the liminal space of travel, travelling subject, and identities. In the liminal space of travel, professional women in teaching and nursing jobs in urban centres perform multiple femininities to suit the space and their personal goals.

CHAPTER 6

Travel Abroad: Recollections of Domestic Workers

In April 1999 I met Leli, a girl from Bajawa, *kabupaten* Ngada, who had just completed a two-year contract working as a maid overseas. She had a stopover to visit her brother, a Catholic priest in Makassar, before catching the next ship to travel back to Flores. During Leli's two-week stay, she frequently visited my boarding house which I shared with her acquaintances (teachers from Flores). I made her a cup of tea, *putar teh*, and we chatted for hours on end. Leli was a shy, petite 20-year-old woman, the youngest of a farming family of seven children. It was obvious how her brother adored Leli, saying how special and good she was to work abroad for the sake of raising the family's income. The term he used, *rela berkorban* or ready to self sacrifice, which is commonly used for an Indonesian war hero, is considered appropriate because she is known for remitting most of her monthly earnings. But, from Leli's perspective, her travel symbolized the beginning of widening roles through personal autonomy. "I know now I can go and do things by myself," she said proudly, summing up her experience of travel abroad. The three of us — Leli, her brother, and I — parted at Port Makassar when we took her aboard the PELNI ship sailing for home in Flores.

Different spaces and subject positions

Unlike this vignette which indicates the importance of subjectivity in the young woman's travel abroad, much research on domestic workers has documented problematic relations between employees and employers in the place of employment (Meldrum 2000, p. 3).

129

Other recent research has highlighted how migrant domestic workers have been subordinated not only by their employers but also by their urban host society (Momsen 1999, p. 1). Among others, Robinson (2000*a*) has studied Indonesian women working as domestics in the Middle East, pointing out the inadequacy of binary frameworks in understanding the complexities of this transnational movement. Recent research on domestic worker migration comprises a range of variations in country of origin, ethnicity, and social background of domestic workers, including Irish, Italians, and lately, Filipinas working in Britain and France (Cox 1999; Narula 1999); Slovenians working in Italy (Barbič and Miklavčič-Brezigar 1999); Filipinas, Indonesians, and Sri Lankans working in Hong Kong, Singapore, and Malaysia (Constable 1997; Tam 1999; Yeoh and Huang 1999*a*; Gamburd 2000); and also Filipinas, Latina, and Chicanas working in the United States and Canada (Romero 1992; Hondagneu-Sotelo 2001; Parrenas 2001).

Travelling abroad to be a domestic worker allows women to experience different spaces, experiment with a variety of subject positions and thus imagine a different "subject's becoming" (Gibson 2001, p. 641). I follow the recent feminist framework which explores the ways in which migrant women negotiate and inhabit multiple subject positions (Silvey and Lawson 1999, p. 127, see also Kofman and England 1997). Women's travel abroad represents traversing home and the state's boundaries and activating different dynamics of relations. This travel allows a young woman to spread her wings farther and at the same time to be viewed as "a heroine" in exile for the benefit of the whole family, as the previous vignette shows. Resisting the romantic view of this type of travel, as detailed by Groves and Chang (1999), this chapter examines the women's experience of spaces including the material conditions at different stages of their journey as they proceed to work overseas as also discussed in Williams (2005).

Domestic service in Indonesia has a long history since the colonial period (Elmhirst 1999; Robinson 2000*a*). It has provided jobs for many unskilled young women. More recently, Eastern Indonesian women have travelled from rural areas to engage in domestic work in global cities, such as Hong Kong, Singapore, and Kuala Lumpur. Since the early 1990s, the number of Indonesian women working abroad has increased to meet the rising demand for domestic helpers in Asia Pacific countries (Hugo 2000). In the mid-1990s, nearly 42,000 Indonesian women went abroad as domestic workers in Asia Pacific countries. Five years later, the annual number departed had more than tripled, reaching 155,879. Between 1992 and 1998 total remittances increased from US$264 million to US$1,252 million, equivalent to an increase from slightly less than 1 per cent to 2.6 per cent of total exports (Hugo 2000, pp. 122–23). By 1999 the total of the previous five years foreign exchange earnings from the official channel of remittances by overseas migrant workers reached US$4 billion (*Bisnis Indonesia* (Indonesian daily newspaper) 1999). The World Bank fact sheet on migrant workers reported that the recorded remittances reached almost US$2 billion in 2001, steadily increasing to US$2.1 billion in 2002, and US$1.49 billion in 2003, however decreased in 2004 to US$1 billion. For 2005, it is estimated that the total remittances reached US$2.5 billion. In reality, the total remittance are much higher since not all in-flow are formally recorded.

Remittances from workers have increasing significance to both the government and the families of individual workers (Heyzer and Wee 1994; Momsen 1999). The state, using its regional apparatus of administration, has actively supported the recruitment drive for overseas domestic workers because of its interest in increasing its foreign exchange earnings. Following the Indonesian financial crisis, more than one million Indonesian contract workers migrated overseas. Three-quarters of these were women working as maids abroad (International Labor Organization 1999). Hugo (2000, p. 109) points out that during the Crisis, overseas migration of women was used as a strategy to cope with the reduction in household purchasing power.

Domestic work in the urban households of global cities is a lure. In Asia Pacific region, more affluent urban households in Singapore, Malaysia, and Hong Kong employ domestic workers from countries such as the Philippines, Indonesia, Sri Lanka, Bangladesh, and Thailand. The ILO's findings on women's overseas migration represent the generally accepted reason that "Asian women migrants opt to work abroad under trying conditions for the good of the family..." (International Labor Organization 1998). Domestic work abroad is attractive for young women because it is low skilled with low barriers to entry, pays relatively well, and often the provision of housing as a live-in worker encourages even more women to do this job (Cox 1989; Tam 1999). The work also allows "migrant women to acculturate to the city and learn new ways of living" (Hondagneu-Sotelo 2001, p. 48) and it pays significantly more than similar work inside the country. The increasing demand for domestic jobs in the Asia Pacific region encourages a rising number of Indonesian women to undertake overseas migration.

Here, I am less interested in the economics of domestic service or in the cultural opposites of "the dynamic social relations of dominance and difference" between employers and their foreign employees (Momsen 1999, p. 1), which carry the risk of homogenizing migrants' experience and erasing parts of their identities (Silvey and Lawson 1999, p. 127). Instead, I focus on the subject and her interpretations of place, particularly the spaces and conditions under which domestic workers experience overseas travel. More specifically, I explore the migrants' shifting subjectivity as a result of their overseas travel (McDonald 1999), because "migrant identities are also constructed through the process of mobility itself in ways that incorporate and blend experiences of multiple places simultaneously" (Silvey and Lawson 1999, p. 125). I situate my work within a broader set of travel frameworks to unpack domestic workers' migration, drawing on an increasing number of studies such as those by Constable (1997) and Romero (1992), whose approach argues against an essentialist view of domestic worker–employer relations:

> Studies that centrally or exclusively focus on oppression, however, tend to overemphasize the passivity and powerlessness of the worker, as well as the dominating power of the employer. Power is viewed too unidimensionally. It is understood as emanating from the employer's superior class position, sometimes reinforced by issues of race or ethnicity, gender, or other factors. The worker is simply cast as victim... (Constable 1997, p. 9)

In this context, I am concerned with the issue of how domestic workers, through their travel, experience multiple spaces which enable them to occupy a variety of subject positions.

For some Eastern Indonesian women I interviewed, the appeal of travelling and working abroad — apart from the money — was the opportunity to escape from family constraints and live in a different community overseas for an extended period. Some simply wished to experience different spaces and places, which in their words was *"memperluas cakrawala"*, which literally means to expand their horizons. Others found it difficult to find suitable employment in the local labour market of East Nusa Tenggara that would guarantee a reasonable income. Still others travelled abroad as domestic workers in a search for personal autonomy, echoing the nurses and teachers going to urban centres.

The style of this chapter differs from the previous ones. I take my cue from Netti's personal map — an exceptionally vivid drawing — which

Figure 6.1: A map of Netti's travel abroad.

tells stories of her personal struggles and triumphs of her journey (see Figure 6.1). On one typical occasion, listening to my informant's story, I asked Netti to remember her travel experience and jot down her memories. Netti sketched quite an interesting drawing of her migration, while she was narrating her journey. I decided to use the unusual cartography of Netti's drawing to structure my representations of the women's travel abroad. The typical journey of a domestic worker going abroad follows several distinctive phases, each representing a different space — leaving home, in-transit, working abroad, and returning home. But first I present the profile of the domestic workers interviewed.

The pursuit, looking for experiences

The increasing popularity of travel for an overseas contract job among Eastern Indonesian women begs further questions of what this travel entails and what it means for them. Travel abroad to enter domestic service is then examined, analysing each stage of the journey by drawing upon the experiences of fifteen returned domestic workers (Table 6.1). They were interviewed informally mainly in their homes, at my boarding house or in public parks during fieldwork in Makassar and Flores between 1999 and 2000. As thirteen of the fifteen women went to Hong Kong, most stories relate to the group going to Hong Kong. As with previous groups of informants, I entered their network through "snowballing" connections. Through my association with a Catholic Religious Order, the Society of the Divine Word, or SVD, I was introduced to a woman known as a "ringleader" — an ex-domestic worker who had become a recruiter. I became acquainted with her group of friends. They accepted me in their circle as a fellow traveller, *perantau*. As we exchanged our life stories, they knew I was originally from Java and had travelled from Australia for my research. As we exchanged our stories and autobiographies, we shared our experiences of living overseas. We could relate to each other to some extent as travellers on a journey. Our common experience as women travellers, sometimes struggling alone to make sense of our new circle of relations, became our mutual bond.

The returned migrants seemed pleased to share their stories and had the time to talk — similar to my encounter with Leli in the vignette — probably because they were on holiday after their contract abroad. More importantly, the trust generated through the network of the SVD Order as my point of entry to the field should not be underestimated. My curiosity about their travel experiences was met with an enthusiastic willingness to tell their travel experiences and talk about themselves.

This group of informants were all single and aged in their twenties, and previously had no particular skills or job experiences. As reflected in Table 6.1, they had similar social and economic backgrounds of middle-to-low income families with a predominantly farming background. Before their migration all had been unemployed, therefore financially dependent on their families. All, except one, had attended secondary school and two of them had studied at the tertiary level. The secondary level of education of my informants was higher than those of women studied by Heyzer and Wee (1994), in which only 30 per cent of the Indonesian domestic workers finished high schooling while the majority had only primary schooling. Nevertheless among those who had completed high school to be overseas domestic migrants, many were rural women, reflecting the scarcity of rural employment (Heyzer and Wee 1994). My informants started their overseas travel between 17 and 23 years old, which is inside

Table 6.1: Profile of domestic workers.

Name	Origin	Family Occupation	Religion	Age (years)	Edu Level	Work Place	Service (years)
Miriam	Ende	Farming	Catholic	23	2	HK	2
Vero	Ende	Fishing	Catholic	20	2	HK	2
Siti	Ende	Weaving	Muslim	22	1	SNG	1
Leli	Bajawa	Farming	Catholic	20	2	SNG	2
Betsi	Bajawa	Farming	Catholic	23	2	HK	2
Linda	Bajawa	Trading	Catholic	21	2	HK	2
Lena	Ende	Farming	Catholic	25	2	HK	2
Susana	Ende	Farming	Catholic	24	3	HK	2
Rita	Ende	Labouring	Catholic	25	2	HK	2
Netti	Ende	Farming	Catholic	27	2	HK	4
Krista	Ende	Farming	Catholic	29	3	HK	4
Agnes	Ende	Fishing	Catholic	26	2	HK	2
Liana	Ende	Labouring	Catholic	23	2	HK	2
Karina	Ende	Farming	Catholic	25	2	HK	2
Mariana	Ende	Farming	Catholic	24	2	HK	2

Note: Edu (Education) 1 = Primary; 2 = Secondary; 3 = Tertiary
Source: Fieldwork.

the 15–25 age group bracket of rural women in Heyzer and Wee's (1994) study. Except for one Muslim woman from Ende who worked for only one year and thus did not complete her contract, all had at least two years experience as domestic workers abroad. Two women had four-year service and two others were on holiday and would be returning for a second term of their contracts.

Travelling abroad to be a domestic worker reveals a personal and metaphorical journey of struggle for subjectivity in changing spaces and relations. This is illustrated in Netti's sketch. Netti's map can be viewed as one mode of cartographic vision which resists the mainstream cartography of objectivity and strives to make women's space visible with a variety of graphic grids and geometries of experiences and feelings (Huffman 1997). However, as Domosh (1997) and others remind us, we need to go beyond understanding the individual experiences, and it is necessary to examine the conditions under which these processes are produced.

When I analyse Netti's map within the local historical context it reveals the terms in which this type of travel is being constructed and performed. In this way the analysis of the informants' experience at different stages of the journey provides a link which enables me to see broader phenomena within travel abroad for the local women. Netti's map contains four clear stages of a journey, which form a circuit:

- Leaving home

- In-transit

- Working abroad

- Returning home

Theorizing domestic contract migration in terms of a broader set of processes of travel allows me to examine how this type of travel provides an opportunity for women to occupy various subject positions. The following discussion of this type of travel traces these typical stages to highlight conditions and experiences of space at each phase of the journey, and it begins by considering the departure from the family home.

Leaving home

Commonly, the departure stage was the first hurdle. It involved one of the most difficult decisions about travelling overseas as it was often the young women's first journey away from home. Their attachment to home was related to a particular phase in their life cycle and, to some extent, a specific subject position as lower status in the family and kinship hierarchy as an unmarried daughter. Often women who worked as maids abroad were characterized by very limited resources, in terms of both their economic and social capital. Although there were a range of experiences during the departure stage among those who had completed their journey abroad, a common thread ran through the beginning of travel experiences — an uneasiness regarding their departure, as evidenced in discussing the stories of individual women.

Netti, Susana and others decided independently to work abroad to earn a reasonable income. When asked for the reason, superficially they used similar narratives of "helping their families financially". However there were other deeper and perhaps more significant personal reasons revealed, which are discussed in the next subsection but also emerge throughout the stages of their travel. They also understood that without any experience, they had little chance locally to secure a suitable job which would guarantee good pay. What thoughts had gone through their minds before finally deciding to go abroad?

Figure 6.2: Leaving home.

Netti's reflection after returning from her contract abroad was shared with me — particularly her thoughts at the start of the journey — as we looked at the sketch she did of her journey (Figure 6.1). Netti's map illustrates a process of changing spaces and relations associated with her overseas travel. This cartography of travel defies conventional mapping in the way that it contains grids of social relations in each phase of travel, and it is linked by personal memories, sentiments and feelings. In essence, the drawing established a view from the inside — which also depicts conflicting thoughts, maps significant events, and attaches a sense of place.

As shown by Netti's map, the stage of leaving home was characterized by a strong feeling of attachment to her family's house *"rumahku"* (my home) forming the place where her memories are stored. A confused girl is enchantingly shown in front of the pier. She is about to make a new step, to cross the *dermaga* (boundary of the port) — a significant place separating land and ocean (see Figure 6.3). The image of a crucial first step crossing the unknown territory pinpoints the importance of sea as a threshold. Sea is a source of reference in relation to others, and it forges connections with outsiders (Graham 1999, p. 72). Netti's important move creating new spaces and forging new, uncertain relations is captured by her drawing of the threshold between home and away. This illustrates her mixed emotions of leaving the family home to enter new scales of relations. There was a concern about community attitudes questioning the bona fides of her occupation, an excitement about a new space, and an anxiety about uncertainties of securing a better economic future.

Figure 6.3: Home — Subsection from Netti's map.

Motivation

Generally, the opportunity to earn a good income to help the family was the main motivation given by most informants — a finding that has parallels with many similar studies on overseas domestic workers (Momsen 1999; International Labor Organization 1998). Yet within this broad generalization of motivation nestled a rich variety of individual reasons. Netti, for example, was part of the first groups of women from her hamlet in the Ende regency in Flores to work overseas. Single, aged 27, and as the second child of a large family of eight, she lived at home with her parents. Her father owned a piece of land — less than half a hectare — for subsistence gardening and her mother was a housewife, helping out in the garden. Netti's eldest brother, who was married with two children, worked as a labourer in the construction industry in Malaysia. He remitted part of his earnings back to the family and thus had helped to keep Netti's family solvent. Netti, like many high school graduates (*lulusan SMA*), had been attracted to the public service which offered the prospect of a secure job within local government. However, she did not succeed in securing any job after leaving school. Despite her initial reluctance and uneasiness about leaving home, Netti's motivation to work as a domestic worker in Hong Kong was presented as primarily economic — to earn a good income so that she could assist in rebuilding her family home, which was ruined because of an earthquake. Her narrative also contains a desire for social mobility to escape the impoverished family way of life as farmers:

> My intention to travel started when there was an earthquake in
> 1992 [in Ende], and our house was destroyed. I wanted to go
> and earn money. We would have liked to start building the house
> straight away, but we didn't have the money. Also, it was always
> the same thing when we lived with my parents. It was even harder
> to ask for some money. My parents grumbled whenever I needed
> money. When I finished high school I was unemployed for a while
> and stayed home. If I wanted to help and do some work in the
> [subsistence] garden, it felt physically too demanding. In the years
> when we were at school, we didn't have to work in the garden. The
> sun was too hot, I could hardly stand it to work there... (Fieldwork)

When I met Netti in 1999 she had achieved her economic goal. Her
home had been completely renovated and become one of the most imposing dwellings in the area. It was reconstructed using bricks and it had
proper roof tiles rather than the common thatched roof and also shiny
floor tiles — an unmistakable sign of wealth and prosperity.

Susana, on the other hand, was a 24 year old and the fourth daughter
of a family with five girls. Similarly, she was determined to improve the
family's finances. Her parents were subsistence farmers. Unmarried, she
was the only one in the family who managed to complete a vocational
high school education to become a kindergarten teacher, while her siblings did not go beyond primary school. Her reason for wanting to be
a domestic worker in Hong Kong seemed simple — the absence of local
job opportunities — and yet it also revealed a hidden a desire to decide
her own life path, beneath her conviction of "the divine provision":

> My experience was that it was hard to find a job after finishing
> high school. I finished a teacher training [vocational high school
> level] and I searched for a job in East Timor [which at the time was
> a province of Indonesia], to Kupang and other places in Flores but
> I could not find any teaching jobs. I came back home and intended
> to study for a diploma so that I could teach religion. But I felt
> that no matter how much more I studied, because I was supposed
> to be a kindergarten teacher, it would still be hard to find a job.

> However if I went back to study in order to teach adults, I was
> a bit unsure of myself... And then I thought more about it. Fi-
> nancially, we could not afford my further studies, as my parents
> were farmers. Then almost every night we heard on the radio that
> they needed domestic workers. I wanted to have the experience of

working abroad. Well, I was not so sure, but it must have been a divine provision. I had gone everywhere, applied for a lot of things but nothing came out of them. Out of the blue, I met a [distant] cousin who had been a domestic worker, yet whom I had not met for a while. That was how it started and then I made up my mind to travel overseas. (Fieldwork)

By working her two-year contract in Hong Kong, Susana achieved her goal of increasing the family income. Nevertheless, when questioned further, both Netti and Susana and the rest of informants indicated varied and deeper personal reasons for their travel. There was desire to experience different spaces — to go beyond their homes and family, "to learn new skills and to meet new people". These were Liana's words. Liana is a happy-go-lucky girl who decided to apply to go to Hong Kong with her best friend Mariana. They were bored with being unemployed and broke so they travelled together to spread their wings and to widen their perspectives (*memperluas cakrawala*).

Travelling abroad to be a domestic worker provides a personal space by, at least temporarily, creating a distance from the family (Barbič and Miklavčič-Brezigar 1999, p. 175). Agnes, for instance, was disillusioned with her boyfriend and sought solace abroad, away from family and friends. Once her relationship with her boyfriend was severed, she avoided meeting people in the local community in case they questioned her about her failed marriage plans. When told by a friend about an opportunity to become a domestic worker, she needed no further encouragement. For Agnes, working overseas was one way of obtaining space and privacy.

Women were also motivated to move from their rural households to urban households abroad because it gave them the opportunity to become "modern" or "to learn a new way of living" among others by gaining familiarity with the urban lifestyle and the latest appliances (Momsen 1999; Elmhirst 1999; Hondagneu-Sotelo 2001). Many women, most notably Liana and Mariana, were pleased to be associated with "modernity". They were proud that they had acquired jeans and a pair of sneakers as material signs of urban sophistication. Jokingly, Liana said she could not care less what local people in her *kampung* must have thought, when she adopted sneakers in *kampung* instead of bare feet. Yet becoming "modern" in their local community had its problems, because the returned domestic workers stood out as being very different or strange (*aneh*).

Among some obvious economic reasons expressed by the informants, a strong motivating factor, evident from the experiences of Liana and Mariana, was the desire to travel to experience different spaces. This impression differs from that reported by Heyzer and Wee (1994), in which East Javanese domestic workers (mainly in the Middle East) considered providing for the family and making a pilgrimage to Mecca as the primary motives:

> They were motivated by concerns for family survival and not by their need to enjoy an independent life or to fulfil their own aspirations. Their decision to migrate as domestic workers was based on their chief concern about the survival of their children and the ability to provide their children with a good life, good education and continuous financial support. Among the rural and urban women who were recruited, the renovation of the existing family home or the building of a house was considered an important factor in their decision to migrate as domestic workers. Equally important is the accumulation of money to buy land and cattle to use for the household's consumption, or to pay off family debt. (Heyzer and Wee 1994, p. 49)

In contrast to the East Javanese women's case, the Eastern Indonesian women's travel for contract domestic work shows a combination of reasons as equally important. While the explanation used often pointed to economic factors such as renovating the family home or financing sibling education as a primary motivation, when unpacking their stories further I found that it was rare that one factor predominated. There were a set of factors closely interconnected, as their stories indicate, triggering their journey which was seen as "a secular pilgrimage or even a rite of passage" to gain training and savings (Momsen 1999, p. 301). Different stages in the life cycle and the cultural context of areas of origin as well as different ways of engaging with the women in the research process may explain the different representations of motivation between East Javanese and Eastern Indonesian women.

Recruitment

Most young women in my study learned about opportunities to work abroad from official radio announcements or from the *kepala desa* (head of the village). The village headmen urging women of the region to apply as part of a local government initiative, represents one formal recruitment process. The women from East Nusa Tenggara in my study went through different recruitment processes. Elsewhere in Southeast Asia, notably Thailand, three basic types of recruitment have been identified: (1) formal recruitment through authorized agents; (2) informal recruitment through unlicensed agents in which a migrant pays the migration fees directly at the time of migration; and (3) "debt bondage" or informal recruitment in which migrants work off the migration fees after arriving at a destination country (Sobieszczy 2000, p. 397). The recruitment experiences of the returned migrant workers who I interviewed do not neatly fall within one category of this framework because the process of recruitment was often a mixture of both formal and informal networks.

Recruitment in Indonesia has been a source of disputes among vested interests — in particular, between the Ministry of Manpower and the licensed employment agencies, known as PJTKI (*Penyalur Jasa Tenaga Kerja Indonesia*), each of which owns their recruitment networks. Recruitment has also become a source of heartache and uncertainty for the domestic workers themselves. The Ministry and employment agencies have divergent ideas about the process of recruitment. Although they all offer plausible arguments to protect migrant workers, they seek to advance their own interests by accusing each other of wrongdoing. This was evident in an article on the disputed role of the Ministry of Manpower published in the daily *Business News*:

> The association of authorised labour export companies and licenced employment placements (*Gabungan Perusahaan dan Pengusaha Jasa Tenaga Kerja Indonesia*) argues that the State Ministry of Manpower's intervention in handling the recruitment of overseas domestic workers overstepped the boundary of its own authority ...
>
> For example in the process of recruitment, the department is not only playing a role as the policy maker, but at the same time as the executor of recruitment processes. Some of the ministerial decisions on the recruitment are viewed as biased against the licensed employment agents... (*Business News*, 5 July 2000) [my translation].

In response to growing pressures, Presidential Decisions, Keppres No. 29/1999 and Keppres No. 49/2000 were passed to create a new institution, Badan Koordinasi Penempatan TKI, a coordinating body for overseas migrant placement. The new body is aimed at integrating the efforts of nine separate institutions — Manpower, Internal Affairs, Foreign

Affairs, Health, Education, Religion, Defence, Police, and the Central Bank. The new institution's task is to assist with the recruitment and work placement of overseas migrant workers and provide services which cut costs and protect the workers (*Bisnis Indonesia* (Indonesian daily newspaper) 1999; Direktorat Jendral Binapenta 2000). The Institution's rationale is reflected in a newspaper article:

> There is of course nothing wrong in principle with sending workers abroad. Indeed during the Crisis, doing so would not only make it possible for Indonesians to earn a decent living abroad but also by sending home their pay, they could help make life easier for the family at home while making positive contribution to the country's balance of trade.

> Also, it must be remembered that there are good employment agents as well as bad ones and one bad case should not be allowed to tarnish the reputation of the employment agency business as a whole...

> For sure, if we are resolved to continue to regard this particular trade [of labour] as sound principle — which it appears we are — it is time we did some serious cleaning up to make sure that it benefits all on both the job providing and the job receiving ends of the deal. (*Jakarta Post* (Daily newspaper), 1 May 1999)

The formal recruitment process is accelerated by the state's efforts to increase the export of domestic services. Once the international migration flows started, private recruitment agencies used the opportunity to recruit suitable workers and to capitalize on their links with their counterparts overseas (Massey, Arango, Hugo, Kouaouci, Pellegrino, and Taylor 1993; Sobieszczy 2000). Heyzer and Wee (1994) explain how the recruitment network spans from the importing countries to Indonesia, permeating down to the villages and, simultaneously, linking them to global cities. The field workers employed by agencies in turn employ assistants to work as brokers, which include returned migrants, market traders or well-known figures in town (Heyzer and Wee 1994, pp. 47–48).

In parts of Flores, many local women were likely to have known a friend or a relative who had worked as a maid overseas. These returned migrants in turn recruit relatives, friends, acquaintances, and neighbours. Susana, for instance, had a cousin who had worked as a domestic worker in Hong Kong. Once Susana's social network included one of the migrant women, it was easier for another family member to follow. Social capital in a form of networks of other migrants comprising friends and relatives was significant in securing an overseas job, and in turn in assisting the migrant worker settling in the job at the destination (Hugo 1999; Hugo 2000).

Undertaking contract migrant work through formal recruitment under the state's instrumentality is notoriously bureaucratic, lengthy, and costly (Hugo 2000, p. 123). The informal process, however, is more effective as many migrants decide to move because they have relatives or friends who are involved in migration (Hugo 1999). By the same token, although Susana had heard of job opportunities on the radio many times — the formal channel — she did not pursue them until she had a personal recommendation from a trusted relative. Most domestic workers interviewed used informal networks, which included friends, relatives and an occasional acquaintance in a recruiting agency. Most believed that a personal reference from an ex-employee would ease the complex process of applying for an overseas job.

The social and economic networks of the individual women to some extent determined the outcome of the job hunting. Susana, despite the initial disapproval of her parents, insisted on pursuing an application once she had been convinced by a cousin of the good pay. This cousin later became a local representative of a maid recruitment agency in Surabaya and sent many more of her relatives and friends abroad. By using this personal connection, the employment agency was able to recruit workers committed to the job. This embeddedness of individuals in social networks generates trust and in turn creates an efficient economic transaction (Granovetter 1985, p. 490). One of Susana's friends also learnt about the information on job availability through a formal channel, but did not proceed until a relative facilitated her application to work abroad:

> One day, the government through the head of the village asked whether there were women interested in working [as domestic workers] in Hong Kong. I was immediately interested and had asked for permission from my parents... but other people talked about me, that I was going to do this and that [bad]. Later however I met my relative who had worked abroad and I was determined then. (Fieldwork)

The lack of accessible accurate information at the grass-roots level regarding the recruitment process often encouraged the women to resort to the trusted informal network to minimize the risk of being exploited.

Thus they dealt only with people they knew, ranging from neighbours, friends and relatives to, most importantly, returned migrants with success stories (Heyzer and Wee 1994). An unauthorized recruiter asking women to pay recruitment fees upfront is often found scouring rural areas. This unlicensed *calo* (middleman) may persuade families to part with their money to obtain a quicker service than that of the long bureaucratic channel (Direktorat Jendral Binapenta 2000; Hugo 2000). Where women are not able to pay in advance, the *calo* is also known to dock the first few months salary of domestic workers (Haris and Adika 2002). Invariably, the group of women I interviewed were careful to avoid unknown *calos* and chose to pass through an informal network which, in turn, converged into the authorized system. Learning to use the limited information and choosing the most practical and safest way to register their interests in the overseas contract job represent a new space of uncertainty for the women.

The women used both informal and formal channels to apply for jobs. Indeed, it is difficult to separate the economic and social factors determining the employment of Susana and other women. Networks of personal contacts do not fit the neat theoretical divisions between economic and social factors and yet it was through this network that individuals often heard about and obtained jobs (Hanson and Pratt 1995). The separation between formal and informal recruitment was blurred, as evident from the women's experience of the recruitment process.

Family/clan's consent

When a woman is ready to formally apply for a domestic job abroad, she has to provide a formal letter of consent from her family. This consent precedes further processing of the necessary legal documents, such as health and security clearances, passport and visa. Contrary to the previous cases of daughters' migration to be nurses and teachers, most parents (in practice, fathers) in parts of Flores from my experience were reluctant to give permission for their daughters to work abroad. This particular overseas travel is legitimized differently, mainly on economic reasons, because of the different status of the job and a transnational scale of migration. Despite the difference in legitimization of travel, similarly an important aspect of a father's role is guardianship of his daughter's virtue. A father has to accept responsibility for the consequences of a daughter's job as a domestic worker in a foreign country. Likewise

Ong (1990) in her study of a Malay village in Sungai Jawa has noted a gender differentiation that is commonly expressed in terms of morality. A man's role is to guard the family's virtue and by extension all village men are responsible for the moral status of village women. The code of morality places men's moral capacity and judgement above that of women. Women have to legitimize travels for work, depending on the professions and scale of migration (to urban centres or overseas).

Locally, the profession suffered with the unfortunate association of the acronym TKW. TKW is an Indonesian acronym for *Tenaga Kerja Wanita* referring to overseas female migrant workers, and particularly those working in domestic service. In some local dialects of Flores (Nage, Kéo and Lio) *teka* (c.f., the pronunciation of TK means to sell, so the community tended to associate TKW with prostitution. A community leader in Ende commented that as a father he would never give his daughter consent for this kind of job because of the association with "selling oneself". He claimed to know of many cases where daughters simply escaped (*lari*) to do the job.

The parents' reluctance also stemmed from the community's negative perception resulting from media representations of this type of job which is linked with physical and sexual abuses. The Indonesian media reported that between 1997 and 1998 Solidaritas Perempuan (Women's Solidarity) — an NGO documenting the plight of domestic workers — recorded 147 deaths, 180 abuses, and 442 missing persons among overseas migrant workers (*Merdeka* (Indonesian daily newspaper) 1998). More recently the media reported a case of twenty migrant women aged between 19 and 27 being allegedly held captive by a Malaysian syndicate in a three-storey building on the outskirts of Kuala Lumpur and forced to become "sex slaves" (*Jakarta Post* (Daily newspaper), 12 July 2000). There were also cases of twenty women aged between 14 and 20 years who admitted forging their ages in passports to work abroad. They were reported to have been physically abused, and one woman was reported to have been raped in Sarawak, Malaysia (*Kompas* (Indonesian daily newspaper), 13 March 2000). Given these media representations of the job and the risks involved, it was not surprising that parents were reluctant to allow their daughters to become overseas workers. Yet, despite the negative representation of domestic work, the family often had little choice because of the potential income and in particular because of the daughter's persistence, as illustrated by Susana's comments:

I planned to go in 1994. However my parents did not agree and they took a lot of convincing. So I had to wait. My parents were adamant that I finish my studies and then find suitable work so that our family would amount to something. My father even cried, when he knew of my plan to work as a maid overseas. I said to him: "please don't cry because I do it to help our family financially." My parents had wanted me to stay studying. In my family, no one really had a good education. I was about to study at the diploma level [tertiary level] and became their only hope. When I changed my mind on studying further [and went abroad instead], they asked me why...(Fieldwork)

Women's agency within the intra-household dynamic emerged in the ways they negotiate to obtain consent to travel, by promising to contribute to the household income. Despite their fathers' opposition, when women are recruited through an informal network they often know someone who has worked abroad and the resulting material wealth they have acquired, thus making easier the negotiation for consent. Some parents were able to see beyond the media reports detailing the horror and hazards of working overseas when confronted with the women they knew who had come home economically much better off. However, *calo* were also known to be aggressively looking for workers in rural areas, meeting the women's parents to ask for their consent and promising to send money to the family at home, in some cases up to Rp600,000 per month (A$150), in addition to the worker's monthly salary (*Kompas* (Indonesian daily newspaper), 13 March 2000). Mostly for the first timers, the family's consent was given unwillingly, indicating the first step of a metaphorical journey of a daughter's struggle for subjectivity and her increasing autonomy. This occurred with Netti's parents who worried about her reputation:

One day my parents said that many had commented on my going away, saying that I had sold myself to prostitution. Here, there is a custom if a single woman goes away by herself, there is something peculiar about it. It is not good. Although it is now getting more common for a woman to travel by herself, going overseas is still a rarity. People inevitably will talk about it. (Fieldwork)

On occasions, the crucially important piece of paper showing family consent had been forged to enable young women to escape from their family home. Some women who forged papers were brought back to their home villages after the family had tracked them down in Java. The requirement of consent to travel for women in general and daughters in particular was evidence of their continued subordinate position in the family hierarchy.

Voyages to Java

Most workers destined for overseas went by ship to transit locations in Java. The tension of separation from their kin commenced at the ports of departure. There they said their goodbyes to families and friends. Many embarked on their first ever journey outside Flores. For some, the trip was the first time they were away from the family as a separate and independent identity. By then it was too late to change their minds as they had already paid for their travel to Java. Netti recalled how she sailed for the first time on board a PELNI ship *Kelimutu* leaving for Surabaya on 9 January 1994. As Netti had left home with trepidation, she was relieved to be in the company of some other women, who were intending to work abroad. They occupied a cramped space in economy class — similar to other inter-island travel stories — and were accompanied by a woman about to undertake her second term contract. In addition to other mundane activities, mainly chatting on a ship which most women do, they started building a network of friends and a support system. The time on the ship was spent learning about what to expect in the in-transit dormitory and how to survive in a foreign land if they successfully negotiated the next stage of their journey.

In-transit: dormitory and training

Once women arrived in Java, they were taken to dormitories located in different cities. These dormitories were known to house hundreds of potential migrants while they waited for placement overseas. As Netti and others recalled, the living conditions in these dormitories provided by employment agencies were overcrowded. It was not surprising that Netti was overwhelmed by a sense of crisis in the dormitory because she had to deal with the low morale of those who had been waiting for some months for a placement overseas.

Netti began to question why she wanted to travel abroad. This question was particularly important given the disapproving tone of the gossip in her local community. She almost convinced herself that it would have been better to have stayed home, but casting herself as the family's saviour maintained her resolve. Not surprisingly, given Netti's experience, the travellers during the in-transit period described themselves as being scared and confused in an overcrowded dormitory.

This in-transit period is also a time when the women were subjected to a series of examinations. They included a medical check-up, to make sure that they were physically healthy and not pregnant, and a character investigation, through criminal records held by the police, to guarantee they had not committed any crime. In addition, the women were supposed to undergo intensive training that accustomed them to domestic tasks, such as cooking, cleaning, and simple sewing. This course was also supposed to include practical work in an urban middle-class home and the acquisition of minimal language skills (basic English conversation). There was no fixed training period because it depended on how quickly the domestic worker could be placed in employment. Often the women were videoed, so that potential employers could appraise their physical appearance. Then the game of waiting started, with the women hoping an overseas employer would select them. In-transit time and space represents the hardest challenge for Netti and others because of its mere uncertainties of the in-betweeness.

On-the-job training: agent and temporary employer

While they were in-transit, the agent sent the women for on-the-job-training. In these homes they were supposed to learn how to use modern household appliances, such as a washing machine, rice cooker and gas stove, which were not available in their home towns or villages. However these appliances were only occasionally available. Most returned workers regarded their on-the-job-training as unhelpful, as noted by one of Susana's friends:

> It seemed that we did not learn anything new. We were not told how long this on-the-job-training was going to be. I persevered for four months, I had to work very hard, washing clothes manually and undertaking other physical labour, scrubbing the floor etc. I almost could not take it. Even abroad was not such hard labour. My [temporary] employer was so fussy. I also had to buy my own food and soap. I complained to the agent to be moved to another household. (Fieldwork)

This stage of the journey attracted most complaints from women because of the uncertainty of the period in transit and the difficulties of
being away from home for the first time. However being away from home
did provide a space for self-reflection and self-reliance. The women experimented with various subject positions, such as an employee, a house
keeper, a carer, a confidante, a single and independent woman, as well
as a lover. Some women, as Netti's moment of doubt evidently showed,
began to reconsider their intention of going abroad during this stressful
phase of the journey. As documented in a newspaper article, a few tried
to escape.

> City police are investigating labor exporting company PT Jatim
> Duta Pembangunan for allegedly confining 276 young women against
> their will for several months as they waited to be sent to jobs
> abroad.
>
> Police believe 240 of the women were confined at a three-story
> Gading Serpong shop house in Tangerang and the rest in a four-
> storey building in Jl. Daan Mogot in West Jakarta.
>
> The authorities became aware of the case when two of the women
> confined in Tangerang were severely injured when they tried to
> escape by jumping from the building. Another woman kept in
> West Jakarta also was hurt when she tried to jump from an upper
> floor...
>
> The company also promised the pre-departure period would include
> training and courses in English. The women said they did receive
> English lessons for two to three weeks before the courses suddenly
> ended. "I've been eight months in the building on Jl. Daan Mogot,
> but the work never came," Malina from Kupang in Nusa Tenggara
> Timur said. She said her parents sold a plot of land to finance her
> departure to the capital... (*Jakarta Post* (Daily newspaper), 28
> April 1999)

Even if a woman was fortunate enough to be able to get a placement
to work in an urban household, it was not necessarily an automatic step
to getting a job abroad. This stage was still a long way from the ultimate journey because the deal abroad might fall through. Despite the
difference in pay, on-the-job training in Indonesia was considered better
than waiting a lengthy period in an agency's shelter because it was considered to be one move forward to their final destination of an overseas
contract job. Surviving during the period in-transit for Netti was not
merely a matter of paying for food but also a case of co-operating with

Figure 6.4: The Dormitory — Subsection from Netti's map.

the employment agency and following their rules, and working with the temporary employer. A series of strategic alliances were needed both with the agency and employer to attain the goal of working abroad.

The significant role of the employment agency in Netti's ultimate journey is depicted in her map as a huge male head representing the "boss" of the company or *PT di Surabaya*, as shown in Figure 6.4. In her drawing, Netti depicted other women in the dormitory much smaller than the man's head. The boss' overwhelming physical presence was obvious from the deliberately enlarged scale figure in the picture. Netti explained that he was quite powerful in deciding their future. Indeed, there was a subtle resentment transmitted in our conversation when she described how he was in charge of placements, and how everyone in the dormitory was heavily reliant on his connections. The remote and un-equal relationship between Netti and the boss was graphically inscribed in the head set distantly apart from the inner circle of the women.

Other women, notably Liana and Mariana, felt vulnerable both when they stayed in the dormitory and when they worked at the employer's home. Many of the women were away from their family for the first time, and felt exposed without the protection of their male kinfolk. Similarly another group of women from Ende regency were very anxious because they had to wait in the dormitory for between three to seven months. All of them related their sense of frustration while in-transit. One of them, Miriam, was subject to sexual harassment by her employer while she was undergoing on-the-job training. Yet she managed to maintain control over the situation (*masih berani*), because she had yet to reach the destination of her travel.

In Surabaya the employer I had for on-the-job training was a young unmarried man. I was only there for one day at his house when he came to me. I was asleep in my room when he tried to open the door to come in, but I had locked it. Then after two weeks he tried again. One day after coming home from work, he asked me to come to his room. He asked me to give him a body massage. I felt that it would have been too brave for me to do this. *I felt brave because I had my strong faith.* I cried in front of him so that he would come to his senses. Perhaps he thought that I had not been aware of where that would lead to, because I was not used to a big city such as Surabaya. But I kept on praying and praying very hard, and finally he gave up and nothing happened between us...

I really had a bad time the first two weeks there and I cried. It could be that he realised it then, how much his behaviour had troubled me. Furthermore, most of the neighbours there already thought that something had happened, because there were only the two of us in the house, just like "husband and wife", they said. I only persevered there for a month and then went back to the agency. I was not able to stay there because there was too much a temptation, although he did not give me any trouble since. He was not too bad actually, but he was a man, so he tried to play around with me. (Fieldwork)

Indeed the risk of sexual harassment was a real fear for all these women when they worked at their employer's homes. One reason for this group travelling together was to minimize this risk. Obviously Miriam did not welcome her employer's sexual advances. Paradoxically her tears, symbolically a sign of helplessness, were strategically used to escape her employer's harassment.

Miriam's seemingly weak appearance in shedding tears, showed her strategy of representing herself both as an "inexperienced" employee and a "religious" woman. Nevertheless she shared with me how she remained resolute at the time of this harassment. Her awareness of her sense of self and her own resources indicates her shifting subjectivity, as a strong, independent woman. She enacted simultaneous roles and identities and occupied more subject positions to suit her multiple locations. Miriam's experience shows evidence of a mobile subjectivity, which produces provisional identities and opens up an unpredictable possibility (Ferguson 1999). This process can be conceptualized as a subject shifting positions and identities, aware that her race, class, and gender identity may be held against her. Miriam was attentive to the multiplicities within herself and invested in as many dimensions of her roles and positions as possible to gain an advantage (Ferguson 1999, p. 161). She indicated a self-confidence and bravery (*berani*) to face the sexual approach of her male employer. As Miriam was located in relation to constantly moving trajectories of power, her mobile subjectivity also changed, as Ferguson (1999, p. 161) claims: "Mobile subjectivities are too concrete and dirty to claim innocence, too much in-process to claim closure, too interdependent to claim fixed boundaries."

Miriam's story shows her drawing strength from her sense of self, particularly from her awareness of her own strengths and weaknesses. She did not merely blame her employer for the harassment. This was evident from her comment that there was too much temptation in the house, so she initiated her move back to the dormitory. Miriam's mobile subjectivity contains a notion of being aware of her shifting identities as appropriate to particular local settings. This subjectivity was mutually constituted in and through the transition of working away from her home village.

Being away from home and family for the first time provided a space for Miriam to experiment and rely on her own resourcefulness. Clearly, an ideal of feminine characteristics of docility and obedience (*tunduk dan patuh*), traditionally accepted in her place of origin, in this case lost its intensity with distance. Therefore this journey offered Miriam a kind of free-floating and fluid choice of subject positions among which her subjectivity moves.

Depending on a woman's perspective, a man's sexual advances may be viewed either as an opportunity or a threat. In both cases women could choose among a variety of strategies. They could choose to be around men or avoid them where possible. It was extremely rare to find a job where women could work together in the same house to prevent sexual harassment. A domestic worker staying at an employer's home is seen as being especially vulnerable. It was unlikely that they had adequate support networks and access to information given the isolation of the individualized work situations (International Labor Organization 1998). While in-transit, these networks enabled women to learn from each other about how to avoid risky situations and to defend themselves, and to exercise their rights as workers in dealing with their temporary employer and employment agency.

Figure 6.5: Employer's Home — Subsection from Netti's map.

Working abroad: knowing how to conduct oneself

The culmination of the journey involved working in the houses of their foreign employers. For Mariana, Liana, Agnes, Susana, Netti and the others, this was the destination of their travel where all their hopes for a better economic future were concentrated. Distance from home allowed this group of women the opportunity to transform themselves and to achieve the financial independence of their dreams. Their personal transformation was reflected in their physical appearance — short hair, trendy T-shirts and jeans, and a pair of sneakers. This freedom was not unbounded however, as their employers not only decided on their work routines but also asserted control over their physical presentation.

Most domestic workers in my study were conscious of the constraints imposed by employers and the expectation to work hard. They learnt this through the informal networks of friends and ex-workers even before arrival. As they were paid good money for their domestic services, indeed they were ready to work hard. When Netti arrived at her employers' home she depicted herself as being in "top gear" (see Figure 6.5). She recollected her arrival, wearing her work uniform provided by the employment agency, her hair was cut short; no lipstick, other make-up or nail polish was used. She described her first day working abroad as being prepared for war — *"siap berjuang"*, which literally means *ready for the battle!* This metaphor of a battlefield for the job site reflects the state officials' perspective that migrant women are economic soldiers deployed to battle against the country's economic crisis (Chin 1997).

Evidently, physical appearance was perceived differently by employer and employee. Some workers were well aware that the first struggle of power relations was reflected in the control exerted by the employer over the employee's physical appearance. In Lena's words: *"Mereka mengatur penampilan kita"*, meaning "they [her employers] took control over our presentation." Others might be ignorant or could not care less. Returned domestic workers, like Miriam, Netti, and Susana, stressed that physical appearance was the essential factor in initially obtaining their job and also a key to getting on well with employers. Both parties engaged in constant negotiations to reach a compromise as to what constituted a desirable appearance because it was in both the employers' and workers' interests to complete the two-year period of a contract with minimal friction. The employees strategically presented and positioned themselves to ease their jobs and please their employers, simultaneously achieving their own objectives. This practise of negotiating between different positions was a part of the women's metaphorical journey.

In Susana's case she believed that she owed her job to "good looks and overall presentation" (*penampilan pribadi*). She believed that her fair skin and bright face were the reasons that attracted her employer to select her from among photographs and videos of potential domestic workers. Susana expressed openly in front of some returned migrants that had she been "dark skinned with very curly hair" (*kulit hitam dan rambut keriting*) — a typical attribute of Florenese — no employer would have given her a position. This opinion was widely accepted by the other ex-migrants, which reflects the uneasy ethnic and regional boundaries reproduced in their perception of being a subject in place, as discussed in Chapter 3.

Furthermore, Susana attributed her success in dealing with her employer to an awareness of knowing *how to conduct oneself* in front of the employer, or *tahu membawa diri* as she called it, which was important in her daily conduct. This is shown by the following excerpt:

> I tried to look happy all the time. And I wore neat, appropriate clothes while working. Therefore I would not annoy them. Even though I was sad at times, particularly when I missed my family, or got told off for some reason... When I could not help it anymore, I had to run off to my room or the bathroom, closed the door and cried there. They did not like to see me crying and unhappy because I was told it brings bad luck for the family. In particular the period close to the Chinese New Year. I was warned "do not to shed a single tear" as it chases good luck away. (Fieldwork)

Thus choice of clothes, physical/facial appearance, and personal control over emotional outbursts were part of performing roles as a strong, calm and collected woman, a desirable subject position in the work place.

Susana claimed it was her self-imposed discipline and choice to appear bright and happy all the time because it made life easier. Her awareness of different roles and positions to suit different space and time indicates shifting subjectivity embodied in her behaviour and embedded in her journey as a domestic worker.

Both employer and employee could equally claim that they were in control of the worker's physical appearance. Not only was Susana aware that she was assessed on her appearance but she also used the same yardstick to judge her employers when they first met. She paid special attention to their countenances (*sinar muka*), because these, she said, most revealed their character.

> I finally arrived in Hong Kong and my employers picked me up at the agency. The man was 45 years and the woman was a few years younger. They married quite late, so their children were still young, a five and a two year old. But as soon as I saw them at the agency *I knew immediately from their faces* that they were good people... (Fieldwork)

Domestic workers had to survive on their own from the day that they arrived at their employer's house. The terms of the contract were part of the wider dynamic of relations between employers and employees. There were both formal and informal instructions on how to undertake domestic work and conduct oneself. When I asked Susana why she had to cut her hair short and was prohibited from wearing jewellery, she could not answer directly. Startled by the question, Susana admitted she had given little thought to the matter. She knew perfectly well that long hair and jewellery were inappropriate because of the regulations set by the employment agency. However, she did not comprehend the reasons for the rules and did not see any need to understand them because she could not change anything. Grappling with words, she said:

> Maybe they did not want us to waste our time looking for lost jewellery. They paid us good money, so of course they wanted us to use the time to work instead of to waste it. (Fieldwork)

Obviously the issues of work safety and one form of femininity in relation to jewellery were not significant in Susana's mind. Indeed, in the employer and employee relationship, control over physical appearance starting at the time of a worker's arrival was considered as just a small inconvenience by some workers. Hondagneu-Sotelo (2001) among others found that the reasons for the restriction in physical appearance is to de-sexualise the worker. Despite this, when a domestic worker first arrived, her feeling of anxiety and confusion over new tasks far outweighed her inconvenience over a rule about personal presentation. Susana's comments below show her main concerns:

> When we got home, they did not even ask me to have a rest or something. First they inspected all my clothes. After that I was asked to cook some rice. I didn't even know how to use the rice cooker, so they taught me. After finishing cooking they told me about all the other routine tasks. The day after I was supposed to wash clothes and do other household chores. But I did not even know how to use a washing machine. I prayed hard again, a decade of the rosary. But still I could not even turn the knob. I said to myself, "I am finished." I wanted to let them know, but I did not know how to say it [because of a lack of English]. I just used the body language trying to convey the message that the washing machine did not want to start. Meanwhile I prayed, and was wondering why the machine was so hard to operate... [laughter] (Fieldwork)

Anxiety among new arrivals stemmed from having to relate in a new social situation, using a new language and undertaking unfamiliar domestic tasks involving modern household appliances. On-the-job training in Indonesia was regarded as not very useful because it occurred in very different environments from the real job. This training and the advice from friends did not prepare Netti, for example, for the cultural shock of living as a recently arrived domestic worker.

Netti expressed her sense of being "out of place" and "scared" when she first arrived at the employer's house in Hong Kong. In particular she was worried about her lack of mobility in the city. She had no experience of riding on a lift or catching a subway. However, she quickly mastered these accoutrements of modern life and capitalized on her independence within the vicinity of the apartment and in urban public space. Anxiety over her immobility was transformed into a sense of achievement. This new-found accessibility was an extension of Netti's travel abroad, and indicates her agency in initiating and expanding her mobility: *"sudah jauh-jauh ke sana, mengapa tinggal di rumah saja?"* or "If I have travelled that far, why would I want to stay at home?" Another domestic worker I interviewed had a completely different experience. Leli stayed inside the home most of the time during her contract. She did not acquire a network of friends, like her counterparts in Hong Kong. Besides, her employers only wanted her to work within the home and they did not require her to go shopping. Also, Leli would rather keep out of the apparent trouble that pervaded life outside the home.

These experiences of different women show a range of degrees of mobility in public places and varied familiarity with attributes of "modernity" in the cities. Although, commonly, these women perceive familiarity with an urban life style and their travel within the city as tantamount to becoming "modernized" (Momsen 1999; Elmhirst 1999), their experience and degree of satisfaction in their work varies enormously, depending on the variety of subject positions they choose to inhabit.

Networks of relations: employers, employees and men

Relations with employers: "Smile is my weapon." A domestic worker often replaced the employer's role in the household as the carer and nurturer. As Table 6.2 shows, the day started when a worker arose at 5.30 a.m. and began to prepare breakfast for the whole family at 6 a.m. Usually domestic work did not finish until almost midnight, when the family had already retired to bed. Employers had a vested interest in domestic workers improving their mobility around the neighbourhood and the city because it enabled them to undertake more tasks. Employers would thus help their domestics to gain their bearings.

Netti, like other domestic workers, was trusted with running the household, taking care of children and elderly parents. She was responsible for shopping for daily food supplies and deciding on the family's menu. Most importantly, Netti had to attend to the baby's needs, except on Sundays which was her day off. Yet there were times on her day off when she could not go out. This happened when the baby was ill. The elderly grandmother had uttered expressions such as: "Your arrival was just before the baby son, so you brought luck to this family, bringing the boy." This emphasized that the baby also belonged to Netti, suggesting that her work was constructed also on the basis of emotional relation. Netti substituted for the mother's role, and undertook all of the associated domestic tasks. This gendered substitution of labour occurred between two women — the employer and the employee — within the daily life of the family (Gregson and Lowe 1994; Yeoh and Huang 1999*a*). Netti expressed satisfaction at being in charge of the baby and of the housekeeping, as an autonomous subject, in a way not normally

Table 6.2: Typical daily chores of domestic workers in Hong Kong.

5.30 am:	Wake up, wash face, brush teeth, get dressed
6.00 am:	Prepare breakfast and get milk/bottle ready for children
6.30 am:	Clean/wash the car while employers wake up, get ready for the office, have breakfast
7.30 am:	Give the children a bath/help with personal grooming of employer' elderly parents, while employers go to the office
8.00 am:	Clean the house/mop floor/dust/wipe, wash clothes sometimes by hand, put clothes to dry, take care of children, plan the menu and go shopping for today's meal
1 pm:	Work in kitchen, prepare/cook lunch and clean up afterwards, sit to have lunch with children and elderly members of the family, wash up dishes
6 pm:	Prepare/cook dinner, more clean up, start on ironing clothes, take care of children, while waiting for the employers to come home
7 pm:	Eat dinner together
9–11 pm:	Clean the dishes, iron clothes, tidy the house

Source: Fieldwork.

acknowledged in her own family and kinship hierarchy at her village in Flores. Although these are still domestic responsibilities, the meanings attached to her tasks performed as an autonomous subject and the social relations with her employers were different from those at home (Laurie 1999).

The relationships between female employers and female domestic workers can be seen as exploitative because the employer overcomes their gender disadvantage by benefiting from the employee's lower class and ethnic inequalities (Rollins 1985; Gregson and Lowe 1994; Robinson 1991). Yet I found the experience of Netti and her counterparts did not necessarily reflect a fully exploitative relationship. This is confirmed by Raharto, Hugo, Romdiati, and Bandiyono (1999) who have found little evidence of abuse and exploitation of the female transnational migrants from Flores Timur. Therefore, the uni-dimensional framework of relations of power between employer and foreign employee is likely not to be sufficient to understand the domestic workers' journey (Romero 1992;

Constable 1997), because there are multi-layered interactions simultaneously enacted and performed by both sides. Clearly, cases of physical
abuse and exploitation which are regularly reported by the Indonesian
media (see Arfah's story, Box 6.1) were but one part of the relationship
which received exposure. Unlike these victims, Netti negotiated her roles
and work and drew considerable benefit from the relationship with her
employer.

Box 6.1: The fate of a migrant worker: Arfah's story.

Arfah (43 years) worked as a domestic worker in Malaysia
and suffered a bad fate. She was physically abused and her
salary was not paid as agreed. She had hot water poured over
her and was hit, resulting in four of her front teeth falling out
and all of her body was scalded and swollen. Her saliva could
not stop running and her left ear could no longer hear, and
around her eyes was black. Worse still, she also suffered psy-
chological damage. Arfah was among hundreds of Indonesian
domestic workers who suffered bad treatment, and there are
even worse cases of rape, or forced prostitution and pregnancy
as a result... (Elsam 1997)[my translation]

During Netti's contract she successfully created a workable relationship with her employers, and was treated well. Every night she ate with
the family at the dining table. She was given her own bedroom, which
included a comfortable bed, table, chair and cupboard. On special occasions, such as Christmas and her birthday, she was given presents. In
fact, her last birthday was celebrated in a restaurant just as a member
of the family, and she received a pair of gold earrings as her birthday
present. Netti also had a special bond with the children *"saya setengah
mati cinta anak itu"* or literally "I loved that baby to death." Obviously,
her success in attending to the everyday needs of the children made her
indispensable. Thus she was offered more money to extend her contract,
which suggested that she was able to exercise some power in the relationship with her employer. Indeed, Netti had consciously ingratiated herself
into the family, constantly performing different roles and identities:

> *Smile was my weapon.* As I did not understand many words in
> Cantonese, they understandably got upset if I did not follow their

instruction to complete the job. Occasionally the elderly grandmother was dissatisfied with a completed task. I sensed it from her expression. Then I could only force myself *to smile*. You could not take things too seriously when they got upset as a result of misunderstanding. If you made a mistake one day, you learnt from it and tried to forget about it the next day...

The baby was so attached to me. She preferred to be with me than her own mother. The family wanted me to stay as long as possible... (Fieldwork)

Everyday relations were punctuated by constant negotiations, as revealed in the previous stories. The women's strategies involve being aware of different incidents, bodily performance such as using smiles and emphasizing a caring identity. Like most aspects of life, mistakes and accidents were unavoidable events in a household's existence, as is shown in Karina's story, one of Netti's friends, who — at the time of the interview — had just came back for a few days from Hong Kong.

The shifting and fluid subject positions and performances through and with space produce results sometimes beyond the women's control. Karina manoeuvred from the subject position of a caring domestic worker to an assertive employee when inadvertently she scorched and ruined a pair of her employer's trousers while she was ironing them. There was no further drama, except that she had to pay for the mistake. She stood up and rang her agent seeking redress, but to no avail. This episode was one that stayed in her mind, indicating a deep resentment at being treated unjustly. Karina cried silently when relating this particular story to me as we sat on the outside porch of Netti's home, so I just had to cradle her in my arms. Given her employers' financial clout, she thought that one pair of trousers would not mean too much. However her monthly salary was docked by 50 per cent to pay for the new trousers. Karina was upset but defenceless because she had not been informed about this penalty. Although she had previously signed a document, she was unaware of its contents. This situation was not resolved to her satisfaction because the agent refused to intervene, although she acted confidently.

The variety of stories emphasize that a range of domestic workers' experiences abroad cannot be distilled into only one version of reality, as they move through different subject positions and widening roles.

Relations with other employees Victoria Park in Central district was the most popular site for Netti and her friends to meet other fellow

Figure 6.6: Victoria Park — Subsection from Netti's map.

domestic workers while working in Hong Kong. Her drawing of the park represents the place offering a different set of social relations where all of the participants are equal. In Netti's words, it was a place and time for letting your hair down. Constable (1997, p. 168) in her study of domestic workers in Hong Kong confirms Netti's story that "activities in the square stand in striking contrast to the activities of the rest of the week". In the park Netti met fellow employees who were from her own region or island for support and fun. There they danced to music from a tape recorder that was brought for that purpose, partying, swapping and sharing food and stories (see Figure 6.6). There was an opportunity to speak in their mother tongue and invoke memories of home.

Like other foreign domestic workers, inhabiting subject positions other than as domestics, including as consumers is an important part of their journeys:

> After working alone in the employer's home all week, on Sunday in Central foreign workers gain strength in numbers. They reestablish and express other facets of their identity, if only for a few hours. As they share news from home, they are no longer "DH" [domestic helpers] but wives, mothers, aunts, sisters, townmates, and school-mates. (Constable 1997, p. 169)

Enacting other subject positions and identities abroad was seen as a part of the new space of the domestic workers' travel. Because of the isolation of the work, Netti made efforts to network with other workers from Eastern Indonesia. Initially Netti was hesitant but then was very pleased to befriend a girl from Flores who worked in a flat within the same block. Women from immigrant groups which are too small to form a community often led a much more isolated life, as suggested by Hondagneu-Sotelo (2001) observing a case of an Indonesian domestic worker in the United States.

Netti's story indicates a small group of Eastern Indonesians working in Hong Kong having initiatives to mutually offer support and to widen their networks. Abandoning her characteristic modesty and shyness, Netti asked permission from her employers to make phone calls to arrange occasional meetings with other domestic workers from her own region. Obviously, it meant a lot to Netti to have some friends to perform a role as companion on the journey and with whom to share experiences and support.

On Sundays, their day off, Netti and her friends would gather to celebrate an Indonesian Catholic Mass, a service provided by an Indonesian chaplain. They also performed a subject position as consumers as they shopped and posed for photographs which significantly changed "the lacklustre image of the humble maids" into a more glamorous image of femininity, "decked out in all their finery" (Constable 1997, p. 168). Then they gathered together in the park to renew friendships. These regular meetings were seen as one of the highlights of being abroad. I saw Netti's enlarged photograph taken in Victoria Park, which was displayed prominently in her home. Similarly, Susana, Liana, and Mariana and others also met on Sundays, their day off, to provide mutual emotional support.

Relations with men As in most aspects of domestic work, social relations had advantages and disadvantages. Leli, for example, refused to go out with men as a practical defence against getting into "trouble" with her employer or with any man. Constraints imposed by employers on the physical appearance of domestic workers may be viewed as to make them less femininely attractive (Hondagneu-Sotelo 2001) and to serve as a warning signal against a worker having romantic relations with men. These constraints were accepted without question by some workers. Leli, for instance, welcomed them.

To minimize the risk of losing her job, Susana admitted being reticent about going out with men while working abroad. The attempt of a temporary employer to harass her while in-transit contributed to this attitude. Susana believed that maids had little chance of meeting a potential husband of some social standing in Hong Kong. Also she was concerned about the cases of two married Javanese domestic workers who had been sent home because they were pregnant. Although two men had approached her, Susana declined their advances because she suspected their motives. Given this experience, she reiterated that her aim was

"to gain experience and earn an income, not to look for a husband."
Recollections of their activities abroad suggested that relations with men
were seen as a threat to their ultimate aim and the women were prepared
to avoid contact with them.

Returning home

The full circle of the women's journey ends where it starts, at home.
Usually coming home was eagerly anticipated by the women and their
families. After travel, their relations with the family at home changed.
The domestic workers were valued for their sacrifice working abroad and
bringing the needed extra income. So now, home is where they can
relax. And, as a recently returned worker commented, it is where she
could sleep as much as she wanted. Apparently the family approved of
her temporary "laziness", such as sleeping in and spending time doing
nothing at home. The returned domestic workers were treated as heroines
by their families because of their role in sending significant amounts of
cash home while on contract. Some of my informants reported sending
over half to three-quarters of their earnings home, especially during the
first period of their contract. This finding is similar to that of factory
women in Malaysia who contributed more than half of their income to
the family (Ong 1987), but much more than that reported by Chin (1997)
who estimates that Indonesian domestic workers sent between one-third
and one-half of their monthly salary to their families.

For many, returning home was also a period of adjustment. Living
in semi-rural areas in Flores was very different from an urban lifestyle in
Hong Kong. While working overseas the women were used to performing
certain daily routine tasks, but in their villages the pace of life was slow
and often unpredictable because of sudden family and community com-
mitments. Pressure from the family to do a second contract was strong,
as Susana admitted.

> My parents did not really force me to return [to be a domestic
> worker] again straight away. But they saw me as being quite suc-
> cessful [financially], so I was advised to go there again. They did
> not force me though. It is my own will to help them [financially]
> and also I am preparing for my own future. So I have now started
> the process of re-applying for a job in Hong Kong. (Fieldwork)

The economic benefit to the family was undoubtedly immense. In my informants' cases the remittances paid for the education of their siblings, housing improvements, land purchases, and the establishment of home-based enterprises. A rare newspaper article on the material success of Indonesian domestic workers in Hong Kong confirmed the experience of my informants. Working as a domestic worker is seen as an opportunity to save money. Even on their day off on Sundays, some women tried to earn additional income by selling Indonesian food, *rujak campur* or spicy fruit salad, among their friends. Some sold other goods such as a Walkman (portable tape player). One married woman from Java undertook four contracts between 1990 and 1998. With the proceeds she was able to send three children through high school, open a small retail store in her neighbourhood, provide Rp20 million (A$5,000) capital for her son's fish business, and buy a utility truck as a result of her remittances (Daniel 2000). Some of my informants contemplated working overseas for a second time to secure their personal financial future, rather than that of their family. Nationally, workers' remittances have been increasing in significance as the government has been vigorously promoting this export of labour to boost the foreign exchange earnings. Not surprisingly, the pressure on the domestic workers to return to work abroad comes from many directions. With the change in their economic position within the family and the community, there is more significantly a subtle change within the women themselves. As the above stories reveal, the women move through a trajectory of power, shifting their subjectivity or the way they see themselves.

Subjectivity can be seen as constituted through experience and the exercise of power. Drawing on Foucault's analysis, power may be defined as:

> existing only in its exercise, operating through the production of a particular knowledge... From this perspective, power is neither one directional, nor does it flow from a single source to shape, direct, or constrain subjects. Rather power is a reciprocal relation to subjectivity, where subjectivity can be defined as individual self-consciousness inscribed in particular ideals of behaviour surrounding categories of persons, objects, practices or institutions. Subjectivity is constituted through the exercise of power within which conceptions of personal identity, gender and sexuality come to be generated. Men and women actively exercise power in positioning themselves within, or finding their own location amongst, competing discourses, rather than merely being "positioned by" them. (Kerfoot and Knights 1994, p. 70)

I map women who travel as subjects taking a path along which they can move in the trajectories of power, along the lines of class, gender, and race (Ferguson 1999). I conceptualize travel as a space of different scales of relations and encounters, which is a space thus instrumental in the contestation and creation of identities. By taking new and wider subject positions while travelling, women's subjectivity is likely to shift along with experiences of multiple spaces. Mobile subjectivity correlates with movement along trajectories of power and resistance, emerging from either proximity or distance and the associated connectedness (Ferguson 1999). To conceptualize subjectivity as mobile is to find a way of imagining a self-awareness of identities grounded in bodily lived experiences in the context of events constantly in motion (Jackson and Palmer-Jones 1999; Ferguson 1999). As Ferguson notes:

> Articulation of mobile subjectivities requires careful attention to the specifics of social and geographical location, to the spaces inhabited by individuals, groups, and relationships. (1999, p. 162)

The mobility of Eastern Indonesian women who travelled abroad to be domestic workers suggests that this is one of the options available to them to actively play the politics of place. Women are engaging in multilevel strategies of making connections with other spaces. The politics of place is reflected in the ways women negotiate power on at least two levels: their bodily experiences on one hand, and the emerging relational identities they create through negotiations of their gender norms, community expectations, and kin relations, on the other. In particular, through transnational travel there emerges a space for widening identities. The concrete, contradictory, and complex conditions of domestics' travel demonstrate their changing senses of self — shifting subjectivities — in a range of relations in different stages of the journey. Some examples from the overseas travel experiences of Netti, Susana and friends illustrate this point. Rather than following the model of the employer exploiting single global immigrant workers (Chang 2000), I suggest that we need to consider the women's experiences that show their resistances as they contest relations in every step of their travels. More research is required on Indonesian domestic workers to address the inadequacy of simply totalizing the women's domestic work under a binary cultural and economic opposition, depicting the workers as victims.

The varied recollections of the women highlight different relational dynamics of their travels. Despite domestic work abroad paying significantly better than any similar job in Indonesia, at each stage women have to negotiate their positions to achieve their goals. Although the travel motives and experiences as domestic workers were quite diverse, however the women shared the gendered meanings within the context of their travel. This transnational mobility is partly a response to the constraint and rigidity of their subject positions and roles at home. As they were situated in the specific historical and cultural context of East Nusa Tenggara, the journey abroad was a significant departure from the everyday routine of island life, to which each attached her own meanings of travel.

There is considerable tension inherent in this type of travel, as a consequence of the maintenance of gendered space in the home island. Mobility abroad has been mainly practised by local men and the surrounding islands, so women show their agency in convincing the family of the propriety of travel as contract migrants. In the process of travel, the women's experience expands from the familiar to the less familiar and to larger scale social systems of international connections (Thrift 1993). Women's travel in this way reflects a negotiation of power at several levels: the body/autonomy, home/community, and the interconnectedness of social groups. Paying attention to the experience of the body and conditions of social relations between the women and their families, the community, the agent, the employers and other employees at each stage of the journey has helped fill a void in our understanding of domestic workers moving through the axis of power.

This chapter has elucidated aspects of the journey abroad for Eastern Indonesian women. However bleak the conditions might appear in the Indonesian mass media, at one level women do gain a measure of autonomy of the body from going through the process of travel abroad. At another level, women are able to make broader connections of various spaces by widening their positions. At the intersection of the effects of bodily experience and crossing boundaries, there emerge different identities. The process of women's shifting subjectivity reflects the simultaneity of complex and multi-layered identities resulting from inhabiting a wider range of subject positions. By bringing women's travel to the forefront in the study of migrant domestic workers' abroad, we can deepen our understanding of the lives of Eastern Indonesian women.

Part Three

Reflections

This part takes the dynamics of Eastern Indonesian women's travels full circle. Within the framework of local social relations discussed previously, this final chapter engages in conceptual discussion of the range of travellers' tales told. Women's mobility reveals not only physical change but also a metaphorical journey creating a critical space that enables mobile subjectivities.

CHAPTER 7

Moving Forward: A Process of Becoming

Mapping women's travel

n this study — mapping Eastern Indonesian women's travel — the journey has arrived at the destination. This final chapter engages with both a conceptual discussion of the previous chapters' themes and a strategic analysis of the specificity of the politics of space and its relation to subjectivity. Here, I show how my engagement with the local specificity of women's mobility in Part Two leads to a discussion of the power geometry of place. This links micropolitics of women's travel with the macropolitics of the region. I have explored the notion of women crossing and negotiating boundaries through the travel stories of teachers and nurses (Chapter 5) and also of domestic workers (Chapter 6), such as Susana, leaving home. Susana's emphasis on the importance of her deportment, her bodily attributes of fair skin and her spatial movement are indications of a subject being aware of multiplicities within herself in terms of her race/region, class and gender identity, moving through trajectories of the geometry of power. She strategically placed herself through *langgar laut*, playing her politics of place. Through travel, Susana and others crossed and negotiated boundaries, creating a space of different scales of relations and power.

My contribution to the research on women's mobility focuses on the relationship between the creation of a transient, liminal space of travel and women's shifting subjectivities. This relationship can then be used to explore the link between space, gender, and subjectivity. I have taken into account the travelling subject, explored women's agency in their mobility, and examined their mobility as more than the product of women's class positions and forces of globalization. I have done so by paying attention to the women's voice, identity and personal meanings of mobility, as suggested by Silvey and Lawson (1999).

As Part Two indicates, Eastern Indonesian women's travels in the context of local/ethnic and class relations contain gender dimensions in which a complex mix of identities shapes their mobility. The specificity of the local space produces and reproduces an association of gender with particular spaces, social categories/hierarchies, activities, landscapes and symbols, in which inter-subjective and collective experiences of the community are negotiated (Bhabha 1994). I have analysed women's travel as a space of shifting gender relations in a range of spatial domains and scales which vary between places and over historical time (Callaway 1993; McDowell 1999; Silvey 2006). Different scales of spatial relations contain real and imagined boundaries, which are crossed or negotiated in women's travel — the archipelagic location of Eastern Indonesia, traditional clan/community relations, the kinship system and household relations, and women's bodies themselves.

In this final chapter, I summarize the crucial strategy of *langgar laut* for the women by drawing on the evaluated meanings of this local concept and link it to their practices of politics of place.

Langgar laut and its meanings for women

Travel in the widest sense of both "getting there and being there" (Clifford 1997, p. 23) allows travellers to confront and question their own identities, as experienced by many of my informants. At home, both gender roles and domestic identities are often accepted and taken for granted. Away from home, however, a woman is outside the assumed domain, thus her roles and identities are isolated from their naturalized context, and so exposed to challenges (Frederick and Hyde 1993). The women's travel stories demonstrate how the women created a liminal space whilst inhabiting wider subject positions and roles in different scales of relations and power.

Travel, in this perspective, can occur anywhere within the continuum of freedom and cultural constraints. Many of my informants' travels fall within this spectrum of adventure and domestic necessity. Some women acknowledged a desire for a surprise in their travels. Others travelled partly to fulfil their domestic obligations or wishes which, in some cases, eventually brings the women back to the familiar home.

The liminal space that the women created and experimented with suggests that it had rather uncertain norms. In this liminal space the distinction between inside and outside a boundary became blurred. In this fluid space, the women might choose an ambiguous subject position, contesting a marked boundary. This transient, in-between space opened up their gender identities, which is closely related to the dominant femininity, to contestations. Women, such as the domestic workers were able to occupy multiple subject positions and perform different identities in their travel. Even though women's travel consistently contains uncertainties inherent in new possibilities, it also, as the travel stories suggest, provides an opportunity to actively decentre the prevailing space and sets of relations.

The metaphoric journey of Self for the women was the essence of their *langgar laut*. Resonating with much of feminist theory, the travel stories confirm that the women are situated within the local specificity at the intersections of ethnicity, place, class, and gender politics. Gender determines that they are subject to surveillance of their propriety, and this surveillance extends particularly to maintenance of space, exclusion, movements and the purity of the body. Each travel story told, set within different grids of women's feelings and experiences, has demonstrated that the physical journey of Self recurs in the women's metaphoric journey of shifting subjectivities. The first step of sea travel — the maiden voyage — allows the emergence of a different subjectivity.

The women's travels indicate how women strive for more power in their struggle to negotiate various boundaries. Power is implicit in being able to choose to be included or excluded in different scales of relations. I have used boundary, both imagined and material, as an analytical concept to understand women's efforts to create different spaces. The women's politics of place, embodied in *langgar laut* and grounded in their material movement, are situated in the larger scale of politics of place.

Decentring of space and relations

Langgar laut indicates that women associate crucial meanings with crossing the bounded land into the freedom of the ocean and beyond. This local term separates Self and Other, and implies the collective identification of being an Eastern Indonesian. This collective identification, containing a sense of marginality, provides a clue to how spaces have been used to produce the identification, and thus the relevance of the historiography of Eastern Indonesia, as presented in Chapter 3. Some of the representations of the Eastern Indonesian boundaries contain the notion of regional subjection, where the "subject was 'made' in and through discourse and practices of governmentality" (Gibson 2001, p. 641). Certainly some Eastern Indonesian women I interviewed were feeling "lacking" as subjects in place. An informant articulated her "inadequacy" as a student from the region now studying in Surabaya. She experienced herself as lacking when exposed to different scales of social relations in a different place. The feeling of inadequacy is partly explained in the context of this exclusionary boundary, as an eastern identity going to the more "sophisticated" west. At the individual level, habits, dispositions, and self-awareness bear the inscriptions of governmentality into the body by extension of the individual identification with the relational collective identity. Travel for this informant evoked a sense of transcending the boundary of marginality. This example provides an insight into how the women, coming from Eastern Indonesia, experienced and negotiated the space of the regional marginality.

The regional subjection of Eastern Indonesia intersects with other discourses on gender and thus shapes and is linked to the dynamics of women's mobility. The excerpts of the women's travel narratives signal a crucial meaning of a movement from a place in the margin, a "lagging" region and a "lacking" identity. The women's stories have shown how women's travel emerges as an active intervention to disrupt their being located at the assumed fixed margin, in the lower hierarchy of region and relation. By travel, women simultaneously go with and against the subjection. Subjection does not only mean a unilateral power relation of domination of the subject; it can also involve multilateral relations where the subject may also generate power (Gibson 2001; Gibson-Graham 2006*a*,*b*).

The central meaning of *langgar laut* for the women lies in their decentring of space and particularly in their acceptance of uncertainty of the boundedness of space. The women's stories indicated that, before travel, they had understood that space was definitely bounded. This was reflected in their maintenance of space with their conformity, *tunduk dan patuh* (obedience) to the boundaries of gendered space. Massey points out that "boundaries are socially constructed phenomena and although they may contain linkages and inter-connectedness between places, they do not embody any eternal truth of places" (Massey 1995, p. 85). Travel creates an experience of transience of unbounded space which undermines what women had previously experienced as the "eternal truth".

Re-imagining identity

The women's travel stories have indicated that they are coming out of what Rose (1999, p. 47) terms "trans-individual identities of class, status, and gender", in which they negotiate the process of the identifications and seep through cracks of "the inscription of particular ethical formation, vocabularies of self-description and self-mastery, forms of conduct and body techniques." Women's travel in its multiple strategic movements demonstrates their crisscrossing the power geometry of place through their re-imagining of identities. Travel opens up this space of different identification for the women.

Langgar laut, then, becomes a powerful material symbol of overcoming one's marginality. I have shown in Part Two, how, through the liminal space of travel, women imagined and performed different identities and subject positions, transgressed and negotiated both real and imagined boundaries. Through exploring the experiences of individual women relocating themselves in liminal and ambiguous space, the women's efforts in negotiating boundaries within the context of their local specificity can be recognized.

Enabling mobile subjectivity

The analyses of the travel stories demonstrates the women's different ways of "being and seeing" the world after travel. The shifting subjectivities are closely related to the women's entering into the liminal and transient space of travel. The "constantly moving subjectivity" of women is also discursive (Baber 1994, p. 50; Lather 1991, p. xix) and is constituted within particular social, cultural, and economic relations. Mobile subjectivity recognizes the context-bound social relations which determine the extent of inclusion or exclusion in constructions of boundaries. For instance, Miriam's story in Chapter 6 demonstrated a woman making sense of her identities and shifting subjectivities in different space. Both as a domestic worker and a daughter living away from home, she remained in charge, *berani*, in facing sexual harassment from her employer. Other travel stories show women's different understandings of social realities and social relations through the subjective lenses of their individual travel experience. As the stories of the teachers and nurses travelling for work in the cities indicate, women manipulate the boundaries of the local gender propriety to their advantage. Thus women's spatial movements open up a space for women to perform multiple subject positions and identities and to negotiate a variety of boundaries. Here, my focus on travellers and their "new image-concept" of mobile subjectivity offers a critical awareness of the multiple contested spaces and relations of women's travel (Pile and Thrift 1995*a*, p. 21).

In the final analysis, women's travel represents their making a step closer to the subjective and imagined centre and transcending margins in the context of local specificity. The women's sense of achievement marked by their mobility indicates their disruption of the boundedness of space and confirms the notion of their decentring space. The domestic workers' travel represents their shift between different fractals of centre/margin (McKay 1999, p. 277). This kind of dynamic binary structure of power is conceptualized as fragmented further into a smaller and smaller centre/margin being split by women's experiences. For instance, domestic workers cross the marginality of the region, locating themselves physically at the centre of global cities. There in the centre, they become marginal in their roles as domestics, while at the same time they occupy a central position in the family income generating activities at home on the margin.

Travel creates a space to play the politics of place, to constantly shift between centre and margin, closer and closer to the imagined and moving centre. Within the range of women's travel experiences there emerges a common theme of strategic movements, in crossing the threshold of the local relations and moving forward to the space of ambiguity and uncertainties of changing and wider scales of relations. Women travellers slip in and out of a range of relations, raising some theoretical issues of identity in various domains, as discussed in Part Two. Within the intersecting gender discourses and the local specificity, I have shown in this study that travel offers a convincing entry to the multiplicity of women's subject positions which in turn enable their mobile subjectivities.

This space of travel is experimental, fluid, moving and indeed travel is a process of becoming, where negotiations of relations are taking place. The liminal quality of travel allows women to recreate identities to gain the best advantage in positioning themselves in various scales of relations and power. The women's willingness to take risks and to experiment with themselves in facing the uncertainty of the journey represents a move forward, and opens up a new space for multiple identities and shifting subjectivities. The women's journey constitutes a new geography of femininity for them.

Bibliography

ABC. 1997. *ABC World Airways Guide*. London: Thomas Skinner.

Abu-Lughod, Lila. 1991. "Writing Against Culture". In *Recapturing Anthropology: Working in the Present*, edited by Richard G. Fox, 137–162. Santa Fe: School of American Research Press.

Ananta, Aris, Evi Nurvidya Anwar, and Diah Suzenti. 1997. "Implication of Indonesia's Future Population". In *Indonesia Assessment: Population and Human Resources*, edited by Gavin W. Jones and Terence Hull, 301–322. Singapore: Institute of Southeast Asian Studies.

Andaya, Barbara Watson. 2000. "Introduction". In *Other Pasts: Women, Gender and History in Early Modern Southeast Asia*, edited by Barbara Watson Andaya, 1–26. Honolulu: Centre for Southeast Asian Studies.

Aoki, Eriko. 1997. "Piercing the sky, cutting the earth: The poetics of knowledge and the paradox of power among the Wologai of Central Flores". Ph.D. thesis, The Australian National University, Canberra.

Appadurai, Arjun. 1991. "Global Ethnoscapes: Notes and Queries for a Transnational Anthropology". In *Recapturing Anthropology: Working in the Present*, edited by Richard G. Fox, 191–210. Santa Fe: School of American Research Press.

Aripurnami, Sita. 2000. "Whiny, Finicky, Bitchy, Stupid and 'Revealing': Images of Women in Indonesian Films". In *Indonesian Women: The Journey Continues*, edited by Mayling Oey-Gardiner and Carla Bianpoen, 50–65. Canberra: RSPAS Publishing.

Baber, Kristine M. 1994. "Studying Women's Sexualities: Feminist Transformation". In *Gender, Families, and Close Relationship*, edited by Donna L. Sollie and Leigh A. Leslie, 50–73. London: Sage.

Badan Pusat Statistik Propinsi NTT. 2001. *Nusa Tenggara Timur Dalam Angka*. Kupang: Biro Pusat Statistik.

Barbič, Ana, and Inga Miklavčič-Brezigar. 1999. "Domestic work abroad: A necessity and an opportunity for rural women from the Goriška borderland region of Slovenia". In *Gender, migration and domestic service*, edited by Janet Henshall Momsen, 164–179. London: Routledge.

Barke, Michael. 1986. *Transport and Trade*. Edinburgh: Longman.

Barlow, Colin, Ria Gondowarsito, A. T. Birowo, and S. K. W. Jayasuriya. 1990. "Development in Eastern Indonesia: The Case of Nusa Tenggara Timur". International Development Issues 13, Australian International Development Assistance Bureau, Canberra.

Barlow, Colin, and Joan Hardjono, eds. 1996. *Indonesia Assessment 1995: Development in Eastern Indonesia*. Singapore: Institute of Southeast Asian Studies.

Barlow, Henry. 1995. "Anna Forbes: A Naturalist's Companion in the Far East". In *Adventurous Women in South-East Asia*, edited by John Gullick, 246–270. Kuala Lumpur: Oxford University Press.

Barnes, Robert H. 1974. *Kedang: A Study of the Collective Thought of Eastern Indonesian people*. Oxford: Clarendon Press.

———. 1980. "Concordance, Structure, and Variation: Considerations of Alliance in Kedang". In *The Flow of Life: Essays on Eastern Indonesia*, edited by James J. Fox, 68–97. Cambridge: Harvard University Press.

Bastin, John. 1995. "Sophia Raffles: Hardship and Travel in Sumatra". In *Adventurous Women in South-East Asia*, edited by John Gullick, 1–43. Kuala Lumpur: Oxford University Press.

Baudelaire, C. 1962. *The Painter of Modern Life*. London: Phaidon Press.

Bauer, Janet. 1984. "New Models and Traditional Networks: Migrant Women in Tehran". In *Women in the Cities of Asia: Migration and Urban Adaptation*, edited by James T. Fawcett, Siew-Ean Khoo, and Peter C. Smith, 269–296. Boulder: Westview Press, Inc.

Berger, Mark T. 2001. "(De)constructing the New Order: Capitalism and the cultural contours of the patrimonial state in Indonesia". In *House of Glass: Culture, modernity and the state in Southeast Asia,* edited by Souchou Yao, 191–212. Singapore: Institute of Southeast Asian Studies.

Berninghausen, Jutta, and Birgit Kerstan. 1992. *Forging New Paths, Feminist Social Methodology and Rural Women in Java.* Translated by Brabara A. Reeves. London: Zed Books Ltd.

Bhabha, Homi K. 1994. *The Location of Culture.* London: Routledge.

Bickmore, Albert S. 1868. *Travels in the East Indian Archipelago.* London: John Murray.

Bilsborrow, Richard E., and United Nations Secretariat. 1993. "Internal Female Migration and Development: An overview". Tech. Rep. ST/ESA/SER.R/127, United Nations.

Bisnis Indonesia (Indonesian daily newspaper). 1999. "Pelayanan TKI jadi satu atap". 19 April.

Blunt, Alison. 1994*a*. "Reading authorship and authority: Reading Mary Kingsley's landscape description". In *Writing Women and Space,* edited by Alison Blunt and Gillian Rose, 63–67. MAPPINGS: Society/Theory/Space, New York: The Guildford Press.

———. 1994*b*. *Travel, Gender and Imperialism: Mary Kingsley and West Africa.* New York: The Guildford Press.

———. 1999*a*. "The Flight from Lucknow: British women travelling and writing home, 1857–1858". In *Writes of Passage: Reading Travel Writing,* edited by James Duncan and Derek Gregory, 92–113. London: Routledge.

———. 1999*b*. "Imperial geographies of home: British domesticity in India, 1886–1925". *Transactions of the Institute of British Geography* 24:421–440.

Blunt, Alison, and Gillian Rose. 1994. "Introduction: Women's Colonial and Postcolonial Geographies". In *Writing Women and Space,* edited by Alison Blunt and Gillian Rose, 1–25. MAPPINGS: Society/Theory/Space, New York: The Guildford Press.

Bondi, Liz, and Mona Domosh. 1998. "On the Contours of Public Space: A Tale of Three Women". *Antipode* 30(3):270–289.

Boyle, Greg. 2002. "Finding God, with the poor, in our poverty. Reflecting on the two standards and our world today.". Creighton University's Collaborative Ministry Office.

Bozzoli, Belinda. 1991. *Women of Phokeng: Consciousness, Life Strategy, and Migrancy in South Africa, 1900–1983*. Social History of Africa, Portsmouth, NH: Heinemann.

Brannen, J. 1988. "Research Note: The study of Sensitive Subjects". *Sociological Review* 36:552–36.

Bubandt, Nils. 1997. "Speaking of places: Spatial poesis and localized identity in Buli". In *The Poetic Power of Place: Comparative Perspectives on Austronesian Ideas of Locality*, 132–162. Canberra: Department of Anthropology, RSPAS, The Australian National University.

Bulbeck, Chilla. 1998. *Re-orienting Western Feminisms*. Hong Kong: Cambridge University Press.

Bureau of Transport Economics. 1999. "Adequacy of Tourism Transport Infrastructure in Eastern Indonesia". Report 99, Bureau of Transport Economics, Canberra.

Business News. 2000. "Sistem Penempatan TKI di luar negeri belum profesional". 5 Juli.

Callaway, Helen. 1993. "Spatial domains and women's mobility in Yorubaland, Nigeria". In *Women and Space: Ground Rules and Social Maps*, edited by Shirley Ardener, 165–182. Oxford: Berg.

Cameron, Lisa. 1999. "Survey of recent development". *Bulletin of Indonesian Economic Studies* 35(1):3–41.

Chang, Grace. 2000. *Disposable Domestics: Immigrant Women Workers in the Global Economy*. Cambridge, Mass.: South End Press.

Chauvel, Richard. 1996. "Beyond the Wallace Line". In *Indonesia Assessment 1995: Development in Eastern Indonesia*, edited by Colin Barlow and Joan Hardjono, 61–74. Singapore: Institute of Southeast Asian Studies.

Chin, Christine B.N. 1997. "Walls of silence and late twentieth century representations of the foreign female domestic worker: The case of Filipina and Indonesian female servants in Malaysia". *International Migration Review* 31(2):353–85.

Clifford, James. 1986. "On ethnographic allegory". In *Writing Culture: The Poetics and Politics of Ethnography*, edited by James Clifford and George E Marcus, 98–121. Berkeley: University of California Press.

―――. 1988. *The Predicament of Culture: Twentieth Century Ethnography, Literature, and Art*. Cambridge, MA: Havard University Press.

―――. 1992. "Traveling Cultures". In *Cultural Studies*, edited by L Grossberg, C Nelson, and P.A. Treichler, 96–112. New York: Routledge.

―――. 1997. *Routes: Travel and Translation in the Late Twentieth Century*. Cambridge: Harvard University Press.

Cole, David, and Betty Slade. 1998. "Why has Indonesia's financial crisis been so bad?". *Bulletin of Indonesian Economic Studies* 34(2):61–6.

Constable, Nicole. 1997. *Maid to Order in Hong Kong*. Ithaca, N.Y.: Cornell University Press.

Cooper, Nancy. 1994. "The sirens of Java: Gender ideologies, mythologies, and practice in Central Java". Ph.D. thesis, University of Hawaii.

Cox, Kevin R. 1989. "The Politics of Turf and the Question of Class". In *The Power Of Geography*, edited by J. Wolch and M. Dear. Boston: Unwin Hyman.

Cox, Rosie. 1999. "The role of ethnicity in shaping the domestic employment sector in Britain". In *Gender, migration and domestic service*, edited by Janet Henshall Momsen, 134–146. London: Routledge.

Cresswell, Tim. 1996. *In place/Out of place: Geography, Ideology and Transgression*. Minneapolis: University of Minnesota Press.

Cunningham, Clarke E. 1964. "Order in Atoni House". *Bijdragen tot de Taal-, Land- en Volkenkunde* 120:34–68.

Daniel, Danof. 2000. "Bekerja di LN Kesempatan besar cari uang". *Media Indonesia*, 10 April 2000.

deJong, Willemijn. 2000. "Women's networks in cloth production and exchange in Flores". In *Women and Household in Indonesia*, edited by Juliette Koning, Marleen Nolten, Janet Rodenburg, and Ratna Saptari, 264–280. Richmond: Nordic Institute of Asian Studies and Curzon Press.

Departemen Perhubungan. 1996. *Sistem Transportasi Nasional*. Departemen Perhubungan.

Dickerson-Putman, Jeanette, and Judith K. Brown. 1998. "Introductory Overview: Women's Age Hierarchies". In *Women among Women*, edited by Jeanette Dickerson-Putman and Judith K. Brown, xi–xvii. Urbana and Chicago: University of Illinois Press.

Directorate General of Sea Transport. 1996. *Transportation Statistics 1996*. Jakarta: Department of Communications.

Direktorat Jendral Binapenta. 2000. "Pengiriman TKI tetap dilakukan untuk mengurangi Pengangguran". *Business News*, 16 June 2000.

Djeki. 1977. "Adat Istiadat Daerah Nusa Tenggara Timur". Tech. Rep., Proyek Penelitian dan Pencatatan Kebudayaan Daerah, Kupang.

Domosh, Mona. 1991. "Beyond the Frontiers of geographical knowledge". *Transactions of the Institute of British Geographers* 16:488–490.

———. 1997. "With 'Stout Boots and Stout Heart': Historical Methodology and Feminist Geography". In *Thresholds in Feminist Geography: Difference, Methodology, Representation*, edited by John Paul Jones III, Heidi J. Nast, and Susan M. Roberts, 225–237. Lanham, MD: Rowman and Littlefield Publishers.

Drake, Christine. 1989. *National Integration in Indonesia: Patterns and Policies*. Honolulu: University of Hawaii.

Duncan, James, and Derek Gregory. 1999. "Introduction". In *Writes of Passage: Reading Travel Writing*, edited by James Duncan and Derek Gregory, 1–13. London: Routledge.

Duncombe, Jean, and Dennis Marsden. 1996. "Can we research the private sphere?: Methodological and ethical problems in the study of the role of intimate in personal relationships". In *Gender Relations* in *Public and Private: New Research Perspectives*, edited by Lydia Morris and E. Stina Lyon, 141–155. London: Macmillan Press.

Dwyer, Claire. 1999. "Negotiations of femininity and identity for young British Muslim women". In *Geographies of new femininities*, edited by Nina Laurie, Claire Dwyer, Sarah Holloway, and Fiona Smith, 135–152. New York: Longman.

Elmhirst, Rebecca. 1999. "Learning the ways of the '*priyayi*': Domestic servants and the mediation of modernity in Jakarta, Indonesia". In *Gender, migration and domestic service*, edited by Janet Henshall Momsen, 241–262. London: Routledge.

Elsam. 1997. "TKW: Nasibmu kini". *Asasi Newsletter*: Analisis dokumentasi Hak Asasi Manusia.

England, Kim V. L. 1991. "Gender relations and the spatial structure of the city". *Geoforum* 22(2):135–147.

———. 1994. "Getting Personal: Reflexity, Positionality, and Feminist Research". *Professional Geographer* 46:80–89.

Errington, Shelly. 1990. "Recasting sex, gender and power: A theoretical and regional overview". In *Power and Difference: Gender in Island Southeast Asia*, edited by Jane Monnig Atkinson and Shelly Errington. Stanford: Stanford University Press.

Evans, Kevin. 1998. "Survey of Recent Developments". *Bulletin of Indonesian Economic Studies* 34(2):5–36.

Ferguson, Kathy E. 1999. *The Man Question: Visions of Subjectivity in Feminist Theory*. Berkeley: University of California Press.

Fernandez, Stephanus Ozias, ed. 1990. *Kebijakan Manusia Nusa Tenggara Timur dulu dan kini*. Ledalero: Sekolah Tinggi Filsafat Katolik Ledalero.

Finnegan, Ruth. 1992. *Oral traditions and the verbal arts: A guide to research practice*. London: Routledge.

Forth, Gregory. 1981. *Rindi: An ethnographic study of a traditional domain in Eastern Sumba*. The Hague: Martinus Nijhoff.

————. 1991*a*. "Nage directions: An Eastern Indonesian system of spatial orientation". In *Social Space: Processings of an Interdisciplinary Conference on Human Spatial Behaviour in Dwellings and Settlements*, edited by Gron Ole, 138–148. Odense: Odense University Press.

————. 1991*b*. "Space and place in Eastern Indonesia". Paper presented at CSEAS, University of Kent (Occasional Paper 9), Canterbury.

————. 1998. *Beneath the Volcano*. The Netherlands: KITLV Press.

Fortier, Anne-Marie. 2000. *Migrant Belongings: Memory, Space, Identity*. Oxford: Berg Publisher.

Fox, James J. 1980. "Models and Metaphors: Comparative Research in Eastern Indonesia". In *The Flow of Life: Essays on Eastern Indonesia*, edited by James J. Fox, 327–333. Cambridge: Harvard University Press.

Fox, James J, ed. 1997. *The Poetic Power of Place: Comparative Perspectives on Austronesian Ideas of Locality*. Canberra: Department of Anthropology, RSPAS, The Australian National University.

Fox, James J. 1999. "Precedence in practice among the Atoni Pah Meto of Timor". In *Structuralism's Transformations: Order and Revision in Indonesian and Malaysian Societies*, edited by Lorraine V. Aragon and Susan D. Russell, 3–36. Arizona: Program for Southeast Asian Studies, Arizona State University.

Frederick, Bonnie, and Virginia Hyde. 1993. "Introduction". In *Women and the Journey: The female travel experience*, edited by Bonnie Frederick and Susan H. McLeod, xvii. Seattle: Washington State University Press.

Frederick, Bonnie, and Susan H. McLeod. 1993. "Adventure, Class and Clothing". In *Women and the Journey: The female travel experience*, edited by Bonnie Frederick and Susan H. McLeod, 1–4. Seattle: Washington State University Press.

Frisby, David. 1985. *Fragments of Modernity*. Cambridge: Polity.

Gamburd, Michelle Ruth. 2000. *The Kitchen Spoon's Handle: Transnationalism and Sri Lanka's Migrant Housemaids*. Ithaca, N.Y.: Cornell University Press.

Ganguly, K. 1992. "Migrant identities: Personal memory and the construction of selfhood". *Cultural Studies* 1:27–50.

Ghose, Indira. 1998. *Women Travellers in Colonial India: The Power of the Female Gaze.* Delhi: Oxford University Press.

Gibson, Katherine. 2001. "Regional Subjection and Becoming". *Environment and Planning D: Society and Space* 19:639–667.

Gibson-Graham, Julie Katherine. 2006*a*. *The End of Capitalism (As We Knew It): A Feminist Critique of Political Economy.* 2nd ed. Minneapolis: University of Minnesota Press.

———. 2006*b*. *A Postcapitalist Politics.* Minneapolis: University of Minnesota Press.

Giddens, Anthony. 1993. *Sociology.* 2nd ed. Oxford: Blackwell.

Gordon, John L. 1980. "The marriage nexus among the Manggarai of West Flores". In *The Flow of Life: Essays on Eastern Indonesia*, edited by James J. Fox, 48–67. Cambridge: Harvard University Press.

Graham, Penelope. 1991. "To follow the blood: The path of life in a domain of Eastern Flores, Indonesia". Ph.D. thesis, Department of Anthropology, Research School of Asia and Pacific Studies, Australian National University, Canberra.

———. 1999. "Seas that unite, mountains that divide: Language, identity and development in Flores". *Anthropologi Indonesia* XXIII(58): 71–81.

Granovetter, Mark. 1985. "Economic action and social structure: The problem of embeddedness". *American Journal of Sociology* 91(3):481–510.

Gregson, Nicky, and Miclelle Lowe. 1994. *Servicing the Middle Classes.* London: Routledge.

Grenville, Stephen. 2004. "The IMF and the Indonesian crisis". *Bulletin of Indonesian Economic Studies* 40(1):77–94.

Grimes, Kimberley M. 1998. *Crossing Borders: Changing Social Identities in Southern Mexico.* University of Arizona Press.

Groves, Julian McAllister, and Kimberly A. Chang. 1999. "Romancing resistance and resisting romance: Ethnography and the construction of power in the Filipina domestic worker community in Hong Kong". *Journal of Contemporary Ethnography* 28(3):235–265.

Guest, Philip. 1993. "The Determinants of Female Migration from a Multilevel Perspective". In *United Nations Expert Meeting on Feminization of Internal Migration*. Aguascalientes, Mexico: United Nations.

Gullick, John, ed. 1995*a*. *Adventurous Women in South-East Asia*. Kuala Lumpur: Oxford University Press.

Gullick, John. 1995*b*. "Emily Innes: Keeping Up One's Standards in Malaya". In *Adventurous Women in South-East Asia*, edited by John Gullick, 147–195. Kuala Lumpur: Oxford University Press.

Gupta, Akhil. 1997. "Discipline and Practice: 'The Field' as Site, Method, and Location in Anthropology". In *Anthropological Locations: Boundaries and Grounds of a Field Science*, edited by Akhil Gupta and James Ferguson. Berkeley: University of California Press.

Hamilton, Roy W. 1994. *Gift of the Cotton Maiden*. Berkeley: Regents of the University of California.

Hanson, Susan, and Geraldine Pratt. 1995. *Gender, Work and Space*. London: Routledge.

Hardjono, Joan. 1994. "Resource utilisation and the environment". In *Indonesia's New Order*, edited by Hal Hill, 179–215. Sydney: Allen and Unwin.

Haris, Abdul, and Nyoman Adika. 2002. *Gelombang Migrasi dan Konflik Kepentingan Regional*. Yogyakarta: LESFI.

Hatley, Barbara. 1997. "Nation, 'Tradition,' and Constructions of the Feminine in Modern Indonesian Literature". In *Imagining Indonesia: Cultural Politics and Political Culture*, edited by Jim Schiller and Barbara Martin-Schiller, 90–121. Ohio: The Center for International Studies.

Hendytio, Medelina K., Vidyandika Moelyarto, Arya B. Gaduh, and Tubagus Feridhanusetyawan. 1999. "Globalization, Institutional framework, policy and legislation: An overview with a gender dimension". Tech. Rep., Center for Strategic and International Studies, Jakarta.

Herbert, Steve. 2000. "For Ethnography". *Progress in Human Geography* 24(4):550–568.

Herod, Andrew, and Melissa W. Wright, eds. 2002. *Geographies of power: Placing scale.* Malden, MA: Blackwell.

Heyzer, Noeleen, and Viviennne Wee. 1994. "Domestic Workers in Transient Overseas Employment: Who Benefits, Who Profits". In *The trade in domestic workers: Causes, mechanisms and Consequences of international migration,* edited by Noeleen Heyzer and Geertje Lycklama à Nijeholt, 31–101. Kuala Lumpur, Malaysia: Asian and Pacific Development Centre.

Hicks, David. 1990. *Kinship and Religion in Eastern Indonesia.* Gothenburg: ACTA Universitatis Gothoburgensis.

Hill, Hal, ed. 1989. *Unity and Diversity: Regional Economic Development in Indonesia since 1970.* Singapore: Oxford University Press.

Hill, Hal. 1996. *The Indonesian Economy since 1966: Southeast Asia's Emerging Giant.* Melbourne: Cambridge University Press.

Hondagneu-Sotelo, Pierrette. 2001. *Doméstica: Immigrant workers cleaning and caring in the shadows of affluence.* Berkeley: University of California Press.

hooks, bell. 1990. *Yearning: Race, gender, and cultural politics.* Boston, MA: South End Press.

Howell, Signe. 1995. "The Lio House: Building, category, idea, value.". In *About the House: Levi-Strauss and Beyond,* edited by Carsten and Hugh-Jones, 149–169. Cambridge: University Press.

Huang, Shirlena, and Brenda S.A. Yeoh. 1996. "Gender and Urban Space in the Tropical World". *Singapore Journal of Tropical Geography* 17(2):105–112.

Hubbard, Phil. 1998. "Sexuality, Immorality and the City: Red-light districts and the marginalisation of female street prostitutes". *Gender, Place and Culture* 5(1):55–72.

Huffman, Nikolas H. 1997. "Charting the other maps: Cartography and visual methods in feminist research". In *Thresholds in Feminist Geography: Difference, Methodology, Representation*, edited by John Paul Jones III, Heidi J. Nast, and Susan M. Roberts, 255–283. Lanham, MD: Rowman and Littlefield Publishers.

Hugo, Graeme. 1997. "Changing Patterns and Processes in Population Mobility". In *Indonesia Assessment: Population and Human Resources*, edited by Gavin W. Jones and Terence Hull, 68–100. Singapore: Institute of Southeast Asian Studies.

————. 1999. "Undocumented International Migration in Southeast Asia". In *Asian Migration: Pacific Rim Dynamics*, edited by Yen-Feng Tseng, Chila Bulbeck, Lan-Hung Nora Chiang, and Jung-Chung Hsu, 15–48. Taipei: Interdisciplinary Group for Australian Studies, National Taiwan University.

————. 2000. "The Crisis and International Population Movement in Indonesia". *Asian and Pacific Migration Journal* 9(1):93–129.

Hugo, Graeme J., Terence H. Hull, Valerie J. Hull, and Gavin W. Jones. 1987. *The Demographic Dimension in Indonesian Development*. Singapore: Oxford University Press.

Instone, Lesley. 1999. "(Un)Natural Narratives: Rethinking stories about the Australian environment". In *Conference Proceedings*, edited by J.A. Kesby, J.M. Stanley, R.F. McLean, and L.J. Olive, 175–180. Canberra: Institute of Australian Geographers.

International Labor Organization. 1998. "Emerging gender issues in the Asia Pacific region". http://www.ilo.org/public/english/region/asro/mdtmanila/training/unit2/asiamign.htm.

————. 1999. "Indonesian Employment Strategy Mission: Aide Memoire". http://www.ilo.org/public/english/region/asro/jakarta/aide.htm.

Jackson, Cecile. 2002. "Disciplining Gender?". *World Development* 30(3):497–509.

Jackson, Cecile, and Ricahrd Palmer-Jones. 1999. "Rethinking Gendered Poverty and Work". *Development and Change* 30:557–583.

Jakarta Post (Daily newspaper). 1999*a*. "Company investigated for confining female worker". 28 April.

———. 1999*b*. "Protecting workers". 1 May.

———. 2000. "20 Indonesian women held as sex slaves freed". 12 July.

Janelle, Donald. 1969. "Central place development in a time-space framework". *Professional Geographers* 20:1–10.

Jones, Gavin. 1995. "Introduction". In *People, Land and Sea*, edited by Gavin W. Jones and Yulfita Raharjo, 1–8. Canberra: Demography Program, RSSS, ANU.

Kaplan, Caren. 1996. *Questions of Travel: Postmodern Discourses of Displacement*. Durham, NC: Duke University Press.

Katz, Cindi. 1994. "Playing the Field: Questions of Fieldwork in Geography". *Professional Geographer* 46:67–72.

Kerfoot, Deborah, and David Knights. 1994. "Into the Realm of the Fearful: Power, Identity and the Gender Problematic". In *Power/Gender: Social Relations in Theory and Practice*, edited by H. Lorraine Radtke and Henrikus J. Stam, 67–88. London: Sage.

Khoo, Siew-Ean, and Peter Pirie. 1984. "Female Rural-to-Urban Migration in Peninsular Malaysia". In *Women in the Cities of Asia: Migration and Urban Adaptation*, edited by James T. Fawcett, Siew-Ean Khoo, and Peter C. Smith, 125–142. Boulder: Westview Press, Inc.

Kobayashi, Audrey. 1994. "Coloring the field: Gender, 'race' and the politics of fieldwork". *Professional Geographer* 46:73–80.

———. 1997. "Introduction to Part 1: The Paradox of Difference and Diversity (or, Why the Threshold Keeps Moving)". In *Thresholds in Feminist Geography: Difference, Methodology, Representation*, edited by John Paul Jones III, Heidi J. Nast, and Susan M. Roberts, 3–9. Lanham, MD: Rowman and Littlefield Publishers.

Kofman, E., and K. England. 1997. "Citizenship and International Migration: Taking Account of Gender, Sexuality and 'Race'". *Environment and Planning A* 29(2):191–4.

Kompas (Indonesian daily newspaper). 2000. "TKW Diperkosa dan Disiksa di Serawak". 13 March.

Koning, Juliette. 2000. "Different Times, Different Orientations: Family Life in A Javanese Village". In *Women and Household in Indonesia*, edited by Juliette Koning, Marleen Nolten, Janet Rodenburg, and Ratna Saptari, 181–207. Richmond: Nordic Institute of Asian Studies and Curzon Press.

Koning, Juliette, Marleen Nolten, Janet Rodenburg, and Ratna Saptari, eds. 2000. *Women and Household in Indonesia*. Richmond: Nordic Institute of Asian Studies and Curzon Press.

Koskela, Hille. 1999. "'Gendered exclusions': Women's fear of violence and changing relations to space". *Geografiska Annaler* 81(2):111–124.

Lather, Patricia A. 1991. *Getting smart: Feminist research and pedagogy with/in postmodernism*. New York: Routledge.

Laurie, Nina. 1999. "The shifting geographies of femininity and emergency work in Peru". In *Geographies of new femininities*, edited by Nina Laurie, Claire Dwyer, Sarah Holloway, and Fiona Smith, 67–90. New York: Longman.

Laurie, Nina, Claire Dwyer, Sarah Holloway, and Fiona Smith, eds. 1999. *Geographies of new femininities*. New York: Longman.

Law, Robin. 1999. "Beyond 'women and transport': Towards new geographies of gender and daily mobility". *Progress in Human Geography* 23(4):567–588.

Lawrence, Karen R. 1994. *Penelope Voyages: Women and travel in the British literary tradition*. Ithaca, NY: Cornell University Press.

Laws, Glenda. 1997. "Women's Life Courses, Spatial Mobility, and Policies". In *Thresholds in Feminist Geography: Difference, Methodology, Representation*, edited by John Paul Jones III, Heidi J. Nast, and Susan M. Roberts, 47–64. Lanham, MD: Rowman and Littlefield Publishers.

Lawson, Victoria A. 1998. "Hierarchical households and gendered migration in Latin America: Feminist extentions to migration research". *Progress in Human Geography* 22(1):39–53.

————. 2000. "Arguments within geographies of movement: The theoretical potential of migrants' stories". *Progress in Human Geography* 24(2):173–189.

Lewis, E. D. 1988. *People of the source: The social and ceremonial order of Tana Wai Brama on Flores*. Leiden: Floris Publications Holland.

Leyshon, Andrew. 1995. "Annihilating space?: The speed-up of communications". In *A Shrinking World? Global Unevenness and Inequality*, edited by John Allen and Chris Hamnett, 12–49. New York: Oxford University Press.

Lips, Hilary M. 1994. "Female Powerlessness: A Case of 'Cultural Preparedness'?". In *Power/Gender: Social Relations in Theory and Practice*, edited by H. Lorraine Radtke and Henrikus J. Stam, 89–107. London: Sage.

Lubis, Mochtar. 1987. *Indonesia: Land Under the Rainbow*. Manila: Solidaridad.

Mahler, Sarah J., and Patricia R. Pesar. 2006. "Gender Matters: Ethnographers Bring Gender from the Periphery toward the Core of Migration Studies". *International Migration Review* 40(1):27–63.

Manning, Chris. 1998. *Indonesian Labour in Transition: An East Asian success story?* UK: Cambridge University Press.

Marcus, George E., and M Fisher. 1986. *Anthropology as Cultural Critique*. Chicago: University of Chicago Press.

Martin, Patricia Yancey. 1992. "Gender, Interaction, and Inequality in Organisation". In *Gender, Interaction, and Inequality*, edited by Cecilia L. Ridgeway, 208–232. New York: Springer-Verlag.

Massey, Doreen. 1984. "Introduction: Geography Matters". In *Geography matters: A reader*, edited by Doreen Massey and John Allen. Cambridge: Cambridge University Press.

————. 1993. "Power-geometry and a progressive sense of place". In *Mapping the Futures: Local cultures, global change*, edited by Jon Bird, Barry Curtis, Tim Putnam, George Robertson, and Lisa Tickner, 59–69. London: Routledge.

————. 1995. "The conceptualisation of place". In *A Place in the World? Places, Culture and Globalisation*, edited by Doreen Massey and Pat Jess, 45–86. New York: Oxford University Press.

Massey, Doreen, and Pat Jess, eds. 1995. *A Place in the world?: Places, cultures and globalization*. Milton Keynes, England: Oxford University Press.

Massey, Douglas, Jaoquin Arango, Graeme Hugo, Ali Kouaouci, Adela Pellegrino, and J. Edward Taylor. 1993. "Theories of International Migration". *Population and Development* 19(3):431–466.

McDonald, Kevin. 1999. *Struggles for Subjectivity: Identity, action and youth experience*. Singapore: Cambridge University Press.

McDowell, Linda. 1999. *Gender, Identity and Place: Understanding Feminist Geography*. Minneapolis: Polity Press.

McKay, Deirdre. 1999. "Imagining Igorots: Performing Ethnic and Gender Identities on the Philippine Cordillera Central". Ph.D. thesis, Department of Geography, The University of British Columbia, Canada.

————. 2001. "Negotiating the contact zone: Exchanging life stories in research interviews". In *Gender and Geography*, edited by Pamela Moss, 187–199. Oxford: Blackwell Publishers.

McLeod, Ross H. 2005. "Survey of recent developments". *Bulletin of Indonesian Economic Studies* 41(2):133–157.

McWilliam, Andrew. 1997. "Mapping with Metaphor: Cultural topographies in West Timor". In *The Poetic Power of Place*, edited by James J Fox, 103–115. Canberra: Dept of Anthropology, Research School of Pacific and Asian Studies, The Australian National University.

Meldrum, Tim. 2000. *Domestic Service and Gender 1660–1750*. Essex: Pearson Education.

Merdeka (Indonesian daily newspaper). 1998. "Ironi Migran". 8 August.

Mills, Sarah. 1991. *Discourses of Difference: An Analysis of Women's Travel Writing and Colonialism*. London: Routledge.

Minh-ha, Trinh T. 1994. "Other than myself/my other self". In *Travellers' tales: Narratives of home and displacement*, edited by George Robertson, Melinda Mash, Lisa Tickner, Jon Bird, Barry Curtis, and Tim Putnam, 9–26. London: Routledge.

Mitchell, Katharyne. 1997. "Different diasporas and the hype of hybridity". *Environment and Planning D: Society and Space* 15:533–553.

Mohanty, Chandra Talpade. 1987. "Feminist Encounters: Locating the Politics of Experience". *Copyright 1* 1:30–44. Special issue on Fin de Siecle 2000.

———. 1991. "Cartographies of Struggle: Third World Women and the Politics of Feminism". In *Third World Women and the Politics of Feminism*, edited by Chandra Talpade Mohanty, Ann Russo, and Lourdes Torres, 1–47. Indianapolis: Indiana University Press.

Molnar, Katalin A. 2000. *Grandchildren of Ga'e Ancestors: Social Organisation and Cosmology among Hoga Sara of Flores*. Leiden: Land-en Volkunde Press.

Mommersteeg, Andrian, and Margaretha Dirkzwager, eds. 1999. *Punu Nange: Cerita dari So'a Flores*. Jakarta: Yayasan Obor Indonesia.

Momsen, Janet Henshall, ed. 1999. *Gender, migration and domestic service*. London: Routledge.

Morgan, Susan. 1996. *Place matters: Gendered geography in Victorian women's travel books about Southeast Asia*. New Brunswick: Rutgers University Press.

Morin, Karen M. 1999. "Peak Practised: Englishwomen's 'Heroic' Adventures in the Nineteenth-Century American West". *Annals of the Association of American Geographers* 89(3):489–514.

Mullings, Beverley. 1999. "Insider or outsider, both or neither: Some dilemmas of interviewing in a cross-cultural settings". *Geoforum* 30: 337–350.

Nagar, Richa. 1997. "Exploring Methodological Borderlands through Oral Narratives". In *Thresholds in Feminist Geography: Difference, Methodology, Representation*, edited by John Paul Jones III, Heidi J.

Nast, and Susan M. Roberts, 203–224. Lanham, MD: Rowman and Littlefield Publishers.

Najib, Laila. 1997. "Pendidikan dan Pasar Kerja: Studi penelusuran ter-hadap siswa lulusan SLTA tahun 1996 di Timor, NTT". Progress re-port, *Eastern Indonesia Population and Development Research Project Newsletter*. Bappenas and Ausaid project.

Narayan, Kirin. 1997. "How native is a 'native' anthropologist?". In *Situated lives: Gender and culture in everyday life*, edited by Louise Lamphere, Helena Ragone, and Patricia Zavella. London: Routledge.

Narula, Rekha. 1999. "Cinderella need not apply: A study of paid do-mestic work in Paris". In *Gender, migration and domestic service*, edited by Janet Henshall Momsen, 148–163. London: Routledge.

Nast, Heidi J. 1994. "Women in the Field: Critical Feminist Method-ologies and Theoretical Perspectives". *Professional Geographer* 46: 54–66.

Newman, David, and Anssi Paasi. 1998. "Fences and neighbours in the postmodern world: Boundary narratives in political geography". *Progress in Human Geography* 22(2):186–207.

Nitchter, Mark, and Mimi Nichter. 1991. "Hype and Weight". *Medical Anthropology* 249 –284.

Oey-Gardiner, Mayling. 1997. "Educational Developments, Achieve-ments and Challenges". In *Indonesia Assessment: Population and Human Resources*, edited by Gavin W. Jones and Terence Hull. Sin-gapore: Institute of Southeast Asian Studies.

Ong, Aihwa. 1987. *Spirits of Resistance and Capitalist Discipline: Fac-tory Women in Malaysia*. Albany: State University of New York.

———. 1990. "State versus Islam: Malay Families, Women's Bodies, and the Body Politics in Malaysia". *American Ethnologist* 258–276.

Ong, Aihwa, and Michael G. Peletz. 1995. "Introduction". In *Bewitching Women, Pious Men: Gender and Body Politics in Southeast Asia*, edited by Aihwa Ong and Michael G. Peletz, 1–18. Berkeley: University of California Press.

Orinbao, Piet Sareng. 1992*a*. *Seni Tenun suatu segi kebudayaan orang Flores*. Ledalero, Flores: Seminari Tinggi St Paulus.

———. 1992*b*. *Tata berladang tradisional dan pertanian rasional Suku-Bangsa Lio*. Ledalero, Flores: Seminari Tinggi St Paulus.

Parrenas, Rhacel Salazar. 2001. *Servants of globalization: Women, migration, and domestic work*. Stanford: Stanford University Press.

Pile, Steve, and Nigel Thrift. 1995*a*. "Introduction". In *Mapping the Subject: Geographies of Cultural Transformation*, edited by Steve Pile and Nigel Thrift. London: Routledge.

Pile, Steve, and Nigel Thrift, eds. 1995*b*. *Mapping the Subject: Geographies of Cultural Transformation*. London: Routledge.

Pollock, Griselda. 1994. "Territories of desire: Reconsiderations of an African childhood". In *Travellers' tales: Narratives of home and displacement*, edited by George Robertson, Melinda Mash, Lisa Tickner, Jon Bird, Barry Curtis, and Tim Putnam, 63–92. London: Routledge.

Pombejra, Dhivarat Na. 2000. "VOC Employees and their Relatioships with Mon and Siamese Women: A Case Study of Osoet Pegua". In *Other Pasts: Women, Gender and History in Early Modern Southeast Asia*, edited by Barbara Watson Andaya, 195–214. Honolulu: Centre for Southeast Asian Studies.

Pratt, Mary Louise. 1992. *Imperial Eyes: Travel Writing and Transculturation*. London: Routledge.

Purnama, Lita. 2001. "Apa kabar perempuan daerah?". *Jurnal Perempuan* 1(17):41–57.

Purwadi, Agung, and Suheru Muljoatmojo. 2000. "Education in Indonesia: Coping with Challenges in the Third Millennium". *Journal of Southeast Asian Education* 1(1):79–102.

Raharjo, Yulfita. 1997. "Women's Role in Demographic Transition and Human Resource Development". In *Indonesia Assessment: Population and Human Resources*, edited by Gavin W. Jones and Terence Hull, 167–180. Singapore: Institute of Southeast Asian Studies.

Raharto, Aswatini, G. Hugo, H. Romdiati, and S. Bandiyono. 1999. *Migrasi dan Pembangunan di Kawasan Timur Indonesia: Isu Ketenagakerjaan [Migration and Development in Eastern Indonesia: Labour Issues]*. PPT–LIPI.

Robinson, Kathryn. 1991. "Housemaids: The Effects of Gender and Culture on the Internal and International Migration of Indonesian Women". In *Intersexions: Gender/Class/Ethnicity*, edited by Gillian Bottomley, Marie deLepervanche, and Jeannie Martin, 31–51. Sydney: Allen and Unwin.

———. 2000*a*. "Gender, Islam and Nationality: Indonesian Domestic Servants in the Middle East". In *Home and Hegemony: Domestic Service and Identity Politics in South and Southeast Asia*, edited by Kathleen Adams and Sara Dickey, 249–282. Ann Arbor: University of Michigan Press.

———. 2000*b*. "Indonesian Women: From Orde Baru to Reformasi". In *Women in Asia: Tradition, modernity and globalisation*, edited by Louise Edwards and Mina Roces, 139–169. Sydney: Allen and Unwin.

Robinson, Kathryn, and Sharon Bessel. 2002. "Introduction to Issues". In *Women in Indonesia: Gender, Equity and Development*, edited by Kathryn Robinson and Sharon Bessel, 1–12. Singapore: Institute of Southeast Asian Studies.

Rodenburg, Janet. 1997. *In the Shadow of Migration: Rural women and their households in North Tapanuli, Indonesia*. Leiden: KITLV Press.

Rojek, Chris. 1994. *Ways of Escape: Modern Transformations in Leisure and Travel*. Postmodern Social Futures, Lanham: Rowman and Littlefield Publisher.

Rollins, J. 1985. *Between Women: Domestics and their Employers*. Philadelphia: Temple University Press.

Romero, Mary. 1992. *Maid in the U.S.A.* New York: Routledge.

Rose, Gillian. 1997. "Situating knowledges: Positionality, reflexivities and other tactics". *Progress in Human Geography* 21(3):305–320.

Rose, Nikolas. 1999. "Governing". In *Powers of Freedom: Reframing Political Thought*, 15–60. Cambridge: Cambridge University Press.

Rutz, Werner. 1976. *Transport Penetration of the Outer Islands*. Panderborn: Ferdinand Schoeningh.

Said, Edward. 1979. *Orientalism*. New York: Vintage.

Sarup, Madan. 1994. "Home and identity". In *Travellers' tales: Narratives of home and displacement*, edited by George Robertson, Melinda Mash, Lisa Tickner, Jon Bird, Barry Curtis, and Tim Putnam, 93–104. London: Routledge.

Saunders, Graham. 1995. "Harriette McDougall: First Woman Missionary to Sarawak". In *Adventurous Women in South-East Asia*, edited by John Gullick, 44–93. Kuala Lumpur: Oxford University Press.

Sayogyo, ed. 1994. *Kemiskinan dan pembangunan di propinsi Nusa Tenggara Timur*. Jakarta: Yayasan Obor Indonesia.

Shah, Nasra M. 1984. "Female Migrant in Pakistan". In *Women in the Cities of Asia: Migration and Urban Adaptation*, edited by James T. Fawcett, Siew-Ean Khoo, and Peter C. Smith, 108–124. Boulder: Westview Press, Inc.

Siikala, Jukka. 2001. "Introduction: Where have all the people gone". In *Departures*, edited by Jukka Siikala, 1–6. Finland: The Finnish Anthropological Society.

Silvey, Rachel. 2000. "Stigmatized Spaces: Gender and mobility under crisis in South Sulawesi, Indonesia". *Gender, Place and Culture* 7(2): 143–161.

———. 2001. "Migration under crisis; household safety nets in Indonesia's economic collapse". *Geoforum* 32:33–45.

———. 2006. "Geographies of Gender and Migration: Spatializing Social Difference". *International Migration Review* 40(1):64–81.

Silvey, Rachel, and Victoria Lawson. 1999. "Placing Migrant". *Annals of the Association of American Geographers* 89(1):121–132.

Sitorus, Felix, and Alexander Weka. 1994. "Kemiskinan dan Pembangunan: Kasus Kabupaten Ende". In *Kemiskinan dan pembangunan di propinsi Nusa Tenggara Timur*, edited by Sayogyo, 40–55. Jakarta: Yayasan Obor Indonesia.

Smithies, Michael. 1995. "Anna Leonowens: 'School Mistress' at the Court of Siam". In _Adventurous Women in South-East Asia_, edited by John Gullick, 94–146. Kuala Lumpur: Oxford University Press.

Sobieszczy, Teresa. 2000. "Pathways Abroad: Gender and International Migration Recruitment Choices in Northern Thailand". _Asian and Pacific Migration Journal_ 9(4).

Staeheli, Lynn A., and Victoria A. Lawson. 1994. "A Discussion of 'Women in the Field': The Politics of Feminist Fieldwork". _Professional Geographer_ 46:96–102.

Stallybrass, Peter, and Allon White. 1986. _The Politics and Poetics of Transgression_. London: Menthuen.

Stoler, A. L. 1977. "Class structure and female autonomy in rural Java". _Signs_ 3(1):74–89.

Strathern, Marilyn. 1991. _Partial connections_. Savage, MD: Rowman and Littlefield.

Suara Pembaruan (Indonesian daily newspaper). 1999. "Peran Ganda Mengandung Bias [Women's double role is biased]". 21 August.

Suryakusuma, Julia I. 1996. "The State and Sexuality in New Order Indonesia". In _Fantasizing the Feminine in Indonesia_, edited by Laurie J. Sears, 92–119. Durham, NC: Duke University Press.

Tam, Vicky C. W. 1999. "Foreign domestic helpers in Hong Kong and their role in childcare provision". In _Gender, migration and domestic service_, edited by Janet Henshall Momsen, 263–276. London: Routledge.

Therik, Tom G. 1995. "Wehali: The four corner land, the cosmology and traditions of a Timorese ritual centre". Ph.D. thesis, Australian National University, Canberra.

Thrift, N. J. 1983. "On the Determination of Social Action in Space and Time". _Environment and Planning D: Society and Space_ 1(1):23–57.

Thrift, Nigel J. 1993. "For a New Regional Geography 3". _Progress in Human Geography_ 17(1):92–100.

Tirtosudarmo, Riwanto. 1996. "Human Resources Development in Eastern Indonesia". In *Indonesia Assessment 1995: Development in Eastern Indonesia*, edited by Colin Barlow and Joan Hardjono, 198–212. Singapore: Institute of Southeast Asian Studies.

—————. 2002. "Tentang Perbatasan dan Studi Perbatasan: Sebuah pengantar". *Antropologi Indonesia* XXVI(67):iv–vi.

Tsing, Anna Lowenhaupt. 1993. *In the realm of the diamond queen: Marginality in an out-of-the-way place*. Princeton, New Jersey: Princeton University Press.

—————. 2000. "The Global Situation". *Cultural Anthropology* 15(3): 327–360.

Tule, Philipus. 2004. *Longing for the house of God, dwelling in the house of the ancestors: Local belief, Christianity, and Islam among the Kéo of Central Flores*. Studia Instituti Anthropos, Fribourg: Academic Press.

Vatter, Ernst. 1932. *Ata Kiwan: Unbekannte bergvolker im tropischen Holland*. Leipzig: Nusa Indah.

Walter, Bronwen. 1997. "Gender, 'Race,' and Diaspora: Racialized indentities of emigrant Irish women". In *Thresholds in Feminist Geography: Difference, Methodology, Representation*, edited by John Paul Jones III, Heidi J. Nast, and Susan M. Roberts, 339–359. Lanham, MD: Rowman and Littlefield Publishers.

Webster, Wendy. 1998. *Imagining home: Gender, 'race' and national identity, 1945–64*. London: UCL Press.

Werbner, Pnina. 1999. "Global pathways. Working class cosmopolitans and the creation of transnational ethnic worlds". *Social Anthropology* 7(1):17–35.

Wilkes, Julie. 1995. "The social construction of a caring career". In *Gender, Power and Relationship*, edited by Beber Speed Charlotte Burck, 232–247. London: Routledge.

Williams, Catharina Purwani. 1999. "Eastern Indonesia: Spatial Integration". In *Conference Proceedings*, edited by J.A. Kesby, J.M. Stanley, R.F. McLean, and L.J. Olive, 595–610. Canberra: Institute of Australian Geographers.

————. 2005. "'Knowing one's place': Gender, mobility and subjectivity in Eastern Indonesia". *Global Networks* (5):401–17.

Wilson, Elizabeth. 1991. *The sphinx in the city: Urban life, the control of disorder, and women*. London: Wirago.

Wolf, Diane Lauren. 1992. *Factory daughters: Gender, household dynamics, and rural industrialization in Java*. Oxford: University of California Press.

Wolf, Dianne L. 1990. "Daughters, Decisions and Domination: An Empirical and Conceptual Critique of Household Strategies". *Development and Change* 21(1):43–74.

Women and Geography Study Group of the IBG. 1997. *Feminist Geographies: Explorations in diversity and difference*. London: Longman Ltd.

Yeoh, Brenda S. A., and Shirlena Huang. 1999*a*. "Singapore women and foreign domestic workers: negotiating domestic work and motherhood". In *Gender, migration and domestic service*, edited by Janet Henshall Momsen, 277–301. London: Routledge.

————. 1999*b*. "Spaces at the margins: Migrant domestic workers and the development of civil society in Singapore". *Environment and Planning A* 31(7):1149–1167.

Index

About the Author
Dr Catharina Williams has been teaching at The Australian National University (ANU) and at The University of New South Wales at ADFA (Australian Defence Force Academy). The nexus of her research and teaching ranges from the geography of Asia-Pacific and its economic development, to gender and migration and social theories. She has had a number of publications in international journals including *Global Networks*, *Asian and Pacific Migration*, and *Anthropologi Indonesia*. In collaboration with researchers at the ANU she has performed consultancies for Australian and Indonesian development agencies. Growing up in Java, Indonesia, with its rich traditions of social lives, she has a passion for alternative economies and towards a more equitable distribution of resources and power among region, gender, race and class.

www.ingramcontent.com/pod-product-compliance
Lightning Source LLC
Chambersburg PA
CBHW021542260326
41914CB00001B/118